APPLIED MARINE HYDRAULICS

Applied Marine Hydraulics

BY PERRY A. STUTMAN

Cornell Maritime Press

CENTREVILLE, MARYLAND

Library of Congress Cataloging in Publication Data

Stutman, Perry A., 1947-
Applied marine hydraulics.

Bibliography: p.
Includes index.
1. Ships—Hydraulic equipment. 2. Hydrostatics.
3. Hydraulic engineering. 4. Marine engineering.
I. Title.
VM470.S78 1988 623.8′7 87-47737
ISBN 0-87033-366-6

Manufactured in the United States of America
First edition

CONTENTS

PART II
Applied Hydraulics: Shipboard Systems

PART III
Troubleshooting

ACKNOWLEDGMENTS

I suppose it is axiomatic that no book is truly original in every respect. I am acutely aware that in the process of accumulating knowledge and judgment in a field, one is inevitably influenced by all sorts of stimuli, sometimes even without being aware of it. These can be from books one has long forgotten even having read, or from casual remarks by colleagues, or from hearing of someone's failed experiments, or whatever.

And so it is with the material found here. The format is my own, but I gratefully acknowledge the help extended to me by many who remain oblivious of the influence they have had on me and whom, in most instances, I have never met. Their names, if I knew them, are too numerous to list. Yet I am deeply indebted to them all.

I also wish to thank those chief engineers who worked with me aboard the ships I sailed, and who gave me the opportunities and the experience with various hydraulic systems.

Furthermore, I am deeply indebted to Arthur Newberry and Gilbert LaDana for their help, encouragement, and criticism that have gone into the development of this text.

But most of all, I thank Sheila. Without her, this book would never have materialized.

INTRODUCTION

Within the last decade and a half, shipping worldwide has been undergoing major changes. Ships, in general, have become larger, with their cargo-carrying ability increasing three to five times over that of their counterparts of twenty years ago. At the same time, much of the familiar deck machinery has begun to disappear as the concept of the ship has changed to compete with other modes of cargo transfer. Ironically, despite the increase in the size of today's modern cargo vessels, the number of crew aboard ship has been reduced by one-third of what it was not more than a decade ago.

With the change in the nature of ships, modern technology has been instrumental in taking up the slack, where men are no longer available to do the job. To keep pace, hydraulic systems have likewise become more sophisticated.

However, as more electrical equipment has been replaced by hydraulic equipment, ships' personnel often find themselves being "left out in the cold." That is, there is a tremendous lack of familiarity with these systems. Keep in mind that for decades the only hydraulic equipment aboard ship was the steering gear; rarely was there any extensive work associated with this system compared with other equipment aboard ship.

Thus, the goal of this handbook is to present both substantial and diverse information on the subject of hydraulics. To accomplish this goal, the handbook is divided into three parts. The first part deals strictly with hydraulic principles. Familiarization with the first part will provide the reader with the necessary foundation to understand the hydraulic circuits discussed in the second part.

The second part of the handbook discusses the operation of those circuits found aboard ship. Although only selected systems are discussed in Part II, they are of sufficient complexity to make applications to other systems fairly easy. Part III on troubleshooting gives helpful hints on diagnosing actual problems that must be resolved to restore system functions.

The Appendices contain additional information, such as basic graphic symbology, working formulas, and tables, to broaden your knowledge of hydraulics. So it is now up to you, by reading and studying the information contained in this handbook, to help unlock those mysteries that have plagued you.

Good luck and good sailing!

APPLIED MARINE HYDRAULICS

PART I

Principles of Hydraulics

CHAPTER 1

BASIC CONCEPTS OF HYDRAULICS

The field of modern hydraulics has its roots firmly planted in the ancient Greco-Roman era. The word hydraulics itself is based on the Greek words *hydōr,* meaning water, and *aulos,* meaning pipe. Many of the ancient concepts, whose examples are still prominent throughout Europe, are as utilitarian now as they were then.

Modern hydraulics encompasses two major concepts: hydrodynamics and hydrostatics. Simply stated, hydrodynamics makes use of hydraulic devices that employ the impact, or kinetic energy, of a liquid to transmit power. Hydrostatics, on the other hand, concerns the use of hydraulic devices being operated when a force is applied to a confined liquid. It is to the second area that this handbook is devoted.

Advantages of the Hydraulic System

Over the past four decades, hydraulic systems have not only become more prevalent, but the advances have been remarkable. In the relatively short period in which major component and design improvements have occurred, hydraulic systems have become excellent alternatives as power transmission systems. These hydraulic systems demonstrate several major advantages over other types of comparable power systems, including:

1. infinite speed control
2. nearly instantaneous reversibility
3. excellent overload protection

4. the ability to stall without sustaining major damage
5. compactness

To acquire a better understanding of these advantages, consider an expansion of these concepts. An electric power transfer system exists in one of two forms. Either the speed of the electric motor is fixed, or numerous variable resistance devices are employed to develop a wide speed range. The latter system is expensive and requires an extensive maintenance program. The hydraulic system controls actuator output speeds by varying the flow rate. As the circuit flow rate is regulated by a simple valve, or specific pump element, control of the flow rate develops an infinite actuator speed range from zero to its maximum.

Although an electrical system can be adjusted to be reversible, the time required to stop, then reverse, the direction of rotation, even in terms of a few seconds, may be considered *too long*. Where these systems can be reversed rather quickly, the extensive amount of equipment required to accomplish reversing involves additionally higher production cost, maintenance, or overall size. In the hydraulic system, the actuators can be reversed by merely changing the direction of fluid flow. Since fluid flow can be handled by fairly simple and compact directional control valves, the change in direction is only a matter of how quickly the position of the valves can be adjusted. Also, most electric devices are significantly affected by inertia during rotation because of the reactive forces in the electrical fields. On the other hand, in hydraulics, because of the near incompressibility of the liquids, there is no need to compensate significantly for inertia.

Since electric equipment, when overloaded, demands higher than normal current flow, the system's fuses or circuit breakers will open. The system stalls, and on occasion mechanical damage or an electrical fire will occur, necessitating costly repairs. Operation of the system can be renewed only when these protective devices are replaced or reset, respectively. On the other hand, relief valves can be used to protect the hydraulic system from damaging overloads by bypassing fluid directly to the sump, while the system remains in passive operation. Once the overload has been removed, the system will be able to continue to operate.

With the application of the principle of force multiplication, small lightweight components can be used to develop high potential energy systems. While there is no standard rule of thumb, hydraulic systems may need only to take up one-fourth the space occupied by comparable electrical systems, with the weight being as much as one-tenth less.

Beyond these listed advantages, as you become more familiar with power hydraulics, you will learn, as stated in the *Vickers Manual* that "no other medium combines the positiveness, accuracy, and flexibility while maintaining the ability to transmit a maximum of power in a minimum of bulk and weight."

Pascal's Law

In every major field of study, credit is given to an individual or to a group of individuals for formulating the basis for that study, or for being the catalyst responsible for initiating further development. Thus, in the case of modern hydraulics much of the credit has been given to Blaise Pascal, a seventeenth-century French scientist, who discovered the principle related to the use of confined fluids in transmitting power, multiplying forces, and modifying motions.

This principle, known as Pascal's Law, simply states that pressure applied to a confined fluid is transmitted equally and undiminished in all directions, acting at right angles to all surface areas (Fig. 1-1).

Although Pascal's work was carried out in the seventeenth century, progress in the use of hydraulics has been a more recent occurrence. Perhaps because of the simplicity of the science, its potential was realized by a limited number of individuals. In fact, there are situations where most of the concepts are so simple, you will find it difficult to accept them and will continue to anticipate pitfalls. Unfortunately, the only pitfalls you will experience are the ones you create by looking for something that does not exist.

Generation of Pressure

One pitfall is the inability to comprehend how pressure is generated. Typically, pressure is defined as force per unit area, and is expressed as pounds per square inch. Mechanical instruments (pressure gauges) are used to indicate the existing conditions of pressure, but the

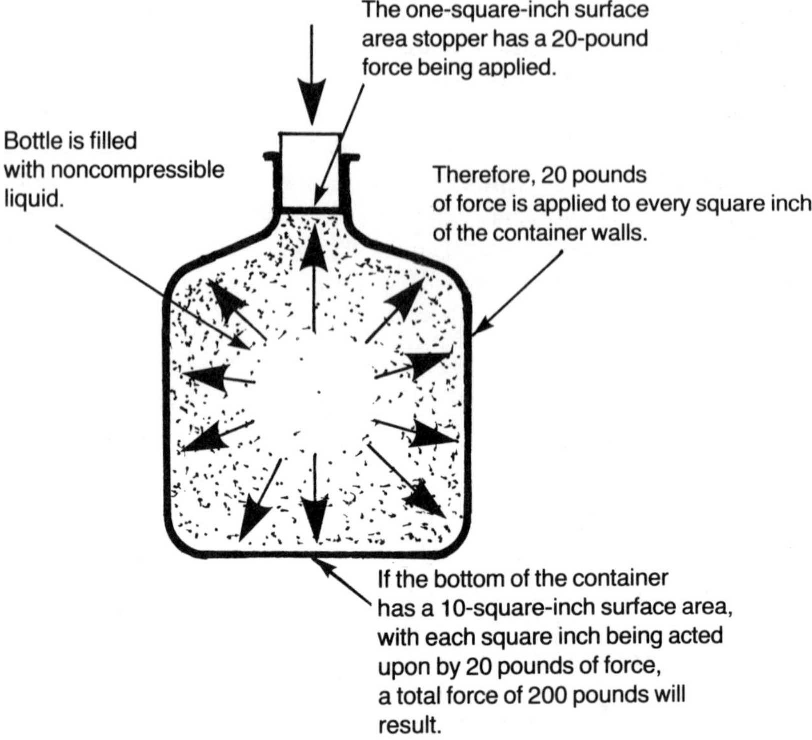

Fig. 1-1. Pressure is distributed equally and undiminished.

realization of how pressure occurs seems to be difficult to understand. Now is the time to dispel any misconceptions you may have, and to realize how pressure is actually generated and maintained.

Within a hydraulic system, where fluid flow exists, pressure is generated as the result of resistance to the flow of the fluid. For the time being, consider the primary resistance to be the load placed upon an actuator. Later on, you will contemplate another *resistance*, the internal friction of the fluid attempting to flow through the pipe. However, before expanding upon these two fundamental concepts, you are going to consider a liquid at rest.

For instance, a cubic foot of water, which weighs 62.4 pounds, acts on the bottom of a cube that covers a surface area of 144 square inches. Dividing the 62.4 pounds by the surface area of 144 square inches, you will find that a one-foot column of water, with a one-square-inch surface area, exerts a force of .433 pounds per square inch per vertical foot. In other words, for each foot of water, a pressure of .433 psi is generated. A 10-foot column of water, regardless of cross-sectional area, exerts a pressure at its base equal to 4.33 psi. Similarly, a 100-foot column of water exerts a pressure of 43.3 psi.

Now, consider the converse. If it is necessary to move water from a zero level to a vertical distance of 100 feet, a minimum pressure of 43.3 psi must be generated at the base of the column in order to support water at that height. With the exception of geographic conditions, it is rare to consider a system necessary to move liquids to that substantial a height. However, it is not uncommon for a hydraulic system to handle loads that are in the magnitude of thousands of pounds of force.

In Fig. 1-2, a cylinder is shown with a piston area of 10 square inches and a total stroke length of 24 inches. It is used to lift a 10,000-pound load, supplied by a 10-gallon-per-minute pump. A check valve is placed at the discharge of the pump to reinforce the concept of pressure, i.e., the generation of pressure that is a result of the load, even though the pump is not in operation. Since the pressure is considered a function of the force divided by the unit area—at a no-flow condition—the indicated data is used to solve for the generated pressure. Thus:

$$P = \frac{\text{force}}{\text{area}} = \frac{\text{pounds}}{\text{square inches}} = \text{psi}$$

$$P = \frac{10{,}000 \text{ lbs}}{10 \text{ in}^2} = \frac{1{,}000 \text{ lbs}}{1 \text{ in}^2} = 1{,}000 \text{ psi}$$

During this static condition, the pressure gauge indicates the 1,000-psi reading with the piston position as indicated at 12 inches above the cylinder bottom. This height results in an additional pressure of .433 psi, if water were in the cylinder. (Because of the resulting 1,000-pound pressure from the load, the additional .433 psi, due to the height of the water, is ignored at this time.) As shown in Fig. 1-2, pressure has only been the result of the gravitational effect of the load.

Effects of Flow Rate

The discussion could end here, if increasing the speed of the cylinder extension did not change the *resulting* oil pressure directed to the

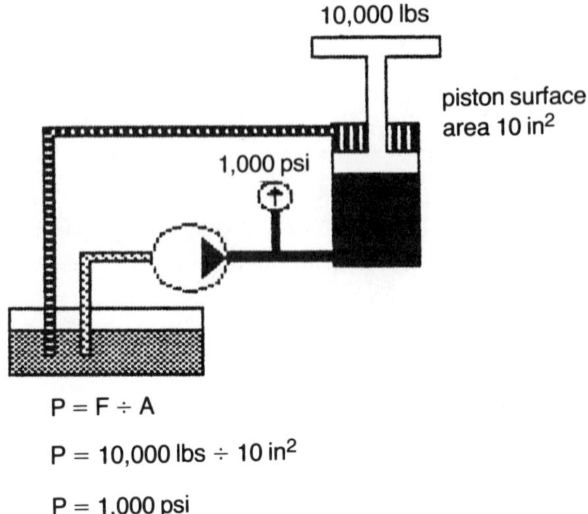

$$P = F \div A$$

$$P = 10{,}000 \text{ lbs} \div 10 \text{ in}^2$$

$$P = 1{,}000 \text{ psi}$$

Fig. 1-2. Under static conditions the load will generate a pressure equal to the force of the load divided by the surface area of the piston.

cylinder. Since the cylinder speed can be observed to increase, there is an accompanying pressure increase. This simple observation could unfortunately lead you to conclude that the rate of cylinder extension is caused by the increase in pressure, when actually it is related to a number of conditions.

To reiterate, pressure is a result of a number of existing conditions, and the changes that occur in those conditions. All of these will be discussed in detail, but it is important at the outset to realize that these conditions, namely, flow rate, piping frictional losses, piping internal diameter, the mass of the load, the size of the actuator, viscosity of the hydraulic oil, among others, will all have an effect upon the resultant pressure.

It should be obvious that when the pump is not operating, zero flow rate exists. The vertical load develops a pressure of 1,000 psi at the pump discharge. What happens to pressure when the flow rate to the cylinder develops at one gpm with a 10,000-pound load on the cylinder being stroked at 23.1 inches? (For now, *time* is not considered.) Clearly, one gallon of oil displaces the piston through its full stroke. Consider this equation: linear displacement of the piston is equal to the volume of oil required to complete stroke.

$$10 \text{ in}^2 \times 23.1 \text{ in} = 231 \text{ in}^3$$
$$1 \text{ gal} = 231 \text{ in}^3$$

With time considered as a factor, note that one minute is required to complete the stroke at the stated pump discharge rate. While the nonoperating pressure has already been established as 1,000 psi, the kinetic operation of the system results in an increase in pressure. The most important factors are the *frictional losses* that oppose the flow of oil making its way to the actuator.

The frictional losses, in addition to the load, include: the internal diameter of the discharge piping; the transitional openings between the components and the piping; the type and number of valves; the number of bends and the sharpness of the bends in the piping; the comparative volumes between the rod and cap ends of the actuator; the fluid flow rate; the viscosity of the hydraulic fluid; the type of piston and rod seals; and whether cushioning-deceleration devices have been installed.

You will find that each of the above frictional losses can be expressed in terms of vertical feet of water. For example, a control valve may be known to produce an equivalent frictional loss of 100 feet of water with a flow rate of 2 gpm. This means that the flow across the valve alone results in a pressure drop of 43.3 psi. Incorporating the figures already established under static conditions, you will note that the pressure at the pump discharge cannot be below 1,043.3 psi. If the pump discharge rate is doubled, the frictional loss quadruples to 400 feet of water, i.e., the pump discharge pressure rises to 1,173 psi.

If all of the other frictional losses are accurately taken into account, it is not surprising to find that the operating pressure for this simple system will be 1,500 to 2,000 psi. Therefore, increasing the flow rate to the actuator increases the speed of actuation. As the speed of actuation increases, the increased flow rate encounters higher frictional losses which *result in higher operating pressures for the system.*

Keeping in mind the actuator speed-pressure relationship, what happens if the valve throttling or pipe diameters are changed? For example, you install a pump to discharge through a large diameter pipe, fitted with a globe valve, that is fully open when the pump is initially started (Fig. 1-3), and in which only the fluid friction opposes the discharge, as the valve is open directly to the tank below. The

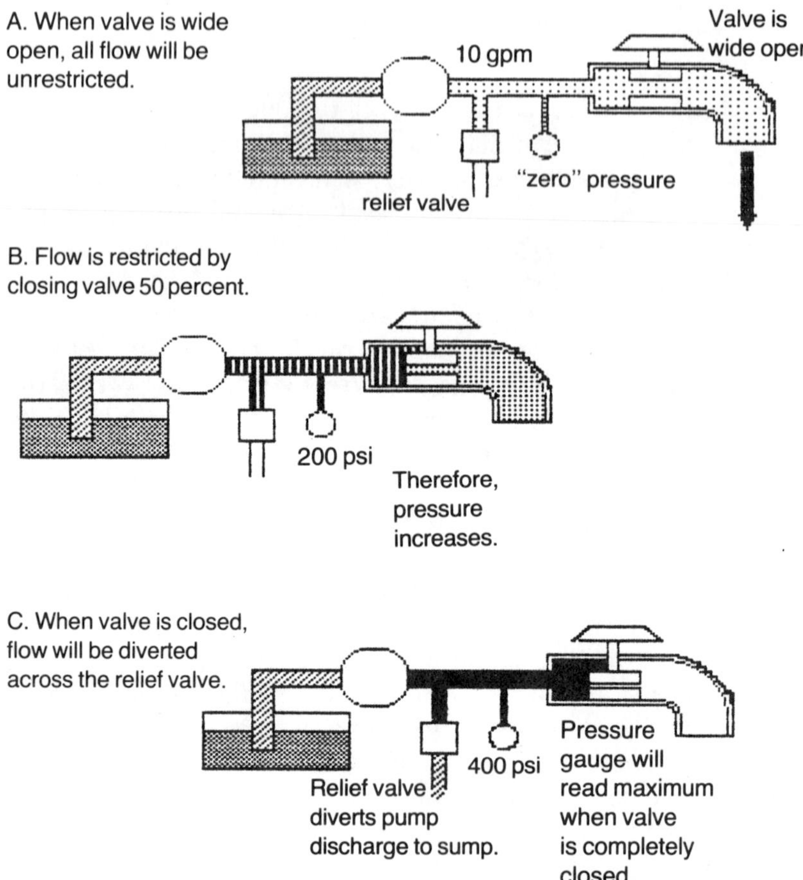

Fig. 1-3. Pressure generated in fluids subjected to flow is due to the restrictions that oppose the flow.

resultant pressure, at the pump discharge, is considered zero. As the valve is closed by 50 percent, the increase in the restriction to flow increases the pressure at the pump discharge. Now with the valve fully closed, the resultant pressure is at its maximum. In other words, as the effective opening of the restriction becomes smaller, an increase in pressure of the liquid results between the point of restriction and the source of flow.

To the same pump, you install parallel to the larger line (Fig. 1-4) a second length of pipe, one-fourth the cross-sectional area of the first. When the valve in the larger pipe is finally closed, oil flow

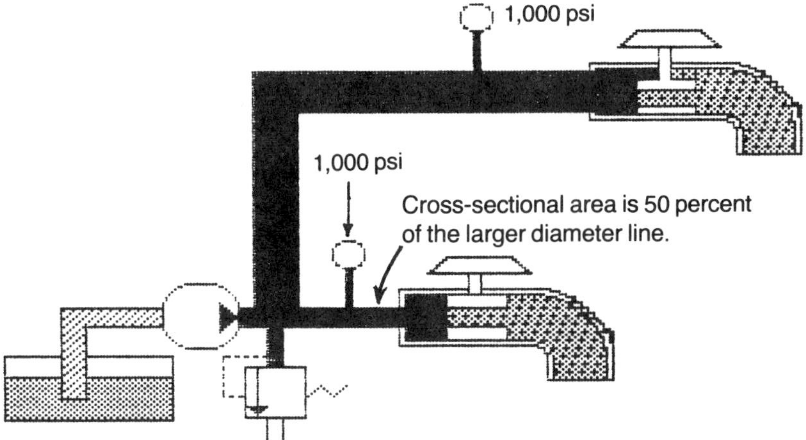

Fig. 1-4. Liquid flow through a pipe one-fourth the cross-sectional area of the larger pipe will have the same effect as closing the larger valve by 50 percent.

is permitted through the smaller line with the second valve completely open. Despite the fact that the second valve is wide open, the pressure is just about equal to that of the first example, where the valve was half open. Therefore, if a high constant flow rate occurs in a small diameter pipe, pressure results well above zero even though no immediately recognizable restriction to the flow exists. Also, if the flow rate to a particular diameter pipe is increased, the resultant pressure must also increase, regardless of the load.

Effects of Liquid Density on Pressure

Water is not the only liquid to be considered in this discussion. The use of oils must also be understood. Typically, hydraulic oils have a density of 55 to 58 pounds per cubic foot. As calculated previously, if the weight per cubic foot of the oil is divided by 144 square inches, the force per square inch per vertical foot can be determined. Thus:

$$55/144 \text{ in}^2 = .382 \text{ psi/ft}$$

and

$$\frac{58 \text{ lbs}}{144 \text{ in}^2} = .4 \text{ psi/ft}$$

Comparing the later figure with that of water, you see that:

1. A 100-foot column of oil will exert a pressure of 40 psi, versus 43.3 psi for a similar column of water.
2. Less potential energy will be required to support a 100-foot column of oil.
3. A pressure of 43.3 psi that supported a 100-foot column will support a column of oil 108.25 feet in height.

Clearly, then, the density of the liquid has an effect upon the pressure generated, and the amount of energy necessary to move or support a liquid column is directly affected by the density of the liquid.

The previous discussion has been centered around a static condition. Now, the dynamic operating condition will be taken into account. As there was the possibility of a misunderstanding about the term "pressure" in the static condition, there may be similar confusion about the terms "flow rate" and "velocity" in discussing the dynamic condition. Therefore, *flow rate* is defined as the volume of fluid passing a point per a given unit of time. *Velocity,* on the other hand, is defined as the time required for a particle to pass between two known points. Obviously, the terms by themselves are easily understood. The problem occurs when and how you apply them. Consider the following conditions and how each relates to the other.

In an open flow system, such as the pump discharging to an open tank, where the gallons per minute (flow rate) from the pump have been increased from 10 to 20 gpm, the velocity of the liquid is observed to increase also.

Now, consider a simple hydraulic system where a one-gallon-per-minute flow rate is established by a pump piped in parallel to two actuators (Fig. 1-5). Each actuator has an internal bore of 10 square inches, and extends to a full 24 inches. Despite each actuator's handling a 10,000-pound load, a one-inch-diameter line is connected to actuator "A"; and a one-half-inch-diameter line is connected to actuator "B." In addition, a pressure gauge is installed at the pump discharge and at the inlėt to each of the actuators. When the pump is not in operation, 1,000 psi is indicated on each of the gauges.

When you start the pump, the indicated discharge pressure rises to 1,500 psi. The actuator connected by the one-inch line begins to extend, while the other does not. In approximately one minute, the first actuator is fully extended, while the second actuator just begins

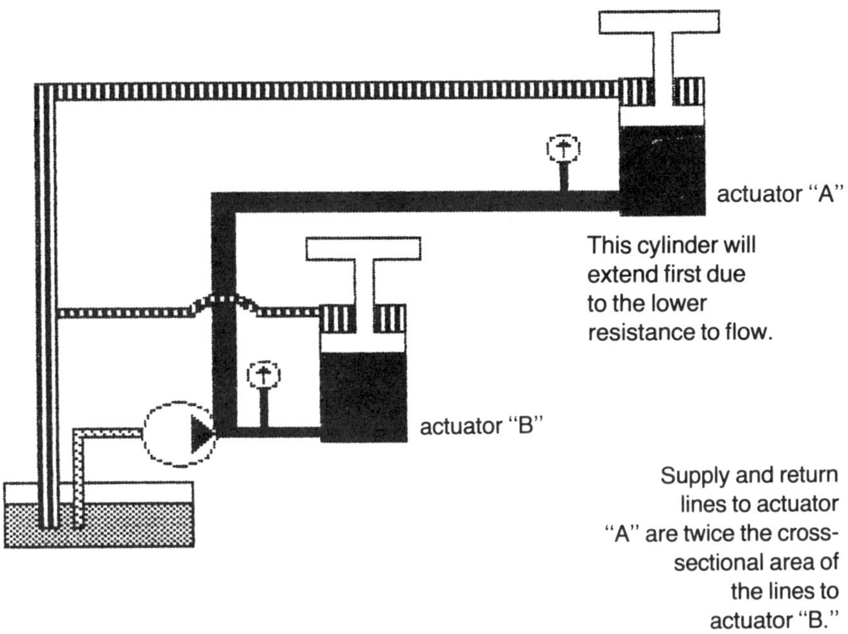

Fig. 1-5. Despite each actuator being of equal size and supporting equal loads, the smaller diameter line will resist the flow so that its cylinder will extend only after the larger line cylinder has extended. The discharge pressure to the second cylinder will be higher, with a higher velocity, despite the pump discharge rate remaining the same.

to extend. For this example, the second actuator is found to extend in one minute as well. This is not as puzzling as it seems.

Fluids flow to the point of least resistance. Since the half-inch line is parallel to the one-inch line, a substantial resistance to flow is created by the smaller diameter line. Once the first cylinder is extended, the second cylinder creates the *least* resistance to flow. Simultaneously, the pump discharge pressure increases because of the increase in the opposition to flow. Since both cylinders are of the same size, and the pump flow rate remains constant, extension for both cylinders takes approximately one minute.

This holds true, as long as enough oil is forced into the cylinders to completely displace the pistons (oil being considered as virtually noncompressible). If both actuators extend in one minute, and the internal cross-sectional areas of the supply pipes are different, the oil velocity through the smaller diameter pipe must be regarded as greater. Thus, while there are instances when the two terms can be used interchangeably, there are many instances in which the one condition exists, but the other does not. Specific reference to the existing operating conditions is therefore essential.

In the above example, a simple arithmetic calculation reveals that a flow rate of one gallon per minute through the one-inch pipe yields a velocity of almost five feet per second. By repeating this procedure for the half-inch pipe, a velocity of almost twenty feet per second is realized. The comparison of these two conditions yields a simple rule of thumb:

> *When the cross-sectional area of a pipe is halved, the velocity of the liquid will increase by four times that of the original velocity.*

Again, please recognize that the concepts of flow rate and velocity need to be kept separate.

Now, consider the following conditions. It is known that each gallon of liquid occupies 231 cubic inches. Each of the cylinders has a volumetric displacement of 231 cubic inches; and each requires one gallon of oil to fully displace the piston within its cylinder. If the flow rate to one of the cylinders is one gallon per minute, the time of actuation is one minute. If the flow rate is increased to 10 gpm, or 2,310 cubic inches per minute, the cylinder is completely extended in approximately 6 seconds. Conclusion: the speed of actuation of any actuator is directly dependent upon the flow rate.

Laminar Versus Turbulent Flow

If, however, the flow rate within the system is increased, as described, the fluid velocity increases proportionally. In attempting to move high velocity fluids through the piping, various problems exist. Designers are aware of these problems, with respect to velocity, and work diligently with the concepts of laminar and turbulent flow.

Laminar flow refers to a condition in which the liquid, flowing through a pipe, occurs in a series of layers that move parallel to each other (Fig. 1-6). Turbulence, on the other hand, describes a condition in which the individual layers do not flow parallel to each other, but, in fact, disturb each successive layer. In order for the designers to determine the theoretical flow conditions through an untried system, a concept known as the Reynold's number is used.

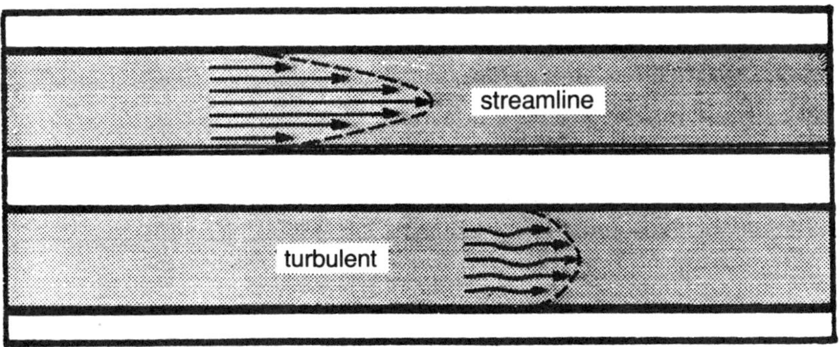

Fig. 1-6. Streamline or laminar flow through a pipe as opposed to the turbulent or nonstreamline flow through the pipe

This number is determined by taking into account the velocity, liquid density, liquid viscosity, and the internal diameter of the pipe; and it is represented by the following formula:

$$\text{Reynold's number} = vDp/\mu$$

where: v = velocity (feet/second)
D = inside diameter of the pipe (feet)
p = fluid density (pounds/cubic foot)
μ = viscosity (centipoise)

Typically, it is found that when the Reynold's number is 2,000 or less, the flow, in practice, is laminar. However, if the number is 4,000 or more, the flow is turbulent. When the number falls between 2,000 and 4,000, the prediction of the flow cannot be determined accurately.

It is reasonable to assume that the laminar flow condition is the most desirable, and a less energy-consuming condition. Once turbulent flow develops within the system, more energy is required to accomplish the same amount of work than was required before turbulence developed.

Where a turbulent condition develops, at least one layer of flow begins to move perpendicular to the lamina and must be reversed to flow in the direction of the source of the flow. As this restricts or cancels a portion of the original energy input, additional energy must be made available to accomplish the same amount of work.

Some of the consequences that will result as turbulent flow continues are:

1. higher overall operating costs
2. overheating of the prime mover
3. overheating of the system
4. improper operation of the system
5. deterioration of the hydraulic fluid
6. cavitation developing at the point of turbulence

CHAPTER 2

HYDRAULICS AS A POWER TRANSMISSION SYSTEM

The first chapter reviewed several misconceptions about hydraulics. Still another misconception is that hydrostatic systems *produce power*. But, as you will see, hydraulic systems *transmit power*. They utilize the energy of a prime mover (electrical motor, internal combustion engine, or manual labor) with the resultant energy transformed by the use of a pump element to the hydraulic medium in order to establish flow through the system. As the oil flows through the system, it, in turn, transforms the energy established at the pump to some output device, in order to perform work.

Force Multiplication

With the following example, you will see how a small input can be used to overcome a larger output by simple transference of the power input. This concept is known as the multiplication of forces, and permits a small compact device to produce a substantial output.

Referring to Fig. 2-1, you can see that a 50-pound force is applied to the end of the lever 10 inches above the centerline of the one-half-square-inch pump piston. The discharge of the pump is directed to the bottom of a 20-square-inch output piston. When the 50-pound force is applied to the top end of the lever, a 500-pound force is developed at the piston (since pressure is equal to the force divided by a unit area). The output pressure, produced by the piston, is calculated by dividing 500 pounds by one-half square inch, or 1,000 psi. As the large output piston is able to move a load in terms of pounds, the maximum load capability is determined by the total force available at the output piston. Considering that force is equal

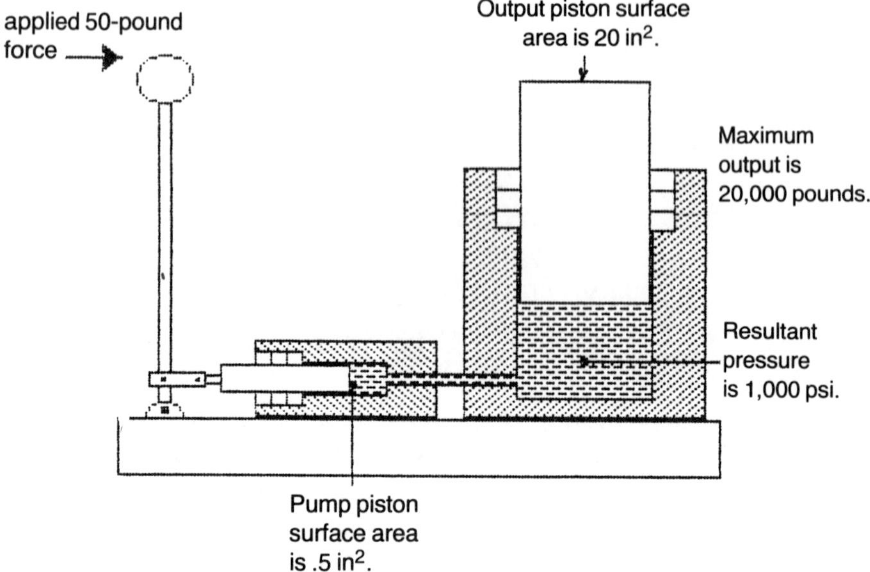

Fig. 2-1. Demonstration of force multiplication

to the existing pressure (in terms of pounds per square inch) when applied to a particular surface area, the total available force output is 20,000 pounds. At first, the conditions set forth in this example seem incredible, but remember that since the output piston is not moved, no work is performed.

To consider the amount of work performed, you need to define work as the movement of a force through a distance:

$$W = F \times D$$

Arbitrarily, the piston position is raised 2 feet. The work performed is determined by multiplying 20,000 pounds times 2 feet to yield 40,000 foot-pounds. It is easy enough to say that the piston is moved 2 feet, but what is actually required to move the piston to that height?

In order to move the piston 2 feet, oil must fill the volume to be vacated by the piston. Thus, the total volume of oil to be displaced is calculated by:

$$\frac{20 \text{ in}^2 \times 2 \text{ ft} \times 12 \text{ in}}{1 \text{ ft}} = 480 \text{ in}^3$$

Therefore, 480 cubic inches of oil must be forced into the cylinder in order to displace the piston. It is simple, of course.

You already know that the pump piston has a surface area of one-half square inch. With a piston stroke length of one inch, a volume of one-half cubic inch of oil moves toward the output piston. Carrying this one step further, the pump piston must be stroked to discharge 960 times.

As you can see, the pump piston moves in one direction to discharge, and in the opposite direction to refill the pump cylinder. Thus a total of 1,920 strokes are made by the operator to move the output piston. If each of the 1,920 strokes takes one second, 1,920 seconds are required to move the output piston 2 feet. Or, in terms of time, the operation takes 32 minutes.

By now it is obvious that a 20,000-pound load can be moved by this simple system. Mathematically accomplishing this task is one thing; but try swinging your arm back and forth for 32 minutes. Your arm will feel like it is the size and weight of a telephone pole. Mechanical advantage is definitely achieved, but not without paying a price somewhere else.

Now, try to speed up the stroking of the pump piston in order to double the flow rate. Without too much difficulty, you realize that the output piston moves the two-foot distance in half the time. Again, note that speed of actuation is directly in response to flow rate.

And so you ask, "Well, what about the pressure?" The answer is a qualified *yes*, the pressure does go up. The pressure increases only as a result of the flow rate, and the attempt to move an increased volume of fluid against a fixed resistance. To reiterate, the pressure increases, but only as a result of the increase in flow rate.

Hydraulic Horsepower

As you've seen, increasing the flow rate affects actuator speed. You have also seen how much work is eventually produced once the actuator moves. Although the power to accomplish this task has not been considered, it cannot be ignored. Power is defined as the amount of work accomplished over a period of time. One horsepower is the equivalent of moving 33,000 pounds through a one-foot distance in one minute, or 33,000 foot-pounds per minute. By dividing 40,000 ft-lbs/32 min by 33,000 ft-lbs/min, the power required to move the load is calculated as .038 hp. By repeating the previous calculation, and substituting 40,000 ft-lbs/16 min, the power required, by decreasing time to move the load, is doubled. Another simple rule of thumb shows that:

> *The horsepower required to move any load will be proportional to the load, but will be inversely proportional to the time that it takes the load to be moved.*

For future reference, remember that one horsepower can also be expressed in the following equivalent terms as:

$$\begin{aligned} 1\text{ hp} &= 550\text{ ft-lbs/sec} \\ 1\text{ hp} &= 746\text{ watts} \\ 1\text{ hp} &= 42.4\text{ btu/min} \end{aligned}$$

The previous examples show the relationships existing among speed of actuation, distance of extension, and force relative to pressure. Thus, hydraulic power is expressed as:

$$\text{power} = \frac{\text{gallons}}{\text{minute}} \times \frac{\text{pounds}}{\text{square inch}}$$

To convert this relationship to mechanical units, the following equivalents are used:

$$\begin{aligned} 1\text{ gal} &= 231\text{ in}^3 \\ 12\text{ in} &= 1\text{ ft} \end{aligned}$$

Thus:

$$\begin{aligned} \text{power} &= \frac{\text{gal}}{\text{min}} \times \frac{231\text{ in}^3}{\text{gal}} \times \frac{\text{lbs}}{\text{in}^2} \times \frac{1\text{ ft}}{12\text{ in}} \\ &= \frac{\text{gal}}{\text{min}} \times \frac{231\text{ in}^3}{\text{gal}} \times \frac{\text{lbs}}{\text{in}^2} \times \frac{1\text{ ft}}{12\text{ in}} \\ &= \frac{231\text{ ft-lbs}}{12\text{ min}} \\ &= \frac{19.25\text{ ft-lbs}}{\text{min}} \end{aligned}$$

This results in the equivalent mechanical power, at a flow rate of 1 gpm at 1 psi. Expressed in terms of horsepower, 19.25 ft-lbs/min is divided by 33,000 ft-lbs/min, or:

$$\begin{aligned} hp &= \frac{19.25 \text{ ft-lbs/min}}{33{,}000 \text{ ft-lbs/min}} \\ &= \frac{19.25 \text{ ft-lbs}}{\text{min}} \times \frac{\text{min}}{33{,}000 \text{ ft-lbs}} \\ &= \frac{19.25 \text{ ft-lbs}}{\text{min}} \times \frac{\text{min}}{33{,}000 \text{ ft-lbs}} \\ &= .000583 \end{aligned}$$

Thus, a one-gallon-per-minute flow rate at one pound per square inch yields a factor of .000583 hp. The total horsepower for any condition then is:

$$hp = gpm \times psi \times .000583$$

This is reduced and expressed as:

$$hp = \frac{gpm \times psi}{1{,}000} \times .583$$

$$hp = \frac{gpm \times psi}{1{,}714}$$

The formula above represents the horsepower of the fluid as it passes from the pump throughout the system. However, if the pump is driven by an electric motor, the horsepower of the motor must be higher, as a motor of 100 percent efficiency does not exist. If a typical electric motor produces only 80 percent of its rated capacity, an electric motor is needed for the system that produces a horsepower 25 percent higher than the required hydraulic horsepower. Thus:

$$hp = \frac{gpm \times psi}{1{,}714} \times 125\%$$

$$hp = \frac{gpm \times psi}{1{,}714} \times 1.25$$

$$hp = gpm \times psi \times .0007$$

While horsepower is useful in understanding the capabilities of hydraulic systems, some of the systems discussed later utilize rotary actuators (hydraulic motors) rather than linear actuators (hydraulic cylinders). Because of the nature of rotary actuators, knowledge of the available torque is as important as knowledge of the hydraulic horsepower of the system.

Torque

There are several ways in which the torque is determined, as well as expressed. When the displacement of the motor is known, the amount of oil, in cubic inches, which is required to rotate the motor once, can be used to calculate torque, regardless of the type of construction. Torque is calculated by the following relationship:

$$\text{torque} = \frac{\text{displacement (in}^3\text{/rev)} \times \text{pressure}}{2\pi}$$

However, if the hydraulic horsepower of the system and the rotating speed of the motor are known, the following formula is more useful:

$$\text{torque} = \frac{63025 \times \text{hp}}{\text{rpm}}$$

Note: torque is defined in terms of inch-pounds rather than foot-pounds. Generally speaking, hydraulic systems, because of their limited physical movement, are designated by inch-pounds.

In developing a system that incorporates a rotary actuator, knowing the torque rate of the motor helps to simplify the job. Torque rate is considered as the torque in inch-pounds per every 100 psi increment. Thus:

$$\text{torque rate} = \frac{\text{torque load (in-lbs)}}{\text{desired operating pressure (psi)} \times .01}$$

One useful condition of the torque rate is in determining the required operating pressure of the system when a particular torque rate of the motor is known. The formula:

$$\text{pressure} = \frac{\text{torque load (in-lbs)} \times 100}{\text{motor torque rate (in-lbs/100 psi)}}$$

CHAPTER 3

HYDRAULIC PUMPS AND MOTORS

The heart of any hydraulic system is the pump. Although pumps generally fall into two major categories, dynamic and displacement, it is the displacement type which is more commonly used in hydrostatic systems. Regardless of the type of pump used, there are misconceptions about the role contributed by these devices, and it is important to understand the function of a pump. Accordingly, a pump is defined as any device which imparts energy to a liquid, in order to move that liquid from one level to another level.

This definition implies that a pump does not produce pressure. Although "pressure" is indicated on the discharge pressure gauge, the pressure results from the flow generated by the pump meeting resistance within the system. Hence, the greater the resistance to the pump discharge, the greater is the resultant pressure, which is limited only by the energy input developed by the prime mover. Consequently, all pumps, when driven at a specific speed, are given a rating according to the flow rate produced at a particular pressure.

Basic Pump Units

Before analyzing the actual pump types, you should be aware of the four typical types of pump power packages, or units, used in hydraulic systems. The most common type is the single-stage pump (Fig. 3-1). This unit incorporates a single-pump element, driven by its prime mover, to generate oil flow through the system. Since there are systems where the rating of a single-stage pump is insufficient to meet the demands for maintaining extremely high pressures, a two-stage pump unit may be preferred (Fig. 3-2). In this unit, two pump

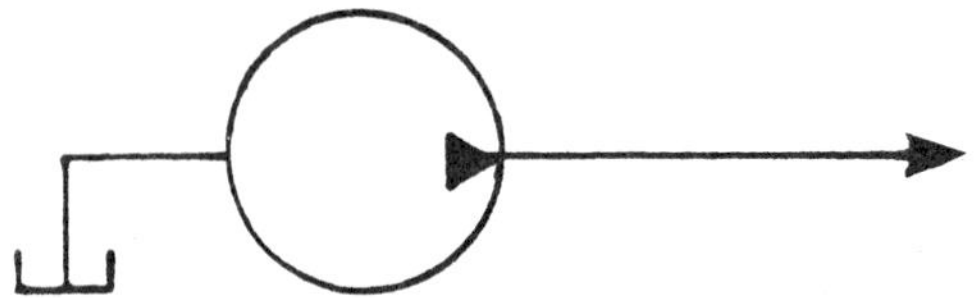

Fig. 3-1. Schematic graphic representation of a single-stage constant flow pump

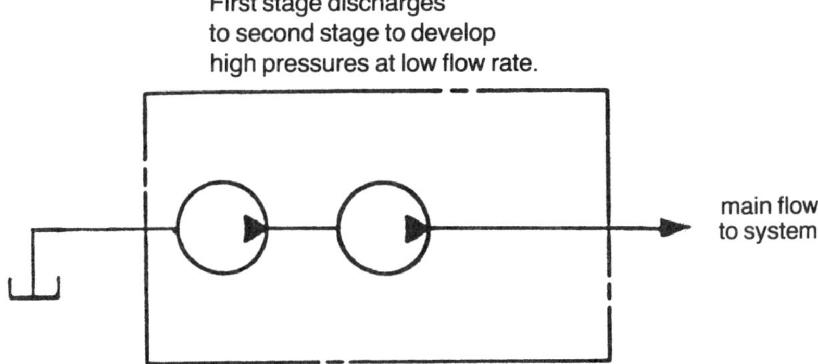

Fig. 3-2. Graphic representation of a two-stage pump unit where the discharge from the first stage becomes the pump intake of the second stage in order to meet high total head conditions

elements are located in one casing and are driven simultaneously by one prime mover. One pump element discharges directly into the suction of the second pump element, which allows pump speeds to be kept within a reasonable range, so as not to promote cavitation. Also, this procedure limits the flow rate, thus preventing any turbulence. Yet it still enables the unit to handle the required load, while remaining a compact unit.

Similar to the two-stage pump is the double-pump unit (Fig. 3-3). This unit also incorporates two pump elements enclosed in the same casing, with both elements driven by the same prime mover. Unlike the previous unit, the discharge from each of the elements combines and discharges into the system in parallel streams. A double-pump unit is used where one pump can easily handle the force of the load, but the additional flow rate may be needed for a short duration when the system requires an increase in actuation speed. Until the increased actuation speed is required, the additional flow rate, from one of the two pump elements, is unloaded directly into the sump, or is recirculated.

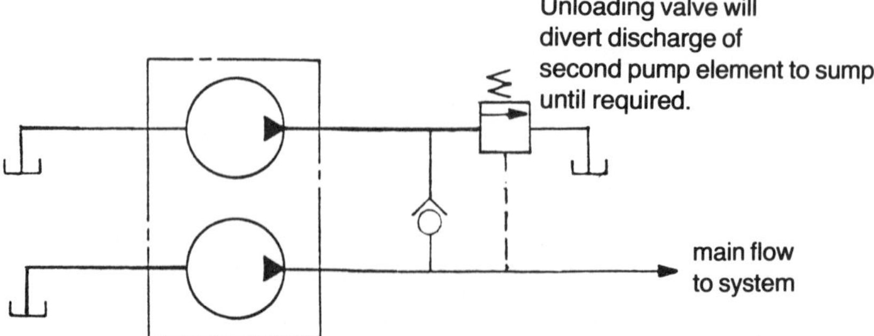

Fig. 3-3. Graphic representation of double-pump unit where both elements operate at the same discharge head but combine their flow rates to double the volume of oil discharged to the system

The fourth type of unit is known as the combination pump (Fig. 3-4). Also driven by one prime mover, this unit is designed with two or more pump elements enclosed in one casing. The discharge from each pump element is used to perform a specific function within the system. This arrangement permits greater efficiency of location, mounting, and space allotment.

Rotary Pumps

Displacement pumps deliver a specific quantity of liquid for each cycle or revolution. These pumps can be further described as rotary and reciprocating. Rotary pumps are devices in which rotation of the driven components results in the displacement of the liquid, while reciprocating pumps incorporate a piston to exert force on the liquid to develop displacement. Generally, one of the following four major types of rotary pumps are incorporated into the hydraulic system:

1. external spur gear tooth
2. internal spur gear tooth
3. vane
4. screw

Spur Gear Pumps

Spur gear pumps are relatively simple, from the standpoint of operation and construction (Fig. 3-5). They incorporate two spur gears

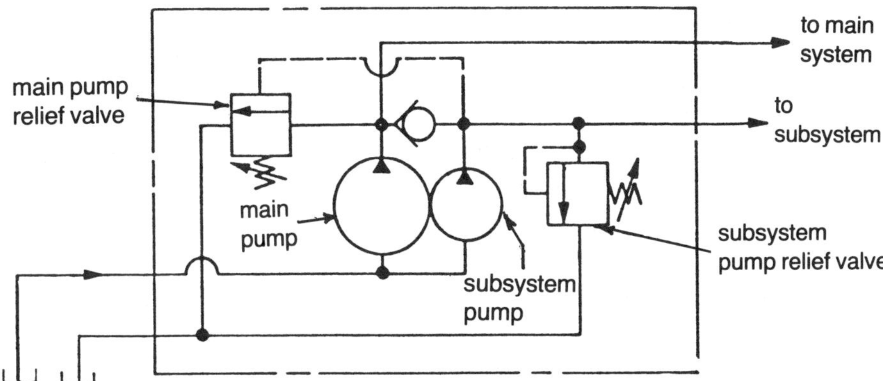

Fig. 3-4. Graphic representation of combination pump power unit where two or more pumps are driven by the same prime mover and the discharge from each is used to perform more than one task within a system

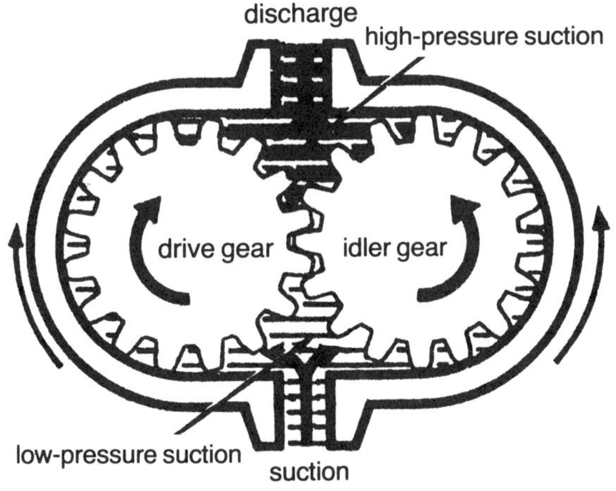

Fig. 3-5. Diagram of simple spur gear pump

that mesh together within the casing, where close peripheral tolerances are provided to aid in the movement of liquids from intake to discharge. One of the two spur gears is driven directly by the prime mover, and is referred to as the driven gear. As the driven gear meshes with the idler gear, the two rotate simultaneously, but in opposite directions. Voids are created between the two consecutive gear teeth, where the major diameter (crest) of each tooth maintains close tolerance with the pump casing. These voids create a number of chambers of specific volumes to be rotated at 1,200 to 1,800 rpm.

As the gears mesh, the liquid is squeezed from the voids, and forced to pass to the point of least resistance, i.e., to the casing outlet.

Since the voids between each set of teeth are virtually sealed at their crests, as well as at the sides of the hub, air initially found in the suction line is forced from the pump when rotated. As long as the height of the suction lift is kept within the accepted limits, oil can pass freely into the suction, and a pressure differential will be created between the pump suction and the source of the liquid. A suction differential is also created by the air being expelled as the gears rotate.

These pumps have proven to be very rugged, reliable, and easy to construct, operate, and maintain. Primarily, the difficulties that occur are related to the wear that develops between the sides of the gear hubs and the casing. Recently, the wear has been compensated for by the use of nylon clearance pieces that are installed on each side of the gear hubs to facilitate easy replacement and repair.

The nature of the spur gears limits the size of these elements. The flow rates are instrinsically limited at the stated revolutions. However, the limited flow rates do not restrict the ability of the pumps to meet the required load-pressure demands as long as this condition is only a matter of the prime mover horsepower, and is within the bursting strength of the casing material. Consequently, the pumps are designed to be used with flow rates of less than 5 gpm. Where systems require higher flow rates, other types of rotary pumps are utilized.

Gerotor Pumps

One alternative to the external spur gear tooth pump is the gear rotor or gerotor pump, also referred to as an internal gear tooth pump (Fig. 3-6). A female gear rotor, with seven teeth or lobes, is free to rotate within the casing. A smaller male gear, with six teeth or sprockets that mesh with the female, has its center located slightly above the horizontal center of the casing, and is directly rotated by the prime mover. Because of this arrangement, the male rotor always has one sprocket entering the area between two lobes of the female rotor, forcing it to rotate. The sprockets, opposite to those meshing with the lobes, form a peripheral seal. Rotation, to both the male and female rotors, creates the rapidly expanding voids on one side of the vertical centerline. Pressures lower than atmospheric result

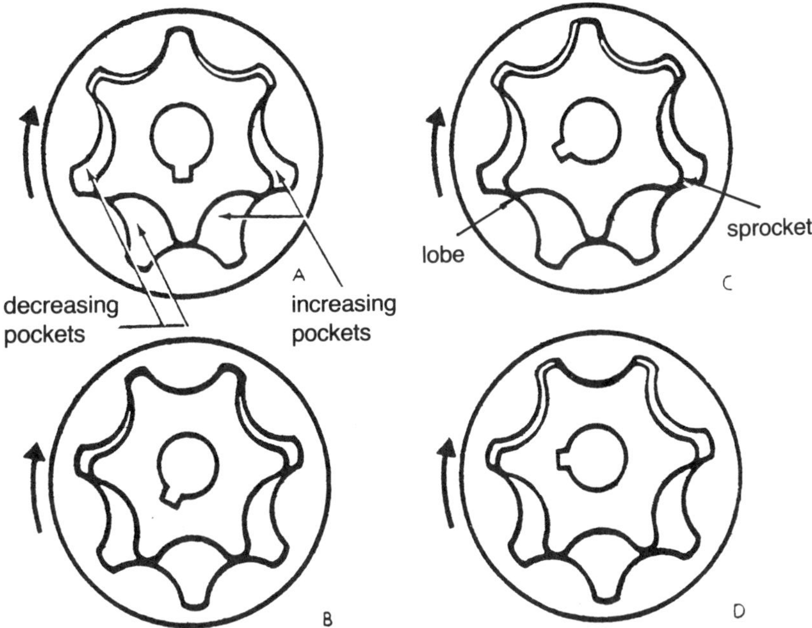

Fig. 3-6. Gerotor (gear rotor) type pump in the various phases of operation as liquid is moved across the pump element

as this action continues. When oil continues to flow and to occupy these voids, it becomes trapped in the areas between the two rotors. As the entrapped oil passes the vertical centerline, it is displaced by the meshing of the sprockets and lobes, and is forced to move towards the casing outlet. The construction, maintenance, and operation of this pump are not very complicated. While the pumps can be built to maintain flow rates near 100 gpm, system pressures of 2,000 psi are ordinarily the maximum limit to which they can be continuously operated.

Vane Pumps

A third rotary displacement type is the vane pump. Although there are three common vane designs—sliding, swinging, and roller—the sliding vane is perhaps the most widely used. Regardless of type, the overall operation of each is basically the same (Fig. 3-7).

In its design, the vane rotor diameter is less than that of the internal bore of the casing, and has a series of equally spaced slots

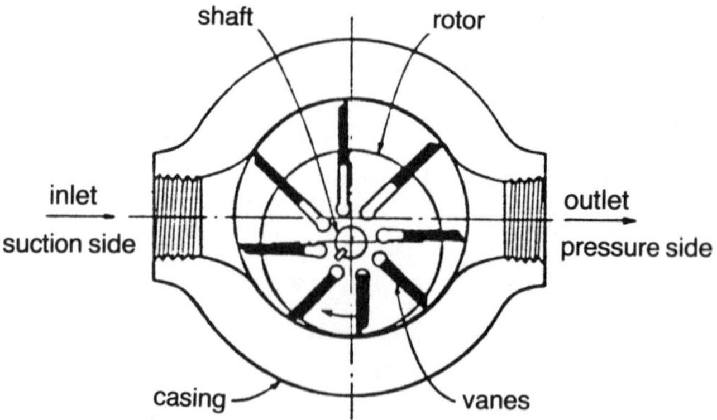

Fig. 3-7. Unbalanced sliding vane pump

that are machined deep enough to accept the entire vane. The geometric center of the rotor is offset, or eccentric, to the center of the casing bore. This allows a tangential point of the rotor to form a close tolerance seal with the casing. As the rotor turns, at 1,200 to 1,800 rpm, centrifugal force is imparted to the vanes, forcing them from their slots when the contour of the casing permits extension. As the vanes pass through the segment of the constantly enlarging "crescent," a rapidly expanding volume is created between consecutive sets of the vanes.

The rapid increase in volume yields a pressure less than atmospheric, so that the oil, stored at atmospheric pressure at the suction, flows to fill the voids. Once a vane has passed to the widest portion of the gap, it has extended to its fullest permissible length. Continued rotation forces the vane to retract into its slot, as the other half of the crescent area begins to diminish in width. The rapidly reducing volume, produced between the vanes, forces the oil from the voids and out of the casing-discharge port.

Reviewing the diagram of the vane pump, notice that equal surface areas exist on both sides of the rotor, yet are exposed to unequal pressures. As a result, extreme side thrust is developed in the direction away from the generated high pressure. This condition, known as *hydraulic thrust,* can result in the premature failure of the bearings, as well as in excessive wear to the casing and rotor. In an effort to eliminate the effects of hydraulic thrust, the balanced vane pump design is preferred in certain systems.

The notable difference between these designs is the elliptical-shape bore of the balanced vane pump versus the concentric shape of the unbalanced vane pump (Fig 3-8). The sides of the ellipse are in close tolerance with two points of the concentric rotor, 180 degrees apart. As a result, four separate but similarly shaped crescent chambers are created, as opposed to the two crescent-shaped areas of the unbalanced vane pump. Rotation of the rotor still produces centrifugal force on the vanes, requiring them to follow the contour of the ellipse. With each of the crescent areas equally divided, two equal, low-pressure volumes oppose each other, as do the high-pressure volumes, to provide hydraulic balance as rotation continues.

In either diagram, notice that the inboard end of each vane slot is in the shape of a teardrop. This permits the discharging oil to be channeled to the inboard end of the vanes to aid in their extension. Otherwise, the vanes, subjected only to centrifugal force, are prevented from fully extending because of the development of extreme pressures increasing oil viscosity and preventing the vanes from maintaining proper contact with the casing. If incomplete contact

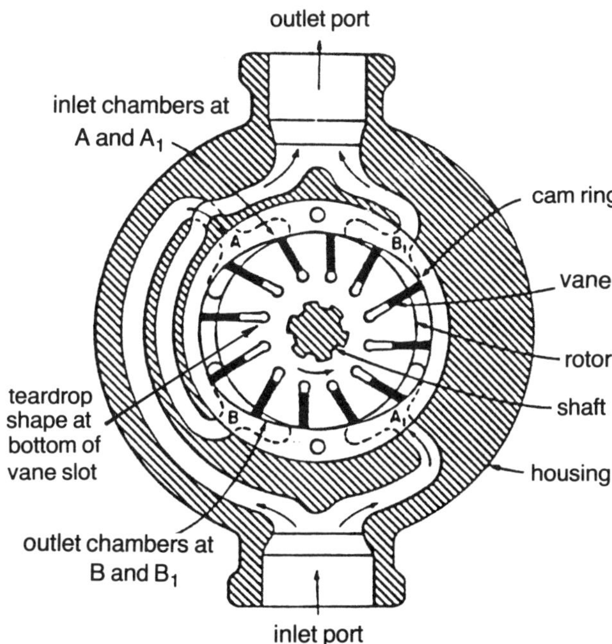

Fig. 3-8. Hydraulically balanced sliding vane pump

exists, the discharge flow rate is reduced, and the pump performance is severely inhibited.

While vane pumps produce flow rates greater than comparable size spur gear pumps, the discharge rates drop in response to increasing pressure gradients; i.e., the pressure increases because of the load-flow-rate increase.

Screw Pumps

The last group of rotary pumps is the screw. Two or three rotors are machined with low- or high-pitch threads respectively (Fig. 3-9). On the double-screw pump low-pitch threads are machined on each rotor, with left-handed threads on one-half of the rotor complementing right-handed threads on the other. With the areas of the major and minor diameters of the threads relatively wide and flat, close, accurate tolerances are achieved so that oil only occupies and flows within the areas created by the flanks of the threads.

As with the spur gear pump, one of the two rotors of the pump is directly driven while the other rotor becomes the idler driven. Because of the binding that may occur between the meshing of the low-pitch threads of this pump and the rotor, timing gears are used to ensure smooth rotation of the rotors. During rotation, oil flows from each end of the rotor toward their center. The flow always develops between the void created by the adjoining sets of threads and the casing. Because of the meshing of the rotors, oil cannot flow along this area of contact. These concepts are extremely important in that the screw pump's greatest advantage is to produce a nonpulsating, linear flow.

The triple-screw pump utilizes a central drive rotor that simultaneously rotates two idler rotors located on each side of the drive rotor. Although the threads on each rotor are left- and right-handed, as they were for the double-screw pump, the high pitch of these threads precludes the need for timing gears. The flow through the casing of the triple-screw pump is similar to the flow pattern for the double-screw pump. Again oil flows from both ends toward the center, in a nonpulsating, linear flow, with hydraulic end thrust eliminated.

Because of the deployment of both left- and right-handed threads on all of the rotors, suction occurs at both ends simultaneously, and discharges at the center of the pump. This prevents end thrust which

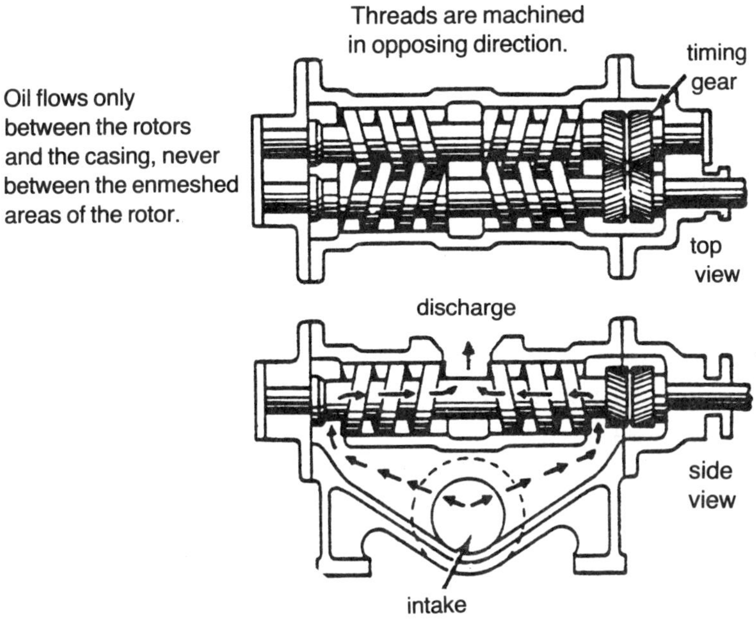

Threads are machined
in opposing direction.
timing
gear
Oil flows only
between the rotors
and the casing, never
between the enmeshed
areas of the rotor.
top
view
discharge
side
view
intake

Fig. 3-9A. Low-pitch, double-screw pump

intake
driven shaft
drive shaft
driven shaft
discharge

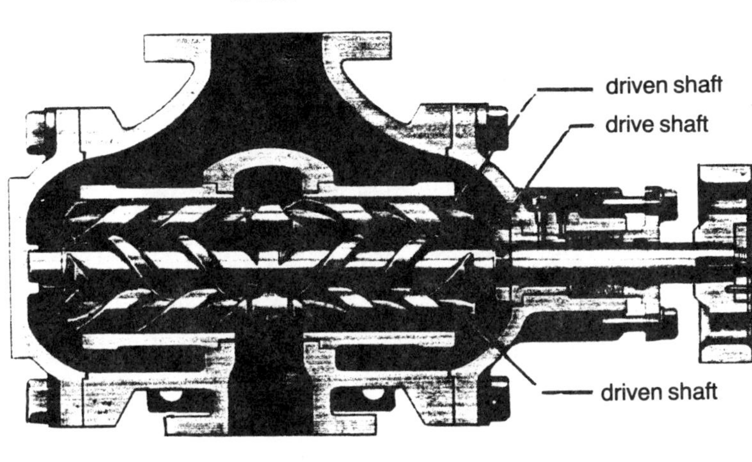

Fig. 3-9B. Hydraulically balanced, high-pitch, triple-screw pump

would result if the threads on each rotor were machined in the same continuous direction. Actually, there is a triple-screw pump in which the threads are machined in a continuous direction along the length of each rotor. In this pump, end thrust is absorbed by the use of a reaction plate installed at the low-pressure end of the rotors. It is necessary for the pump discharge to be led, via a small-diameter line, to the opposite side of the reaction plate, on which the rotor bearings are supported, in order to provide hydraulic balance for the pump.

While all three types of these screw pumps are considered to be of extremely high capacity, 350 to 500 gpm, the reaction-plate-balanced pump is reserved for a system in which the load pressures may be as high as 3,000 psi. The other two pumps are found in systems where the load pressures are less than 600 psi.

All of these rotary displacement pumps have a few concepts in common. First, they are used in constant flow systems, i.e., they will take suction from an oil reservoir and discharge to the system where the direction of oil flow is provided by directional control valves. Second, the vacuum created at the suction is limited to 10 inches of mercury. This seemingly low vacuum is adequate to provide sufficient suction lift. Yet, it also reduces the tendency for pump cavitation to develop, which can result from elevated oil temperatures accompanying a corresponding reduction in vapor pressure upon entering the pump casing. Third, the oil velocities associated with these pumps have the following recommended range limits:

suction velocities—2 to 4 feet per second
discharge velocities—7 to 20 feet per second

From a comparison of constant flow pumps, the physical diameter of the pump suction must be larger than that of the discharge. It is reasonable to consider that the quantity of oil entering the pump must equal the quantity being discharged. If the inlet-discharge port sizes are reversed, void areas, or gas pockets, can develop in the liquid passing through the pump. Upon entering the higher-pressure areas, the gasses will be compressed and rupture. As these gas bubbles rupture, they create pressures as high as 60,000 psi, forming pits on the surfaces of the rotating elements (a process known as cavitation).

Turbulence increases and impedes the otherwise smooth flow through the pump, adding to the operating time of the system. System efficiency drops, as more power is required to perform the same amount of work before this adverse condition was allowed to develop. Also, the energy normally imparted to the fluid exists as heat, and the pump efficiency drops, in turn, increasing the operating difficulties of the system.

Variable Displacement Pumps

Not all systems are adaptable to constant flow pumps. Certain systems require a relatively high flow rate, yet must not be adversely affected by instantaneous reversal in the direction of fluid flow that results in "water hammer." At elevated operating pressures, a variable capacity, reversible flow pump provides better operating characteristics. The following discussion deals with the more common variable displacement pump units: radial piston, axial piston, and bent axis piston.

Radial Piston Pumps

A radial piston pump is a device in which the pistons are positioned perpendicular to the drive shaft axis (Fig. 3-10). Since several manufacturers produce these pumps, the nomenclature of the parts vary widely, even though the overall operation for radial piston pumps is essentially the same. An attempt is made here to indicate the different terms, where applicable.

Internally mounted to the casing is a cylindrical-shaped device, fitted in line with the shaft, and drilled with four axial ports. This device, known as the central cylindrical valve (pintle), is provided with radial exit ports near each end of the main axial ports. These ports channel the flow of oil to and from the system. They also allow flow through the pintle to and from the pump cylinders.

Around the central cylindrical valve is fitted the cylinder body (cylinder block), which is driven by the prime mover. Machined with its cylinders perpendicular to the pintle, the cylinder ports pass through a plane, aligned with the axial ports of the pintle.

Pistons (plungers), fitted into each cylinder, may be attached to devices, known as slippers, by pins (otherwise, the pistons maintain contact with the reaction ring through centrifugal force). The slippers, in turn, are fitted into a circular slot, machined within the

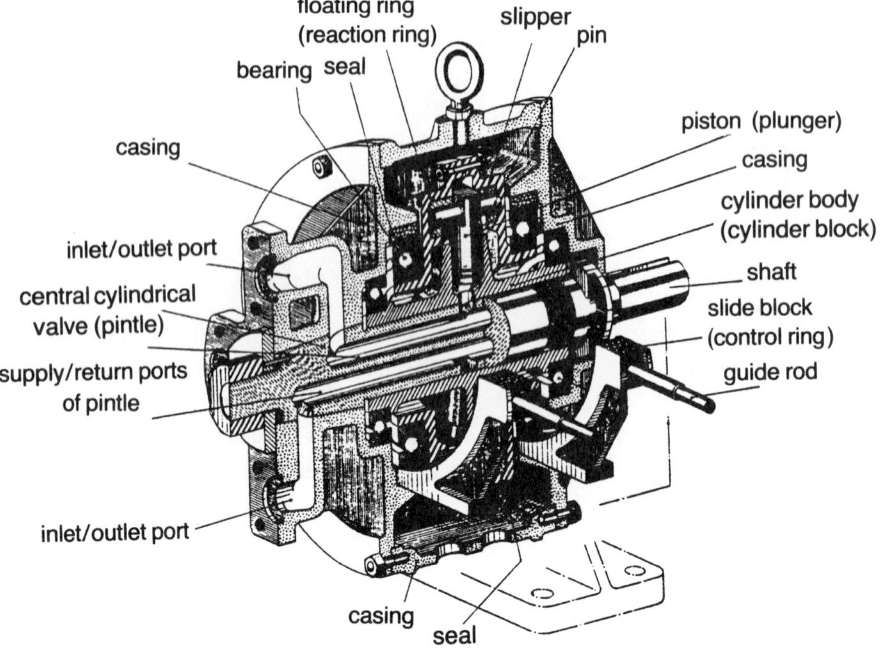

Fig. 3-10. Radial piston pump internal component arrangement

floating ring (reaction ring). The floating ring can be manipulated through the horizontal plane by an externally controlled device, known as the slide block (control ring).

The cylinder body, driven by the prime mover, rotates about the central cylindrical valve, forcing the pistons to rotate about this point as well. The outboard ends of the piston follow the contour of the floating ring groove because of the slippers (or centrifugal force). Central positioning of the ring, with regard to the central cylindrical valve, forces each of the pistons to be at neutral stroke within their respective cylinders. Hence, since no stroke of the pistons occurs, the flow to and from the pump is nonexistent (Fig. 3-11A).

To complete the explanation of this pump operation, consider the following conditions. The cylinder body rotates clockwise (Fig. 3-11B) and the slide block moves the floating ring to the left. Each piston passes the right-hand horizontal center of the pump as the cylinder body rotates. The pistons will now have travelled as close as possible to the pintle (Fig. 3-11C). As the cylinder openings pass over the lands (that separate the egress ports of the pintle), no flow

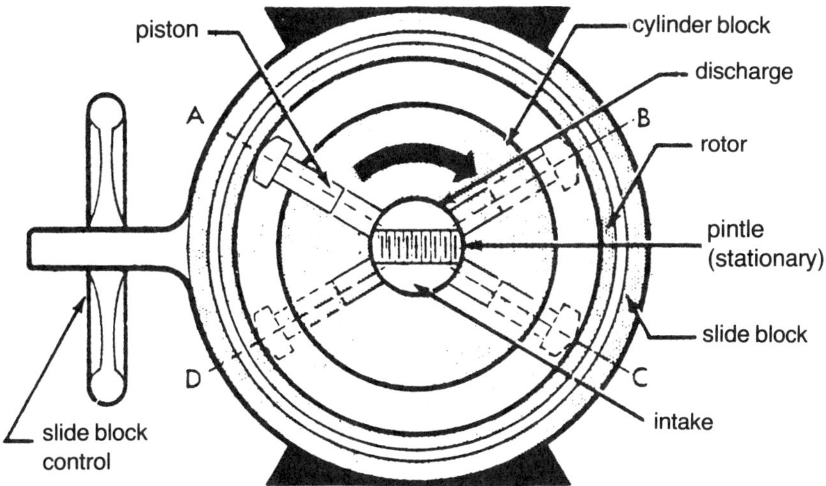

Fig. 3-11A. Diagrammatic representation of radial piston pump in neutral stroke—no flow operation

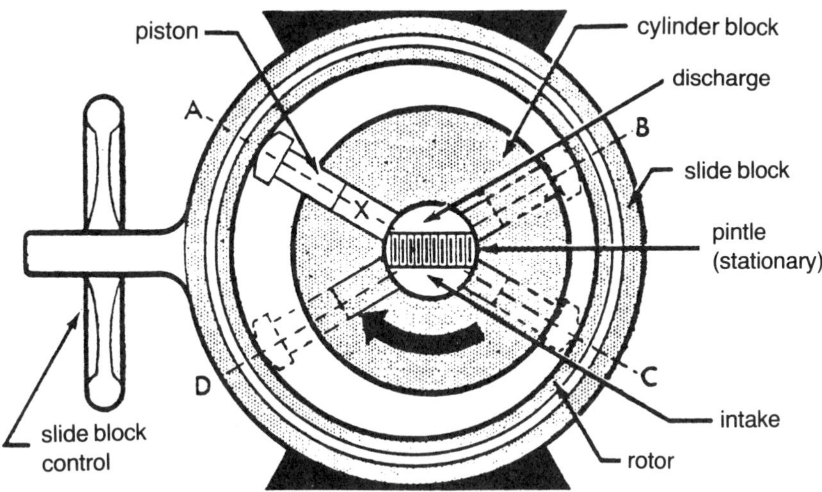

Fig. 3-11B. Diagrammatic representation of radial piston pump with control ring displaced to the left. As pistons rotate clockwise, pistons A and B are forced toward the center, discharging the oil in the cylinders.

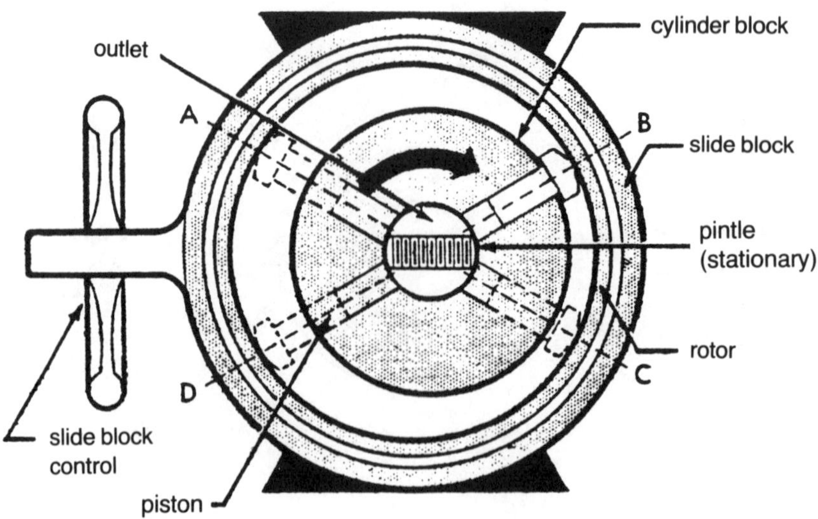

Fig. 3-11C. Diagrammatic representation of radial piston pump with pistons C and D moving away from the pintle and the cylinders filling with oil as the volume of the cylinders increases, producing a "low" pressure return

in or out of the cylinders occurs, as there is no relative piston movement, as well as no available opening between the pintle and the cylinders.

With the floating ring position still to the far left, the pistons move away from the pintle as rotation continues clockwise. This action results in a low-pressure condition developing within the cylinders, until the pistons reach the left-hand horizontal center. At this point, the pistons have moved as far from the pintle as possible. Continuing to rotate in the same direction, the pistons begin to move toward the pintle. This action creates a high-pressure condition in which the cylinder volumes become rapidly reduced. The established position of the floating ring causes oil to flow toward the lower half of the pump, and forces it to flow away from the upper half.

By moving the floating ring to the far right (Fig. 3-11D), the relative piston motion is exactly the opposite to that just described. The direction of oil flow, with respect to the pump, is reversed as well. It should also be understood that by varying the position of the ring between neutral (midstroke) and maximum displacement, the flow rate varies in proportion to any intermediate position selected. By varying the flow rate, the pressure of the system varies

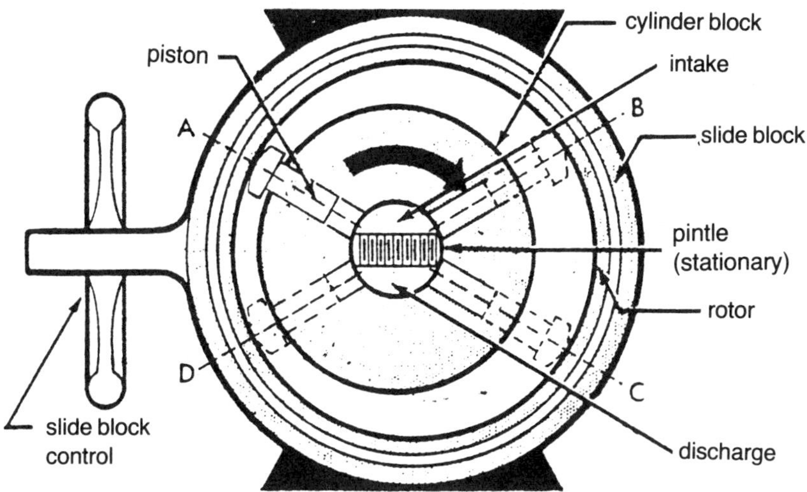

Fig. 3-11D. Diagrammatic representation of radial piston pump with control ring displaced to the right to change direction of flow with respect to the pump; the upper half of the pump now providing low-pressure return with the lower half producing high-pressure return

in proportion to any intermediate position of the floating ring, and the magnitude of the existing load.

As noted, all radial piston pumps do not require the use of the slipper method of maintaining the piston position with regard to the floating ring contour. Instead, centrifugal force, resulting from the high-speed rotation of the cylinder body, is sufficient for the pistons to maintain contact with the reaction ring. With this one exception, the operation of all radial piston pumps is the same as previously described.

Note that of the pumps discussed, pressurized oil flow to the load is *squeezed* from the internal rotating element of the pump. As long as the internal leakage is considered small, this condition is favorable from the standpoint that it maintains a continuous flow of oil across the components in motion. This condition is also true of radial piston pumps *except* when this pump is in neutral stroke. Then the leakage is insufficient to maintain adequate internal lubrication. Consequently, to be properly lubricated, this pump must be placed on stroke. This presents operational problems because the position of the load is changed when the pump is stroked for lubrication. Not only is the load position changed, but an operator is required to place the pump on stroke at regular intervals. The problem of lubrication, posed by the radial piston pump, does not exist with the axial piston pump. As a result, the radial piston pumps described are not frequently used with most modern, pressure-closed systems.

Axial Piston Pumps

The axial piston pump consists of a cylinder barrel driven by the prime mover with the cylinders machined parallel to the shaft (Fig. 3-12). The pistons are generally connected by ball and socket joints to the socket ring. This ring (or plate) is rotated by a universal joint incorporated with the shaft; so that as the ring rotates, it is also permitted to tilt. In order to control the tilt angle of the socket ring, the ring is fitted into the tilting box in a manner that permits the socket ring to rotate freely as the tilt angle changes. The tilting box is permitted to tilt, yet not rotate. This action is accomplished by the use of horizontal pins (or trunnions) pressed into the casing; so that the tilting box tilts without coming in contact with the shaft. External manipulation of the tilting box angle results in the same angle being transferred to the socket ring. A device, referred to as the valve plate, is fixed to the forward end of the casing. The valve plate, machined with semicircular grooves, separated by lands, to either side of the vertical centerline, is used to guide the flow to and from the pump.

To understand the operation of the pump, first consider that the top of the tilting box is positioned toward the valve plate. This action results in the crowns of the pistons assuming an angle similar to that of the tilting box, with respect to the valve plate (Fig. 3-13). By rotating the cylinder barrel clockwise (as viewed from the valve plate end), the pistons that pass across the left-hand semicircular groove are forced to move toward the valve plate. The pistons on the right-hand side are forced to move away from the valve plate, as the cylinder barrel rotates. Because of the relationship of the components, oil is forced to leave the pump on the left-hand side and return from the load on the right.

With the direction and speed of rotation of the cylinder barrel remaining constant, the tilting box angle changes to the perpendicular, with respect to the drive shaft centerline. All of the pistons are forced to move to their midstroke or neutral position within their

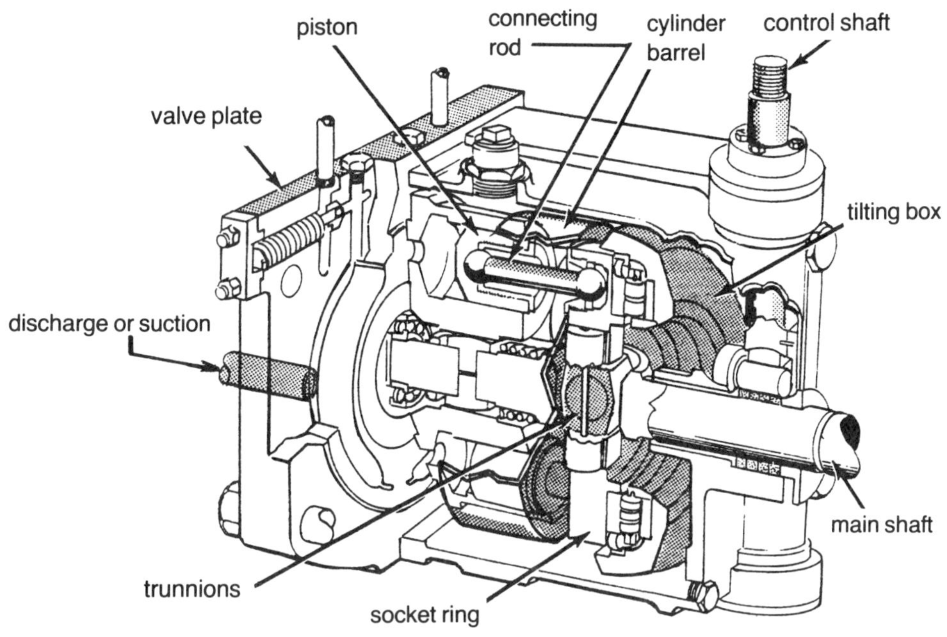

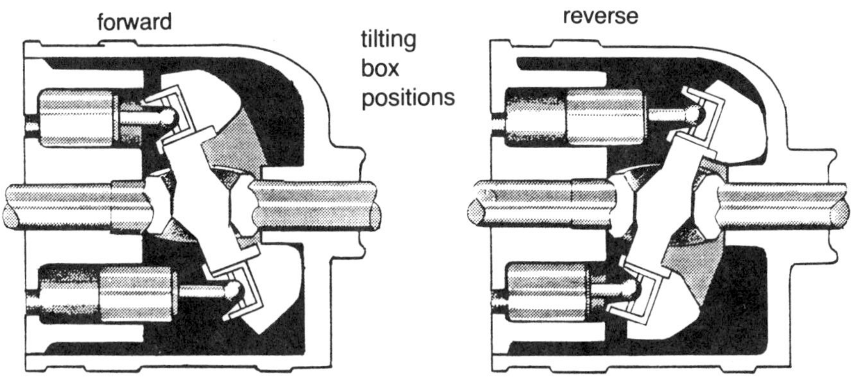

Fig. 3-12. Variable stroke, variable displacement, axial piston pumps

respective cylinders. This action eliminates reciprocation of the pistons, and zero flow exists at the tilting box angle. By changing the tilting box angle beyond zero stroke and away from the valve plate, the pistons develop an angle again with respect to that of the tilting box. The pistons, still following clockwise rotation, now recede from

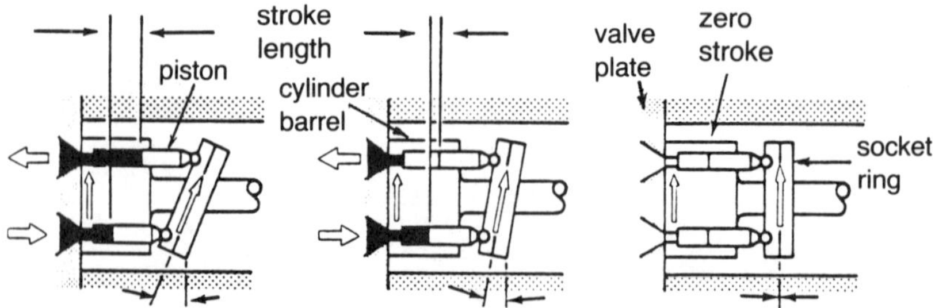

Fig. 3-13. Tilting of the tilting box with constant speed of rotation and direction of rotation to develop variable delivery (courtesy Vickers)

the valve plate on the left-hand side, and are forced toward the valve plate on the right-hand side. In other words, the direction of fluid flow is reversed by initiating a change in the angle of the tilting box opposite the original angle. By steepening the tilting box angle, piston stroke length is increased proportionally. The flow rate is also increased proportionally as the piston stroke increases.

A condition unique to the variable displacement pump is that seven, nine, or eleven pistons are used (Fig. 3-14). To explain why this is significant, consider an axial piston pump that is designed with eight pistons. At some point during the revolution of the cylinder barrel, two of the active pistons are located directly over the lands used to segregate the two semicircular grooves. As the pistons are at the extremes of their strokes, as well as not being aligned with either groove, the oil in the cylinders is unable to pass from the cylinder barrel. Therefore, only six of the eight cylinders are active at this instance.

As the cylinder barrel rotates a few degrees, the pistons that were positioned over the lands become aligned with their respective semicircular grooves. At the same time, the pistons that pass over the lands next have not as yet passed from the semicircular grooves. This means that all eight pistons are active at this instance. With the constant change from eight to six and back to eight active pistons, pulsations are developed by the pump. By reducing the number of pistons to seven, only one piston is always exposed to the lands.

When the number of pistons is reduced to seven, for example, the piston diameter is increased by one-tenth of an inch. This also

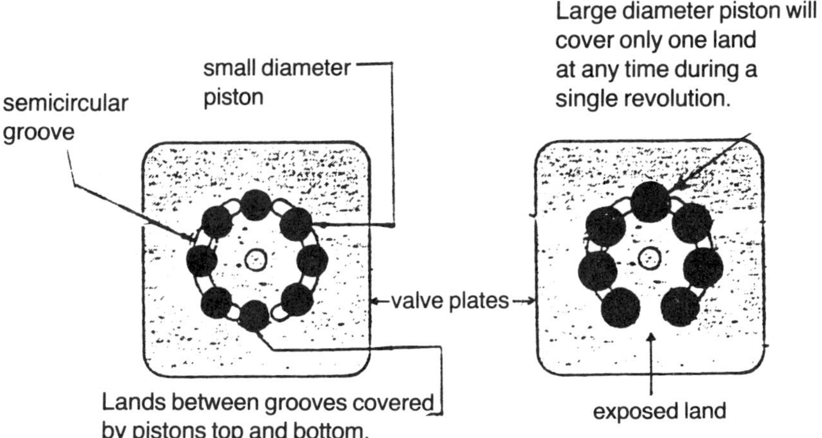

Fig. 3-14. Diagram showing the relationship of even numbered pistons versus the larger diameter odd numbered pistons to relate how capacity is affected as rotation occurs relative to the valve plate of an axial piston pump

means that the capacity of the pump is increased. For comparison, the pump stroke is held at a maximum of 1.25 inches.

Initially, the eight one-inch pistons are found to produce a displacement of 7.85 cubic inches per revolution. Since it has already been stipulated that an average of two pistons cease to discharge during one revolution, the effective discharge is six cubic inches per revolution.

Likewise, the pump with seven 1.1-inch-diameter pistons has a theoretical displacement of 8.3 cubic inches, with one of these pistons effectively lost during discharge. By subtracting the displacement of the lost piston from the total displacement, the displacement of the remaining six pistons is 7.4 cubic inches per revolution. Therefore, the capacity of the pump is improved by using an odd number of pistons.

As previously stated, regardless of the length of the pump stroke, lubrication of all internal parts is possible. First, you should realize that to have proper lubrication, continuous flow of the lubricant must exist. The construction of the radial piston pump floating ring, at neutral stroke, prevents the continuous flow of oil, because of the design of the floating ring. On the other hand, the axial piston pump produces an entirely different lubricating condition.

Within the axial piston pump, the flat face of the cylinder barrel is forced against the grooved side of the valve plate in order to provide the required seal. As oil pressure rises in the system, the interface gap between the cylinder barrel and valve plate increases by a few ten-thousandths of an inch. With oil flow present across the gap, a hydrodynamic wedge forms to prevent the rubbing of these surfaces during rotation. With the pump on stroke, and flow occurring through the pump, a minor, but continuous, flow develops across this interface. The question arises as to what happens when the pump is placed in neutral stroke.

First, it is necessary to eradicate an erroneous assumption. When the pump stroke is increased, the system high side pressure increases (the system pressure will be higher on the side provided with flow, while the side returning oil simultaneously to the other side of the pump will be the return or low side). Thus, you may have assumed that at neutral stroke, zero pressure simultaneously results on both sides of the pump. However, at neutral stroke, the pressures on both sides of the pump are merely equal, and should be expected to be no less than 100 psi in any pressure-closed system. Consequently, the pressure gradient across the components to the casing is sufficient to maintain a minimal continual leak-off between the cylinder barrel and valve plate. The leak-off collects in the casing, and must be permitted to drain into the service tank. If the oil is only allowed to collect in the casing, it will eventually become heated and churned to the point where lubrication will still not be available.

Even though the leak-off is an intrinsically desirable condition, it must also be considered as an internal leak for the system. If allowed to continue unchecked, the system will lose enough oil so that it is no longer operating properly. In most modern, pressure-closed systems, a constant flow replenishing pump is provided automatically to force oil back into the main system, to compensate for the leak-off.

Bent Axis Pump

The third type of variable displacement pump is that of the bent axis (Fig. 3-15). In the construction and assembly of the axial piston pump, the socket ring/tilting box are physically limited as to how far they can tilt; otherwise, the tilting box will rub on the rotating shaft. In the construction of the bent axis pump, the socket ring is

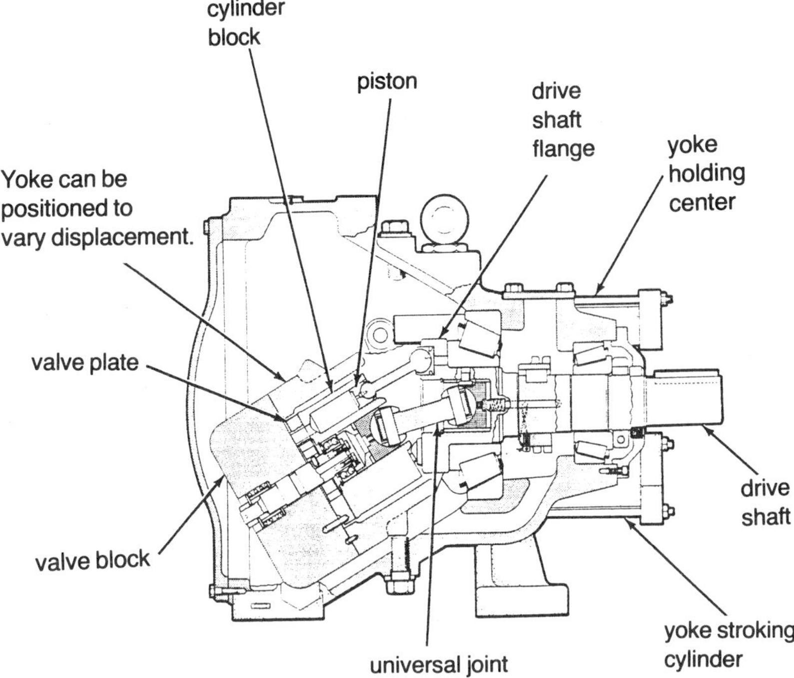

Fig. 3-15. Bent axis, variable displacement, variable stroke pump (courtesy Vickers)

replaced by a device which maintains a permanent perpendicularity with the shaft. By the use of a universal joint, the entire cylinder barrel is pivoted through the horizontal plane to develop the piston stroke. By changing the angle of the barrel, with respect to the shaft axis, the stroking of the pistons is achieved. By *swinging* the cylinder barrel, a greater angle of deflection can be developed than that of the axial piston pump tilting box. Therefore, displacement of a bent axis pump, with the same rotational speed, piston diameter, and the number of pistons provides a greater discharge rate than that of a comparable axial piston pump.

Hydraulic Motors

Thus far, prime consideration has been given to the imparting of energy to a device in order to establish flow. In the field of electricity, the flow of electrical current is induced by rotating a wire coil, such as a wire-wound rotor, through a magnetic field. While this device is known as a generator, its function is to pump electric current through the system. Similarly, when electricity is passed through a wire-wound rotor, mounted in a magnetic field, the interaction will produce rotation of the rotor, and represents a simple description of an electric motor.

In the field of hydraulics, parallel conditions exist. Fluid flow through the system is established by a pump, driven by a prime mover. However, if fluid flow is provided to an element, physically similar to that of a pump, rotation of that device develops. Thus, any device which accepts the energy, transported by liquid flow, to develop rotation, is considered to be a hydraulic motor or a rotary actuator.

Although the theoretical difference between a pump and a motor is relatively simple, the physical differences are somewhat more involved (Fig. 3-16). It is theoretically possible to take any one of the pump elements previously described and use it as a hydraulic motor. Despite this contention, the following discussion will center on the vane and axial piston type motors.

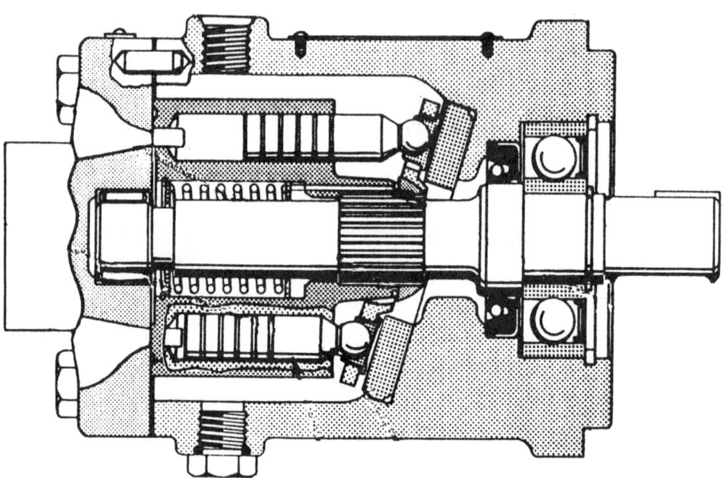

Fig. 3-16. Noncompensated, fixed displacement, axial piston motor

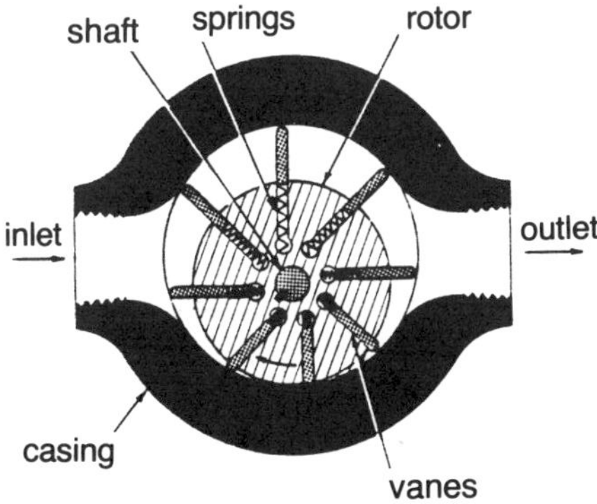

Fig. 3-17. Sliding vane hydraulic motor with spring-loaded vanes

The Vane Motor

Recall the physical makeup of a vane pump. The basic idea of using this device as a motor is to allow the oil to flow into the casing, through what has been the discharge port (Fig. 3-17). As oil flows among the set of vanes, the resulting force causes the vanes to move away from the source of flow. Rotation continues because each vane length is different, and a force differential develops. The reactive force transfers to the slotted rotor, which responds with rotation of the shaft.

As rotation proceeds, the crescent inlet area increases in width. The vanes continue to extend, and as the surface area of each vane increases, the potential energy of the flow input exerted on the vanes is diminished. Although the fluid pressure drops, the increase in exposed area of the vanes yields an effective force, approximating the force that was initially developed when the oil first began to enter the motor casing.

In order for rotation to continue, each vane must be able to seal off its chamber. Once rotation has been established, centrifugal force keeps the vanes in contact with the casing. [The only problem that exists is determining what causes the vanes to initially extend.] Recall that high speed rotation of the pump rotor resulted in centrifugal force being transferred to the vanes and forced them to extend and maintain contact with the casing.

In the vane motor, however, gravity allows the vanes at the top of the motor to slide back into their slots. If the oil flow to the motor were to occur with any of the vanes retracted, the oil will merely bypass the vanes. As a result, the oil flows directly to the exhaust without rotation of the motor being developed.

One solution to this problem is to install springs at the bottom of the vane slots to keep them in contact with the casing. Once rotating speed picks up, centrifugal force, plus oil under pressure also being fed to the bottom edge of the vanes, force them to maintain casing contact. Once rotation has been insured, the various operating characteristics of the motor can be predicted, such as rpm, torque, etc.

As stated previously, speed of actuation of any actuator, whether linear or rotary (hydraulic motor), is dependent upon the flow rate to the actuator. The motors operate for longer durations than the linear actuators, because the operation is limited by the length of the cylinder. Therefore, it is equally important to determine the ability of the motor to exhaust the oil, i.e., determine its displacement.

For example, the pump supplying fluid flow to the motor has a 5 gpm discharge rate. The exhaust of the motor is equipped with a valve that can be throttled to limit the exhaust to 1 gpm. The effective speed of the motor, therefore, is proportional to the exhausting of the 1 gpm, since this represents the current ability to pass oil across the motor.

When the motor displacement is known, i.e., the number of cubic inches of oil required to develop one complete revolution, multiplying that factor by the effective flow rate yields the current rpm. Although the motor speed had been decreased by throttling the exhaust, resistance to the input flow has increased the supply pressure. In addition, the total force on the vane translates into increased torque.

Generally speaking, the application of the vane motor is limited to low torque, high speed conditions. For conditions other than this, the size and weight of the vane motor is extreme and, therefore, its application limited. Usually, piston motors are more frequently used, where the size and weight of a vane motor is unsatisfactory.

The Axial Piston Motor

Physically, an axial piston motor is not significantly different from its counterpart, the axial piston pump (Fig. 3-18). The major physical difference, for a constant displacement motor of this type, is that a swash plate replaces the tilting box. The swash plate is a fixed, angled

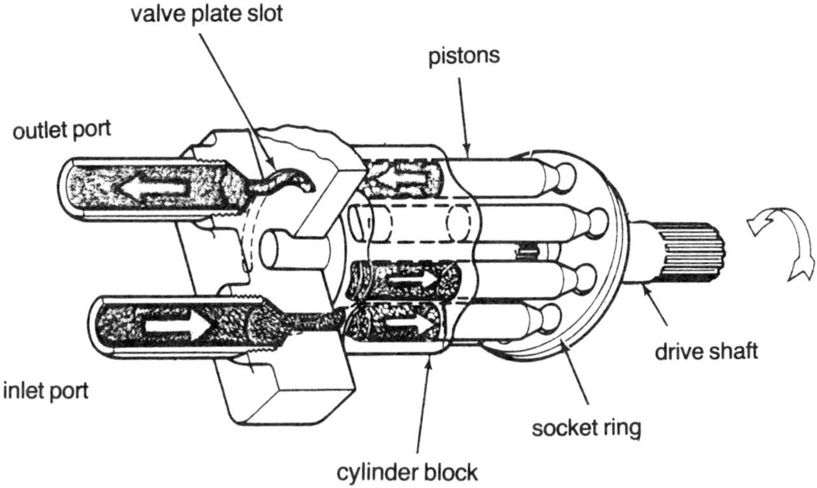

Fig. 3-18. Fixed displacement axial piston motor

wedge on which the socket ring rotates, similar to the function provided by the tilting box. With the swash plate angle fixed, the top of the socket ring will be farthest from the valve plate; therefore, the pistons are fixed at full stroke. With the piston displacement being fixed, a constant flow rate across the motor will yield a constant output speed of the shaft. Only by varying the flow rate is the motor speed changed.

To understand the operation of this motor, consider that oil flow, under pressure, occurs in the left-hand portion of the valve plate (as the motor is viewed from the valve plate end). As the oil passes into the left-hand semicircular groove, it is distributed to fill all of the cylinders currently in position with that groove. The piston, nearest the bottom of the casing, is physically closest to the valve plate.

As oil fills the cylinder, force is exerted at a right angle to each of the piston crowns. Since this force reacts in a plane parallel to the axis of the piston, the piston is forced toward the swash plate. As the piston moves away from the flow, it is also forced to follow the inclined plane. Therefore, the piston not only moves away from the established flow, but must also move up. Since all the pistons are confined to the cylinder barrel, each piston is forced to follow the path of that semicircle. As the pistons move up, rotation of the barrel develops in a clockwise direction.

As the pistons pass the upper land, further rotation of the cylinder barrel forces them to rotate toward the bottom land, and move toward the valve plate. This action causes each piston to empty its cylinder, so that as the pistons pass the bottom land, each is able to accept additional oil flow and continue the cycle.

By reversing the direction of oil flow to the motor, the right side of the valve plate receives the flow. The pistons on the right are forced to move toward the swash plate. As before, they must now move toward the top of the motor as they follow the incline, producing counterclockwise rotation.

By controlling the flow rate, and the direction of flow to the motor, the motor speed and direction of rotation are controlled. Therefore, the simplest power unit is the combination of the capabilities of an axial piston variable-reversible flow pump with that of a fixed displacement axial piston motor.

You might ask, why not use the variable-reversible flow pump as the motor and the fixed displacement motor as the pump? To answer this question, take a look at a system where this has been arranged (Fig. 3-19A).

As you see, the hydraulic motor shaft is fitted with a wire rope drum. The wire rope is reeved through a set of blocks on an angled boom in order to raise and lower a load. By varying the angle of the motor tilting box, the speed of rotation will be affected. Although there is no doubt that speed change by this method results, there may also be some unsuspected conditions that need to be pointed out.

When the tilting box angle of the motor is increased from neutral stroke, the motor rotates. Placing the motor tilting box back in neutral stroke stops the motor rotation, but suspends the load in midair. Keep in mind that all of the pistons are now equidistant from the valve plate.

A major problem is now created, for this alignment is the same as if the pistons were replaced by a smooth surface disk, perpendicularly fixed to the shaft. Gravitational force, acting on the load at the end of the wire rope, is transferred through the wire rope, to the drum and along the motor shaft, to rotate the cylinder barrel. Despite the availability of the pressurized oil flow acting on the pistons, aligned as a flat disk, the oil cannot hydraulically lock the pistons in place. This would permit the cylinder barrel to slip, and the load to fall. When the power unit is arranged so that the pump tilting

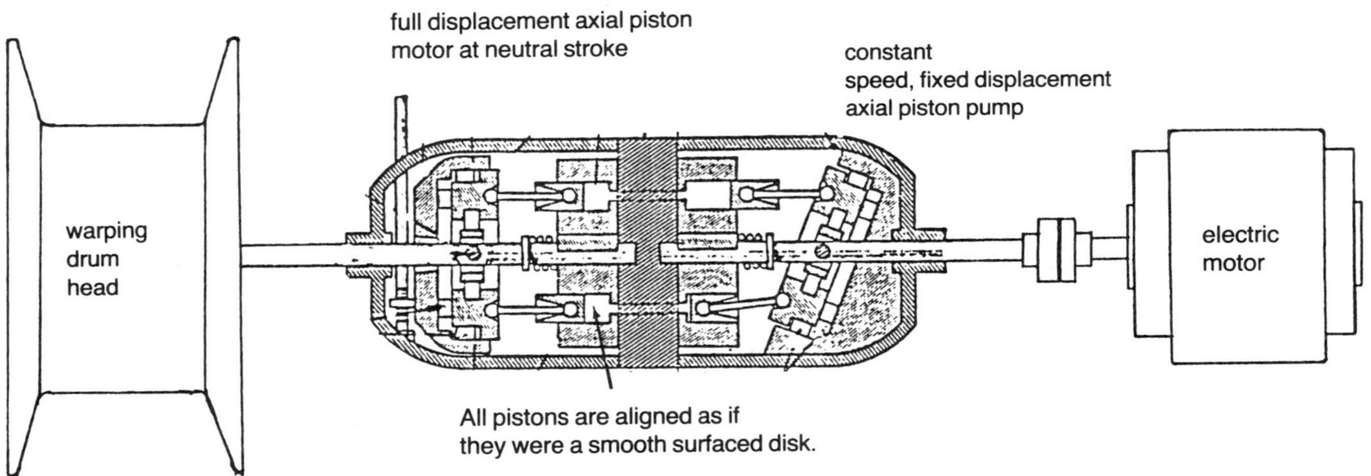

Fig. 3-19A. Hydraulic motor/pump combination showing fixed displacement pump attempting to drive a fully variable displacement motor. Despite motor rotation being stopped with the motor at neutral stroke, the pistons are aligned as though they were a flat disk. The pressurized oil flow from the pump cannot develop sufficient fluid friction to prevent the load, affected by gravity, from allowing the cylinder barrel to rotate and permit the load to drop.

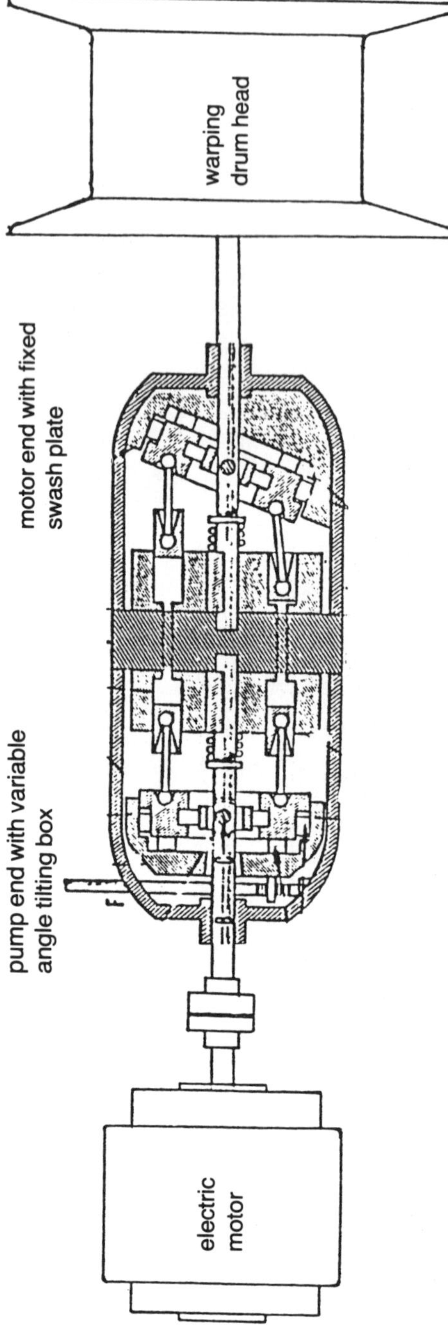

Fig. 3-19B. Hydraulic pump/motor combination, where the pump stroke is varied. When the pump tilting box is modulated, to control flow rate and the direction of flow, the motor end will be prevented from rotation by the hydraulic lock created when the tilting box is placed in neutral stroke.

box is varied and the motor displacement fixed, the control becomes more positive (Fig. 3-19B). As the pump is placed on stroke, flow from the pump is directed to one side of the motor to rotate it in the direction necessary to lift the load. When the tilting box angle is decreased, the motor speed is slowed in proportion to the tilting box angle and the flow rate of the pump. When finally placed at zero stroke, the motor stops.

Compare the pump piston position with that previously described for the motor. The pump pistons now present a flat disk perpendicular to the shaft axis, just as the pistons of the motor had been in the previous example. However, as gravity attempts to pull the load down, the motor pistons attempt to force oil to flow toward the pump. The pump pistons are unable to accept any flow, as they are all aligned in a vertical plane. As no flow can exist between the motor and the pump, the motor pistons are only able to develop an increase in hydrostatic pressure, proportional to the load. Most important, the load remains hydraulically locked in place.

Therefore, controlling the direction of rotation of the motor by the use of a reversible angle motor tilting box is impractical, as well as dangerous. The control of the motor's speed (zero to maximum rpm) is also considered as impractical by the manipulation of the motor tilting box. To understand this, first consider that the tilting box angle is zero; therefore, no reciprocation of the motor pistons occurs. As the angle of the theoretical tilting box is increased just beyond neutral stroke, the motor begins to rotate.

Because of the shallow angle of the tilting box, the length of the piston stroke is extremely short. Therefore, the volume of each cylinder to be filled by the entering oil will occur at a very rapid rate. This means that rapid reciprocation of the pistons will yield high-speed rotation. If the tilting box angle is increased, the piston stroke length is increased, and the volume of the cylinders is also increased. If the flow rate to the motor remains constant, the time required to complete the stroke is increased, accompanied by a decrease in the rotational speed of the motor, and contrary to what would be expected.

Motor Pressure Compensation

While the results of the motor tilting box control produce speeds contrary to expected reactions, it does not mean that a variable angle tilting box motor is never used. At first, this statement may appear to contradict the previous discussion. However, keep in mind that when a motor with a variable angle tilting box is used, placing the tilting box angle at zero will not only create a zero rotational speed, but will also permit the load to rotate the cylinder barrel. Therefore, a permanent minimum angle is physically imposed on the motor tilting box.

For example, consider that a two-degree angle results in a piston displacement, so that 2.3 cubic inches of oil flow produces one revolution. With a 10-gpm flow rate provided to the motor, the rotating speed of the motor is 1,000 rpm. Mathematically, this can be represented as:

$$\text{rpm} = \frac{10\,\dfrac{\text{gal}}{\text{min}} \times 231\,\dfrac{\text{in}^3}{\text{gal}}}{2.3\,\dfrac{\text{in}^3}{\text{rev}}} = \frac{2310\,\dfrac{\text{in}^3}{\text{min}}}{2.3\,\dfrac{\text{in}^3}{\text{rev}}} = 1000\,\frac{\text{rev}}{\text{min}}$$

When the tilting box angle of this motor is increased to maximum, a displacement of 10 cubic inches of oil rotates the motor one revolution. The motor rpm at this angle, with a 10-gpm pump flow rate, is:

$$\text{rpm} = \frac{10\,\dfrac{\text{gal}}{\text{min}} \times 231\,\dfrac{\text{in}^3}{\text{gal}}}{10\,\dfrac{\text{in}^3}{\text{rev}}} = \frac{2310\,\dfrac{\text{in}^3}{\text{min}}}{10\,\dfrac{\text{in}^3}{\text{rev}}} = 231\,\frac{\text{rev}}{\text{min}}$$

As you can see, the motor speed drops from 1,000 rpm to 231 rpm as the angle of the tilting box is increased.

At first, this concept may not be easily accepted. For initially, you learned that by increasing the angle of the pump tilting box, the flow rate from the pump increases. Thus, with an increased flow rate to the motor, the motor rotational speed will increase. Now, when the motor tilting box angle is increased, the motor speed drops off.

The explanation is very simple, and by reviewing the two previous calculations, it is easy to see why. Recall, also, the relationship of the tilting box angle of the motor and its relationship to speed.

First, consider the hydraulic horsepower for the current pump output. If the pump produces a flow rate to the motor of 10 gpm at 2,000 psi, the hydraulic horsepower is calculated as follows:

$$\text{hp} = \frac{10 \text{ gpm} \times 2{,}000 \text{ psi}}{1{,}714} = \frac{20{,}000}{1{,}714} = 11.7 \text{ hp}$$

Now the torque produced is calculated at the two previously calculated speeds. First, high speed:

$$\text{torque} = \frac{63{,}025 \times 11.7}{1{,}000} = \frac{737{,}392.5}{1{,}000} = 737.4 \text{ in-lbs}$$

Follow the same procedure for the low speed condition:

$$\text{torque} = \frac{63{,}025 \times 11.7}{1{,}000} = \frac{737{,}392.5}{231} = 3{,}129.2 \text{ in-lbs}$$

Mathematically, you have seen that when a constant flow rate is maintained to the motor, manipulation of the motor tilting box angle changes not only the speed but the available torque as well. In addition, the calculations show that the available torque changes inversely with the speed. Rule of thumb: *as the motor speed is decreased, the torque is increased, as long as the flow rate and pressure are not changed.*

In certain systems, this concept is useful, e.g., when a high motor speed is initially desired to take the slack out of a line used to haul up a load. Then, an increase in torque can be automatically provided to continue to raise the load, without stalling the motor.

It is obvious that the operator can make the necessary tilting box angle adjustment to compensate for the wide range of operating loads. However, extreme over- and under-compensation can result. Consequently, an automatic motor compensator is used to accomplish this task, as load variations occur.

You've already seen that by increasing the angle of the motor tilting box, the speed of rotation decreases with a proportional increase in torque. All you need to do, then, is to provide some device that reacts automatically to changes in the load to give you the required speed-torque relationship as the load increases.

For the discussion, an axial piston type motor with a tilting box is used. Also, the tilting box has a minimum angle that is never decreased less than two degrees from the vertical (Fig. 3-20). A small linear actuator is positioned, with respect to the tilting box, so that its angle will be increased as the actuator extends. Oil flow to this compensating actuator is manipulated, so that as oil flow under pressure to the motor increases, the compensating actuator extends proportionally, causing the tilting box angle to increase.

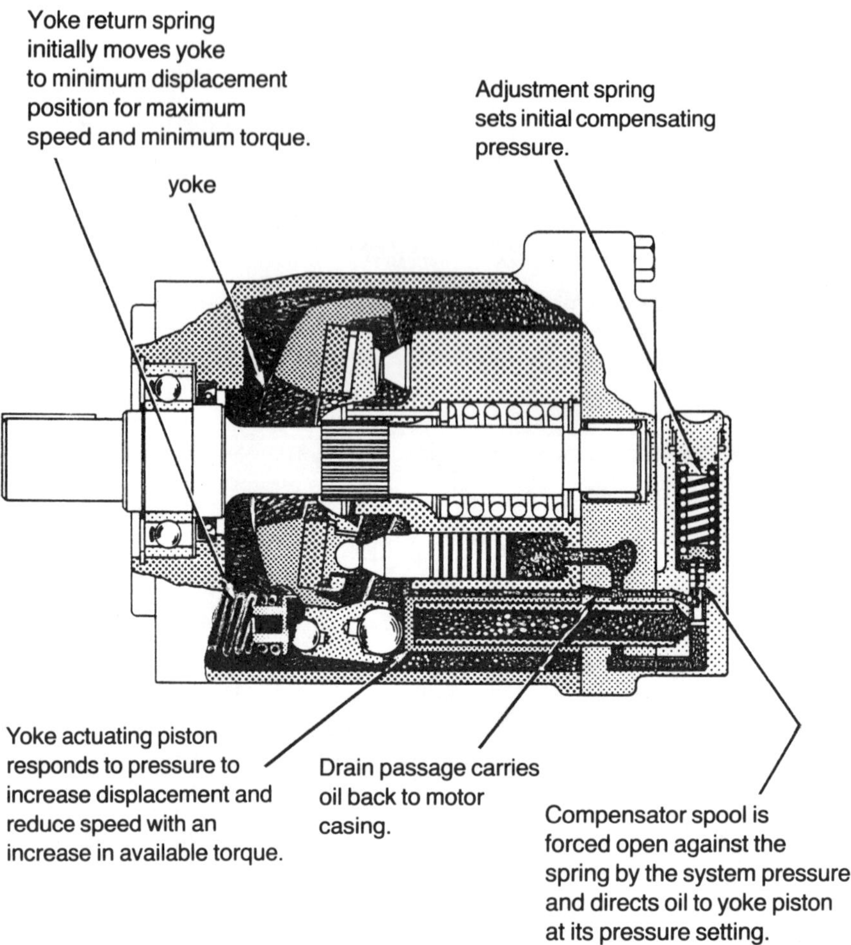

Fig. 3-20. Axial piston type motor equipped with pressure compensator. Actuation of the compensator will increase tilting box angle to reduce rotational speed and increase torque.

One method used to control the supply of oil to the compensating actuator is the use of a spring-loaded, hydraulically piloted spool valve. A high-pressure port is provided from the main oil supply when the motor is rotated to haul in the load. As load on the motor increases, resistance to rotation also increases. This increased resistance causes the steady high flow rate of the pump to increase in pressure. The compensating spool valve shifts to admit more oil to the compensating actuator. Simultaneously, the quantity of oil bled from the actuator is diminished. As oil pressure to the actuator increases, the actuator is forced to extend; and the angle of the tilting box increases. As previously explained, the speed drops with higher torque available to handle the load.

Conversely, as the load decreases, resistance to rotation also decreases. The ability to increase flow rate across the motor results in a drop in high side pressure. The reduction in pressure permits the compensating spool valve to be shifted downward by the spring. This action permits oil to bleed off from the compensating actuator, allowing the pressure in the actuator to decrease. The tilting box return spring reduces the angle and allows the speed to increase, and the torque to be reduced.

Pump Pressure Compensation

Up to this point, three conditions have been related to the control of the hydraulic motor system:

1. motor speed range
2. direction of rotation
3. pressure compensation for torque control

One last control system is considered, i.e., pressure compensation of the pump. This is done in order to limit excessive power demands on the prime mover while the system is operated under extreme load conditions.

One method currently employed is similar to that utilized for motor pressure compensation. The main difference between these two systems is that the tilting box angle will be steep when oil pressure to the compensating device is relatively low (Fig. 3-21).

Again, as high side pressure increases with load, the piloted spring loaded spool valve shifts against its compression spring. This action admits more oil to the compensating actuator than is allowed to bleed off. As the actuator is forced to extend, the tilting box angle decreases, reducing the length of piston stroke. Following this action, the pump flow rate is reduced. The oil pressure to the high side of the system is reduced proportionally until a balance is achieved between the hydraulic pressure (a function of load) shifting of the compensating spool valve and the compression of its spring. A reduction in resistance to oil flow reduces high side pressure, and the previous actions are reversed to allow the pump to resume its designated flow rate.

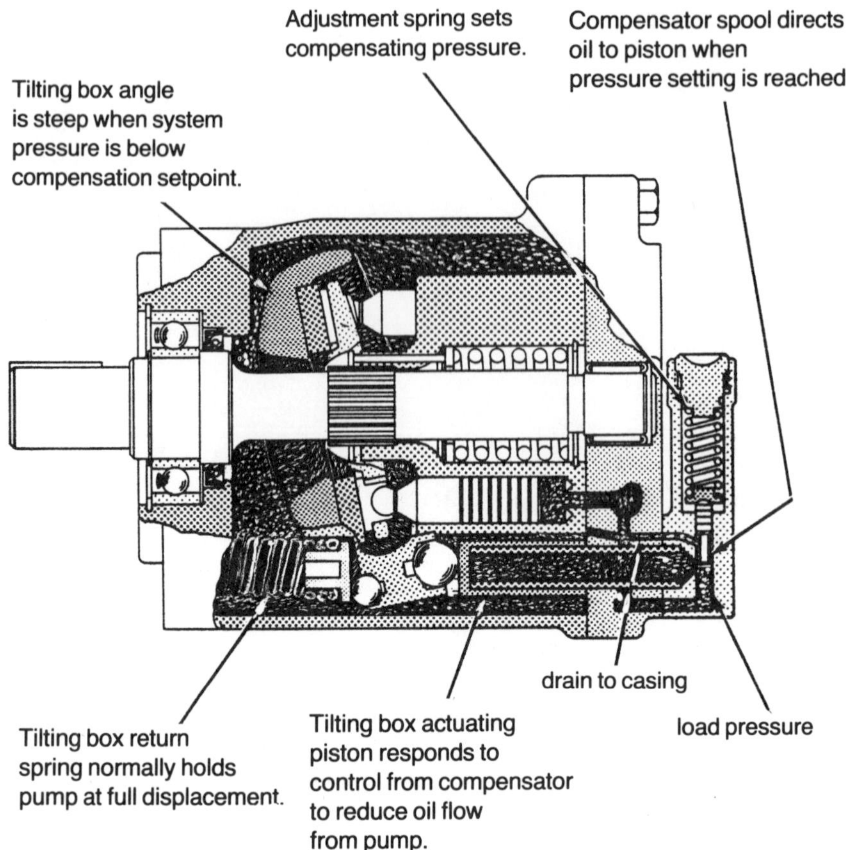

Fig. 3-21. Axial piston pump equipped with pressure compensator

Torque Motors

As you have just seen, compensating hydraulic motors are needed to adjust the torque to load conditions. Other motors are needed where high torque is required to be maintained under all loads (Fig. 3-22). These devices, referred to as limited rotation torque motors, are not required to develop high speeds; therefore, overall size is not a prime limiting factor.

The Vane Torque Motor

The vane torque motor is a relatively simple device. A small diameter concentric rotor is positioned in the geometric center of the larger

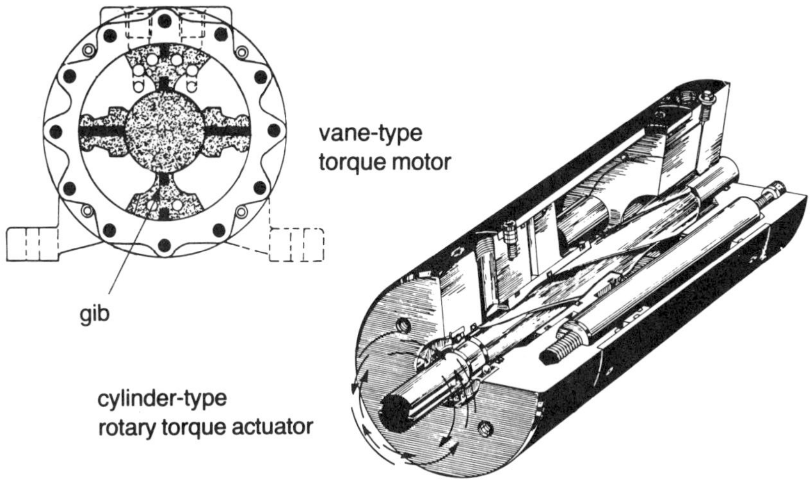

Fig. 3-22. Vane and piston type torque motors

bore concentric casing. Vanes, permanently fixed to the rotor, are designed to maintain a close clearance with the casing, by the use of sealing "gibs," in order to develop specific internal chambers. The large surface area of the vanes permits oil pressure to be transferred as a force perpendicular to the center of rotation. The motor casing is ported, or channeled, so that complementary sides of each vane are exposed to high-pressure oil, while the opposite sides are relieved of oil. The generated pressure differential across the vanes promotes rotation. Therefore, when oil at equal pressure is present on both sides of the same vane, the rotor will be hydraulically locked in place.

The Internally Opposed Torque Motor

The second torque motor is vastly different from the vane type. Internally opposed pistons are fitted in a long narrow cylinder, and are not permitted to rotate. Exiting each end of the cylinder is a transfer axle, machined with external helical threads on the interior ends. Around each interior end the hollow piston is fitted, machined internally with complementary helical threads. The cap ends of these pistons are therefore opposed to each other. As oil under pressure enters the void between the two pistons, the outboard side of each piston is simultaneously bled of oil. Linear internal guides prevent the pistons from rotating as they move away from each other. The linear movement of the pistons produces rotation of the axles as a result of the interaction of the mating helical threads.

With the cylinder secured, the axles at each end rotate independently as the pistons continue to move away from each other. Reverse rotation is developed when high-pressure oil, acting on the outboard side of the pistons, forces the pistons to move toward each other as the center is bled of oil.

CHAPTER 4

LINEAR ACTUATORS

Although the motor (rotary actuator) is used in many hydraulic systems, the piston-cylinder unit, or linear actuator, is the workhorse in the majority of these systems (Fig. 4-1). Generally, actuators fall into three categories:

1. the ram
2. the differential piston
3. the telescoping

The Ram Actuator

Although the term "ram" can be applied to almost any linear actuator, it is differentiated from the piston type in that it is virtually the same diameter throughout its length. Since oil under pressure acts on only one side of the ram, hydraulic systems of this type are considered only to produce *push*. To retract a ram, another cylinder needs to be installed on the other end, or gravity retraction has to be employed where the rams are installed vertically. Rams are used where extreme load conditions and side thrust present operational problems to the system.

The Differential Piston Actuator

The most common type of linear actuator in use is the double-acting differential area piston. The cylinder bodies for these actuators are either solid, bored forgings, or are built up from standardized components. While the solid type of construction presents fewer long-term leakage problems, its universality is very limited. Although

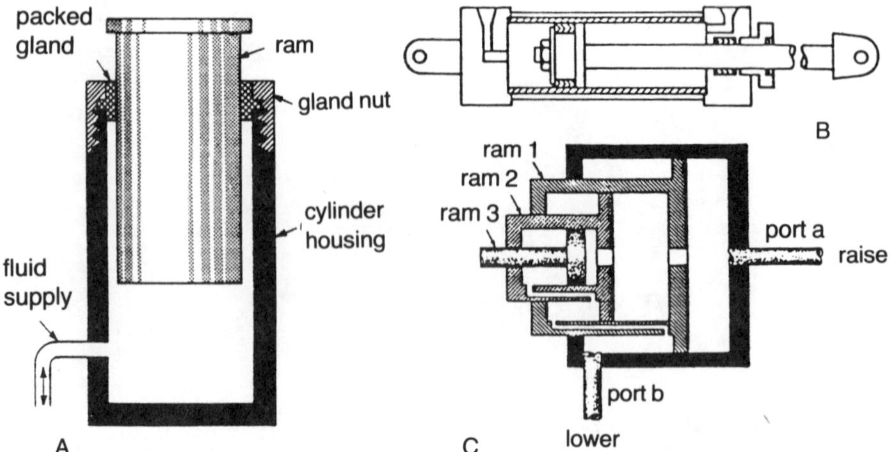

Fig. 4-1. Major types of linear actuators: (A) ram type (B) piston/cylinder type (C) telescoping type

suitable for more rugged use than the built-up cylinder, it must be designed for a specific use.

The built-up type, on the other hand, is composed of individual components that can be assembled in any number of configurations to satisfy design considerations. Also, if any of the individual components sustains major damage it can be replaced, rather than the entire unit having to be replaced (Fig. 4-2).

Essentially, the cylinder or tube is fitted with a piston, whose rod is screwed or bolted to the piston. End caps are installed on the tube ends, with suitable seals, and are fixed in place by stay or tie rods.

Notably, the end caps, for either the rod or cap, provide the flexibility of both construction and installation. While there are many installation combinations of trunnions, clevises, and control devices, only the basic concepts are discussed below.

Trunnions are large diameter pins, used where extensive forces are to be encountered. They permit the limited pivoting of the cylinder during its extension-retraction operation.

Clevises are fork and blade devices. They are installed at either end of the cylinder to provide attachment to the load, and flexibility of movement during extension-retraction, such as pivoting or sway.

The end caps may be equipped with devices that decelerate or cushion the piston as it reaches the end of its stroke (Fig. 4-3). The basic idea is to reduce piston speed, i.e., inertia, as the piston ap-

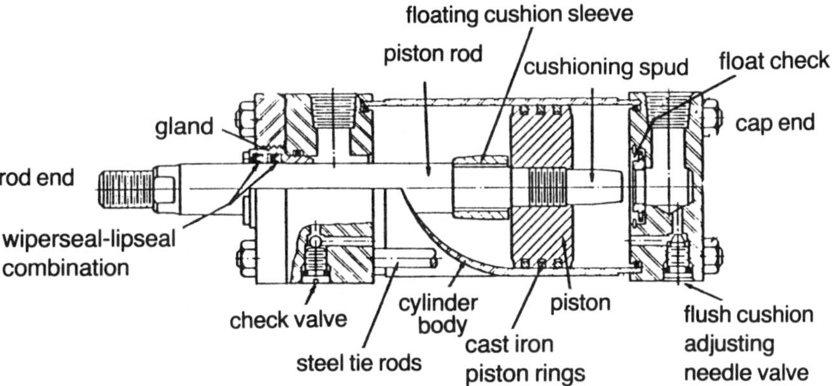

Fig. 4-2. Fully assembled, or built up, linear actuator

proaches the end of its stroke. To accomplish this, the cap end of the piston is fitted with a short spud, larger in diameter than that of the rod. If necessary, the rod is also enlarged to a diameter similar to that of the cap end spud. Internally, recesses in the end caps accept the enlarged diameters. Two ports are provided, one fitted with a needle valve to adjust and restrict oil flow, the other with a check valve to permit oil to free-flow into the cylinder as the piston initially moves.

During extension, oil is permitted to enter the cylinder across both ports, and at first moves the piston slowly. As the spud is forced clear of its recess, full oil flow to the cylinder continues through the recessed inlet and allows extension-retraction under normal speed conditions.

During retraction, full oil flow exhausts, at first through the recessed outlet. As the tapered end of the spud enters the recess, exhaust oil flow is gradually restricted, and piston deceleration begins. Once the spud has fully occupied the recess, the only oil flow is across the needle valve. The needle valve restricts the exhausting oil flow, with a reduction of piston speed being a result of the lower effective exhaust flow rate. The exhaust flow rate, substantially less than the available input, dampens the piston inertia and prevents the piston from "slamming" into the end cap.

The Telescoping Actuator

Generally, this actuator is applied to the lifting of loads that decrease as the cylinder is extended, such as the bed of a dump truck. Three

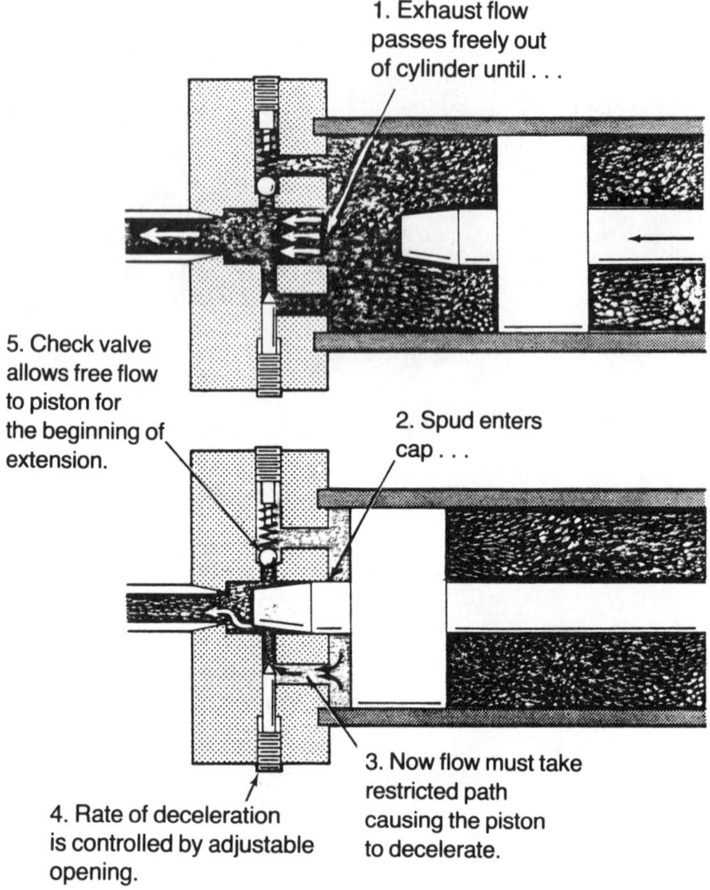

Fig. 4-3. Cushioning/decelerating devices applied to linear actuators

to five sleeves, of different diameters, are installed with each successively smaller sleeve inside of the next largest sleeve.

As oil under pressure enters the retracted cylinder, the largest diameter sleeve extends first, since the force output is the greatest. Once it has fully extended, the next largest sleeve extends, and so on, until complete extension has occurred. Retraction occurs in the opposite fashion, as the smaller output force is easily overcome.

Aside from its limited application, one problem that develops with telescoping actuators is the sealing of the numerous sleeves. Dirt and grit are always damaging to cylinder operation. Although these problems are not reserved for telescoping cylinders alone, they become magnified with this device.

To limit the scoring of cylinders in general, rod wipers are often used. These are nothing more sophisticated than a synthetic rubber, flexible collar fixed to the cylinder on the rod end. As the rod retracts, and passes through the collar, it is "wiped" off, keeping grit from damaging the rod packing.

CHAPTER 5

DIRECTIONAL CONTROL VALVES

Directional control valves, as the name implies, are used to control the direction of oil flow through hydraulic systems and the actuators. Although they share this common function, directional control valves vary considerably in their construction and design. Usually, they are classified according to their principal characteristics, such as:

1. type of internal valve element—sliding spool, rotating cartridge, and poppet (ball or piston).
2. methods of actuation—manual lever, electric solenoids, hydraulic or pneumatic pilot actuation, and cams.
3. number of paths that the oil will take over the entire operation of the valve, such as: two-way, three-way, four-way, etc.
4. size—nominal pipe size connection or rated gpm flow.
5. connections—pipe thread, flanged, or stacked.

Check Valves

The simplest of all directional control valves is the check valve (Fig. 5-1). It generally permits free flow in one direction while blocking or restricting flow in the opposite direction. Although certain check valves are pilot-actuated to block the flow at specific elevated pressures, the majority open and close as a result of pressure differentials acting on the valve. With this type of check valve, oil, entering in the free-flow direction, pops the valve element open. If the inlet flow is lost, or reverse flow to the valve is higher at the outlet, the valve is forced to close. To provide proper closing of these valves, under all operating conditions, the check valve is frequently equipped with a light coiled spring to insure positive closing.

Another type of check valve commonly used in hydraulic systems is the double-check valve (Fig. 5-2). A simple form of this type of

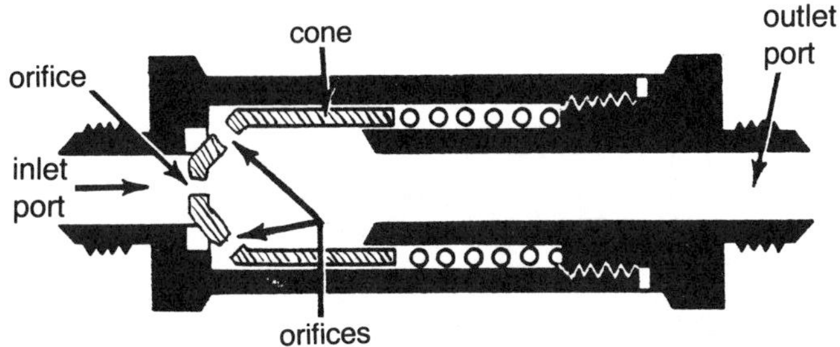

Fig. 5-1A. Poppet type check valve

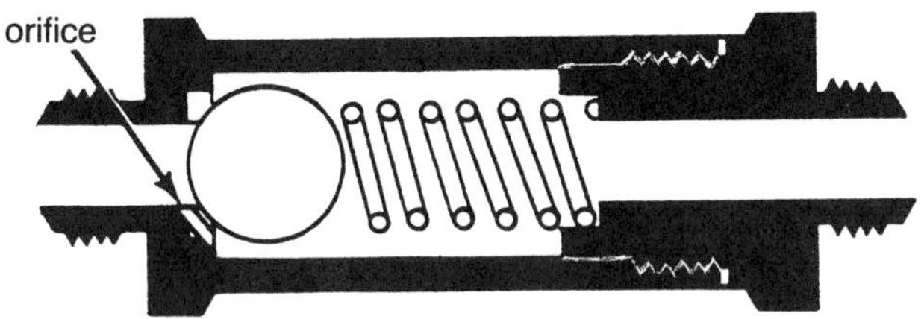

Fig. 5-1B. Ball type check valve

check uses a single-valve element that shuttles away from the high-pressure flow in order to block it from passing out of the low-pressure port. It may also be designed with two valve elements connected to a common outlet. In either case, double-check valves are used in systems where high-pressure oil is required to actuate a subsystem, regardless of the direction of the high-pressure oil flow through the main system.

The majority of directional control valves are manipulated to change the direction of the flow through the system. These valves generally fall into one of two main categories: the sliding spool, and the rotary cartridge.

Sliding Spool Valves

It is common to control the position of these valves manually or by mechanical means. Although the sliding spool has greater versatility, there are circumstances in which only the rotary cartridge valve can be satisfactorily employed.

To understand how these valves work, consider the operation of a simple three-position, manually controlled, four-way, center-closed sliding spool valve (see Style "A" in Fig. 5-3). With this valve, three conditions of the direction of flow are possible:

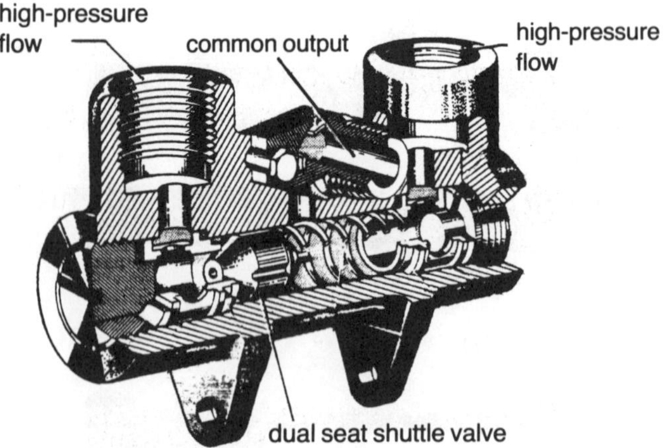

Fig. 5-2. Double-check valve used for dual rotation pressure closed systems

1. from the pump to the actuator, for extension
2. from the pump to the actuator, for retraction
3. centering of the valve—to stop the flow

Note that the spool has four piston areas, appropriately spaced, on the spool shank. Also, keep in mind that port A of the valve is generally aligned with the cap end of the actuator, port B with the rod end, port P with the pump discharge, and that port T is always connected to the tank. By centering the valve, the piston areas, or lands, are positioned to cover the ports in the valve body marked A and B. This position leaves the pump discharge port P blocked off, with flow from the pump no longer able to flow to the actuator.

By shifting the valve spool to the left, oil flow from the pump is aligned to the cap end of the actuator, with the exhaust oil flow from the rod end aligned directly to the tank. By shifting the spool to the far right, the flow across the valve is reversed, as well as the direction of the actuator.

While the operation of the spool valve is relatively simple, certain design variations provide the basic valve with flexibility in its application to the various systems. For instance, spring centering, detention, numerous center envelope configurations, and two, rather than three, valve positions are a few of the typical design variations.

Spring centering is achieved by the installation of a coiled spring at each end of the spool. By moving the control lever, the spring is easily compressed in one direction, allowing the valve spool to shift.

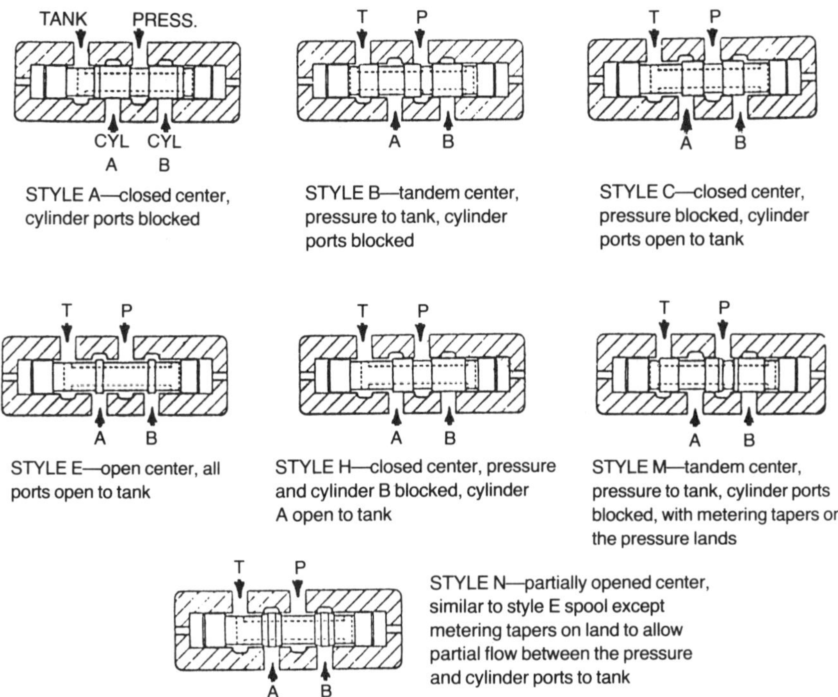

Fig. 5-3. Examples of directional valve spool and body configurations

When the operator releases the lever, the spring forces the valve spool back to its centered position (Fig. 5-4A).

Although spring-centered valves satisfy a particular need, such as safety, the valves can be manipulated to bridge two envelope positions. Since this may prove to be hazardous, if not inefficient, the valve can be assembled with "detent" (Fig. 5-4B); i.e., for each operating position of the valve, the spool is held in that specific position. One way that this is accomplished is for one end of the spool shank to be notched for each required valve position. A spring-loaded poppet slips into the notch and maintains, as well as gives the operator the "feel" for, each positive position of the valve.

Valve-centering configurations give the valves their diversified applications. For instance, a center-closed valve is satisfactory where a single system is operated for a short duration. However, if the system is to be operated for an extended period, the pump in this system is subjected to cavitation under the no-flow condition. Or, the pump discharge is unnecessarily forced across the relief valve.

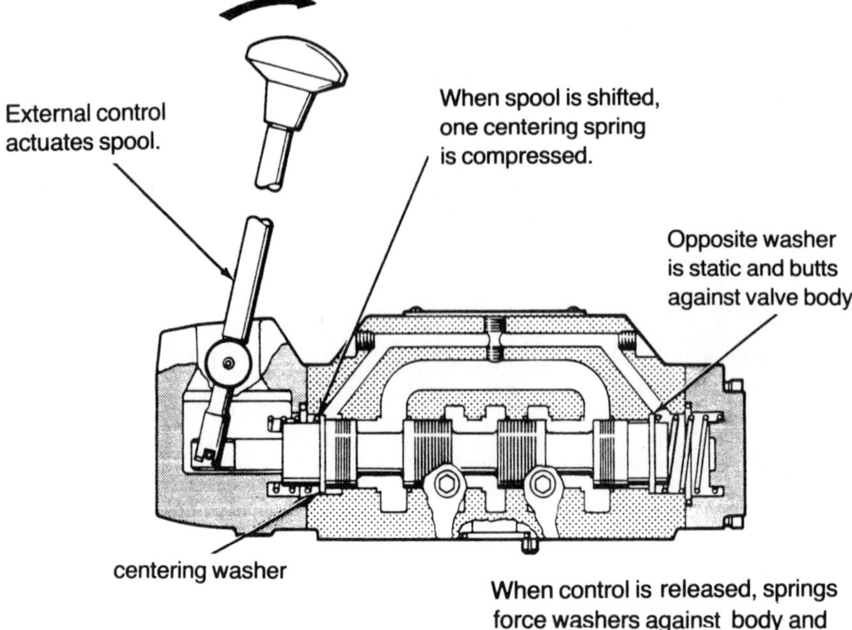

Fig. 5-4A. Spring-centered, manually operated directional control valve

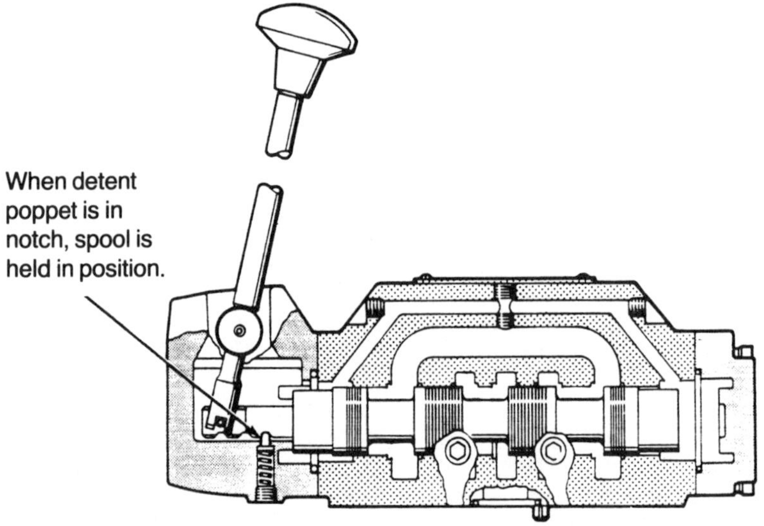

Fig. 5-4B. Detented, manually operated directional control valve

An open-centered valve, on the other hand, such as the tandem-centered valve, would be more adaptable. The design of the spool, when placed in its centered position, still blocks flow from the actuator to either the A or B port. The pump discharge, however, is continually recirculated to the tank. This not only maintains discharge pressure well below the relief valve setting; it also helps to keep the pump from heating up.

When more than one control valve is required for multiple subcircuit operation of the system, additional piping is required to hook up all of the valves. One method used to avoid this cumbersome piping tangle is the use of two or more open-centered valves. With the proper open-centered configuration, individual valve units can be stacked or bolted together to form a compact valve manifold. In this arrangement, when one of the valves is centered, oil flow to the other valves is still available to permit directional operation of the other subcircuits.

Generally, it is found that the valve spools from a manufacturer are interchangeable with the valve bodies regardless of the spool configuration. This provides for any number of ported control arrangements to be developed for a specific need.

In addition, there are other open-centered arrangements available by obtaining the necessary spool and exchanging it. And, the valve can be assembled to meet the required needs of the system without the need for expensive specialized manufacturing.

Furthermore, two-position controls can be obtained, for example, by using a three-position valve and by exchanging the spool (Fig. 5-5). While a two-position valve can be controlled manually, it is more common to use an alternate method. In most systems, this valve requires constant repositioning to prevent unnecessary overloading of the system, requiring constant operator attention. Therefore, cams, electric solenoids, or fluid pilot action, often initiated by some operating condition of the system, are more satisfactory. This is particularly true where immediate or continual actuator reversal in the system is required.

Rotary Cartridge Valves

The rotary cartridge type of directional control valve performs the same functions as the manually or mechanically actuated sliding spool valve (Fig. 5-6). It is somewhat simpler in design, in that a

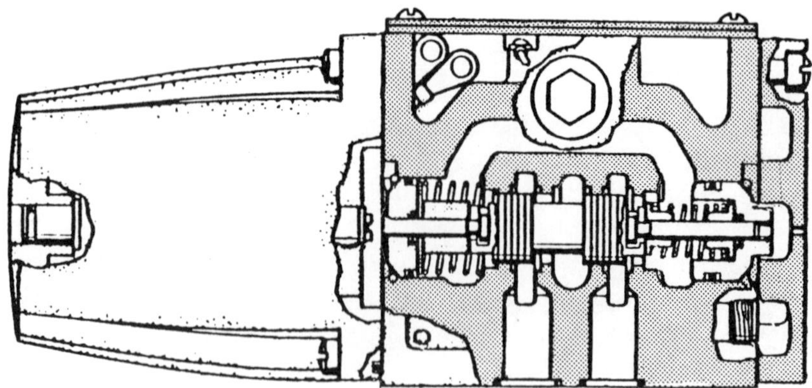

Fig. 5-5. Two-position or offset type of solenoid-actuated directional control valve

round cartridge, drilled with ports, is inserted into an acceptable ported valve body. A control lever is fitted externally to the cartridge shaft to control its position. When the cartridge ports are aligned to the body ports, oil is guided through the cartridge in the required direction. These valves can be designed with center positions similar to the sliding spool, in addition to being spring-centered or detented.

You will find that rotary valves require an additional intermediate linkage in order to provide cam, solenoid, or fluid pilot control. Consequently, valve control, other than manual control, is reserved for sliding spool valves.

Solenoid and Fluid Pilots

Solenoid and fluid pilot actuated valves are similar in operation to each other. A three-position solenoid-controlled valve has an electric solenoid positioned at each end of a sliding spool. When one of the solenoids is remotely energized, the resulting magnetic force is sufficient to move the solenoid plunger, acting on the end of the spool, to shift it against the opposing coiled spring. When the solenoid is de-energized, the compressed spring forces the spool back to its centered position. Energizing the opposite solenoid shifts the spool in the opposite direction to obtain the change in direction of oil flow across the valve.

The fluid pilot actuation (Fig. 5-7 and Fig. 5-8) is similar to that of the solenoid valve from the viewpoint of being energized and de-

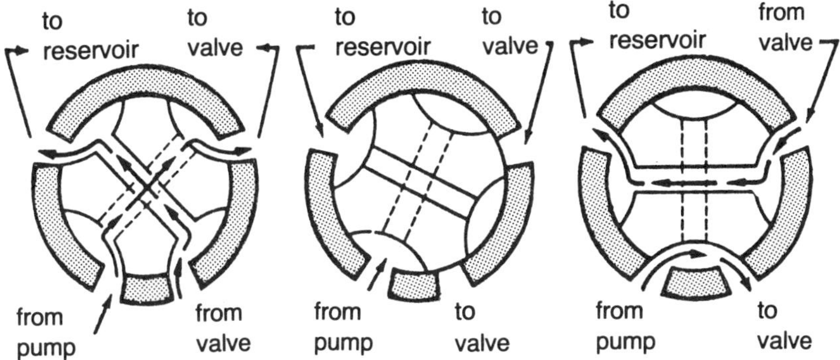

Fig. 5-6. Rotating the spool of a rotary type valve to control the direction of flow

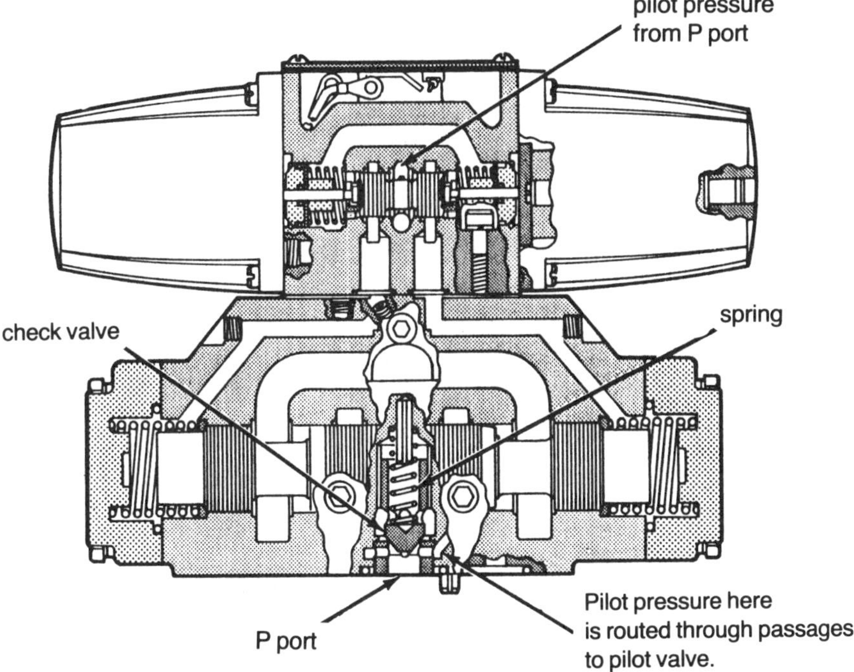

Fig. 5-7. Fluid pilot actuated valve

energized. As the pilot pressure to one end of the spool increases above the oil pressure acting on the opposite end, the spool shifts in the direction of the lower force. Once the spool shifts, the main system flow occurs as previously described for any other directional control

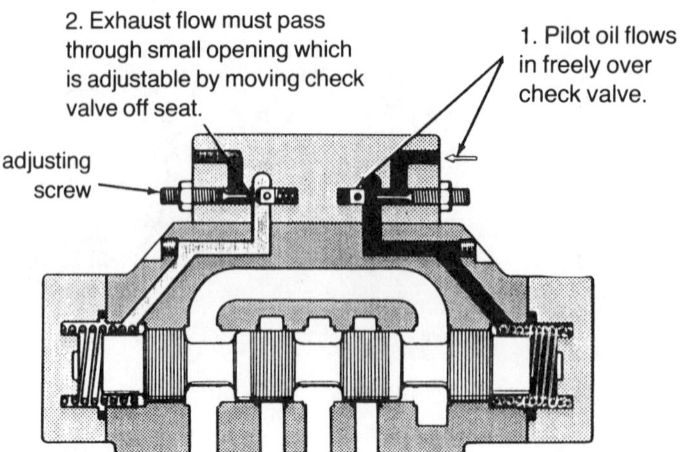

Fig. 5-8. Hydraulically piloted directional control valve (courtesy Vickers)

valve. When the pilot-actuating pressure is released, the coiled springs recenter the spool.

In certain systems, a solenoid-controlled pilot valve is used in series with a larger directional control valve. For example, a small, three-position spool is directly acted upon by the solenoids. The pilot spool manipulates the high-pressure pilot oil to the ends of the larger directional control valve spool to control its position. This type of operation is necessary where high fluid flow rates and pressures of the system are encountered. As the force output by the solenoid alone would be inadequate, the solenoid in question would require an exceptionally large coil or electrical input. Therefore, the combined solenoid pilot valve exists as a more feasible arrangement.

Certain remotely operated directional control valves are only two-positioned. To control the two specific operating conditions of directional flow requirements within the system, these valves may be single solenoid, single pilot, or cam operated, and are generally referred to as offset valves. Since there are only two valve spool positions, the single-actuating force moves the spool in one direction. When this force is relaxed, a coil spring forces the spool to move in the direction of the actuating device.

CHAPTER 6

PRESSURE CONTROL VALVES

Pressure control valves are devices which react to pressure conditions within the hydraulic system to maintain proper control. Before discussing specific pressure control valves, it is important to review the basic concepts discussed in Chapter 1 concerning the generation of pressure.

You will recall that pressure generated anywhere within the hydraulic system is primarily a function of the flow rate and the load opposing the flow. These two basic conditions have a direct bearing on the operation of any pressure control device.

Compression springs are generally used to establish the setpoint, or the actuation pressure, of these devices. The springs, therefore, oppose the resultant force of the existing oil pressure that will operate these valves.

Since the pressure conditions are to be controlled, the setpoint, or operating pressure, of these devices will be referred to as the controlled variable. The controlled variable is defined as: a quantity or condition of the controlled system that is directly measured and controlled.

The flow rate, as has been pointed out, can be manipulated to vary the operating pressure conditions; it will be considered the manipulated variable. The manipulated variable is defined as that quantity or condition of the control agent which is varied by the control device so as to affect the value of the controlled variable.

The control agent is the oil entering the pressure control device. The quantity of oil is varied by the pressure control to yield the desired level. Hence, the pressure becomes the controlled variable developed by the flow rate being manipulated by the control device.

Pressure control valves, therefore, function in response to the flow rate and the opposing loads. Regardless of their designated functions, all pressure controls will react in the same manner. The more common types of pressure controls to be discussed in this chapter are designated as:

1. pressure relief valve
2. compound relief valve
3. sequence valve
4. counterbalance valve
5. unloading valve
6. pressure-reducing valve

Pressure Relief Valve

The function of the pressure relief valve is to establish the maximum operating pressure for the system. It diverts some or all of the oil flow back to the service tank when the designated pressure (control variable) has been exceeded. As a rule of thumb, the setting of these valves causes them to begin opening when the pressure reaches a point 10 percent above the designed normal system operating pressure.

The simplest type of relief valve is connected directly to the pump discharge by a pipe "tee." The valve body contains the valve disk and seat (or ball valve and seat), where a spring is used to hold the disk in a normally closed position (Fig. 6-1). As the flow rate through the line increases without suitable response from the loaded actuator, the pressure increases. As the pressure is uniformly distributed throughout the line, it will act proportionally on the valve disk throughout the increase. Once the resulting force of the oil exceeds the spring force, the valve disk will rise, allowing the oil flow to be diverted to the service tank.

With the simple relief valve, the disk barely lifts off of its seat when the oil pressure barely exceeds setpoint. By "cracking" the valve open, a relatively small quantity of oil will be diverted to the service tank. If the pressure rises well above setpoint, the valve disk will lift proportionally higher, allowing a greater quantity of oil to be diverted to prevent an additional rise in pressure. Unfortunately, by the very nature of this response, the valve creates its own problems.

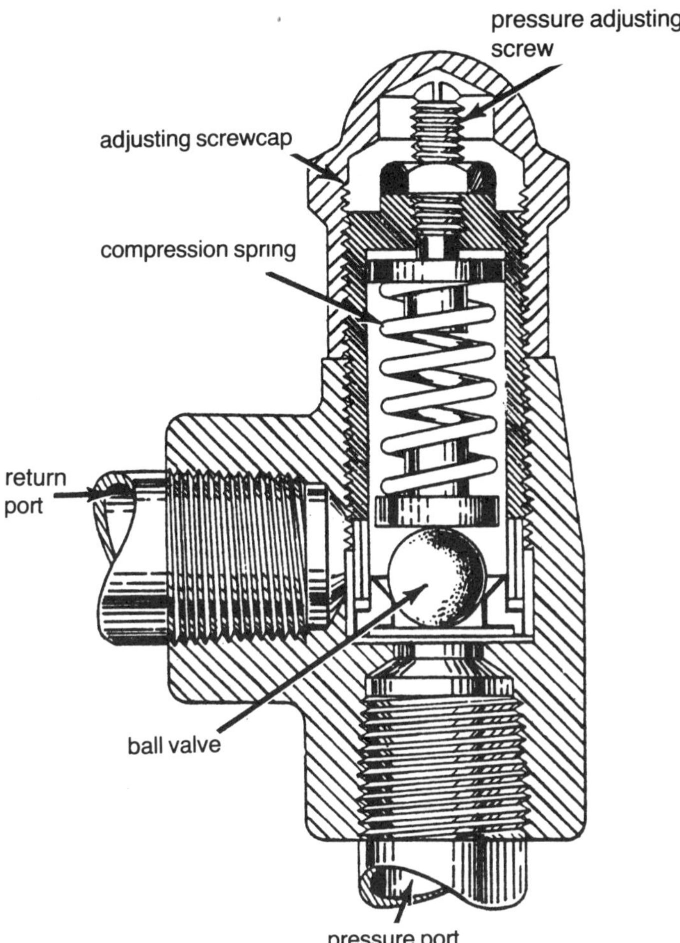

Fig. 6-1. Simple relief valve

When the flow rate/load conditions are only sufficient to "crack" open the valve, it closes quickly once the excess oil has been diverted. If the cause of the excess pressure condition has not been corrected, rapid opening and closing of the valve will be repeated. If allowed to continue, this effect, known as chattering, will either damage the valve seating surfaces or develop "water hammer," as the vibrations are transferred throughout the system.

The valve damage occurs in the form of the valve seat cracking, or the peening of mating surfaces, between the seat and disk. The slight gap that forms allows oil to continually bleed across the valve, even though the valve has been reseated. The immediate effect is excess energy consumption, and reduced flow to the actuator. The long-term effect will require the valve to be reground or replaced as erosion of these surfaces continues.

The alternative condition, known as "water hammer," results when high velocity fluid comes to an abrupt stop. Normally, the energy possessed by the oil flow is transformed into useful work. During the condition of water hammer, the energy is rapidly dissipated as the internal energy is suddenly reversed until the "energy wave" is blocked by a sharp bend or closed valve. Once blocked, the energy wave reverses again until the next block is attained. This continues to occur until all of the energy has been dissipated. The constant change in direction of the energy wave literally pounds on the piping, developing a sound similar to the pipes being struck with a hammer. If allowed to continue, it can lead to the cracking and fretting of pipe joints or other vibration-related damage.

Compound Relief Valve

To prevent chattering on large, high flow systems, a balanced piston or compound relief valve is preferred. The object of this combination valve is to "pop" the valve wide open when setpoint has been achieved. This action, referred to as pressure override, allows the valve to reach its full open position immediately, when setpoint has been reached (Fig. 6-2).

From the diagram in this illustration, you can see that oil is permitted to flow freely through the body of this compound or balanced piston relief valve. Under normal operating conditions, a piston valve blocks the flow of oil to the service tank. When the valve is in its closed position, oil is permitted to bleed across the piston through a small control orifice, to the chamber above the piston. A small poppet valve, held closed by a variable force spring, keeps the oil trapped in this chamber until setpoint pressure has been reached. The valve will not open as long as the pressures above and below the piston are the same, with force balance being achieved. A coiled spring, equivalent to 20 psi, assures that the piston valve remains closed as long as oil is trapped in the upper chamber. Once the small poppet valve is unseated, oil escapes from the upper chamber to the service tank via the drain port in the center of the piston valve. The pressure in the upper chamber is now less than the pressure below

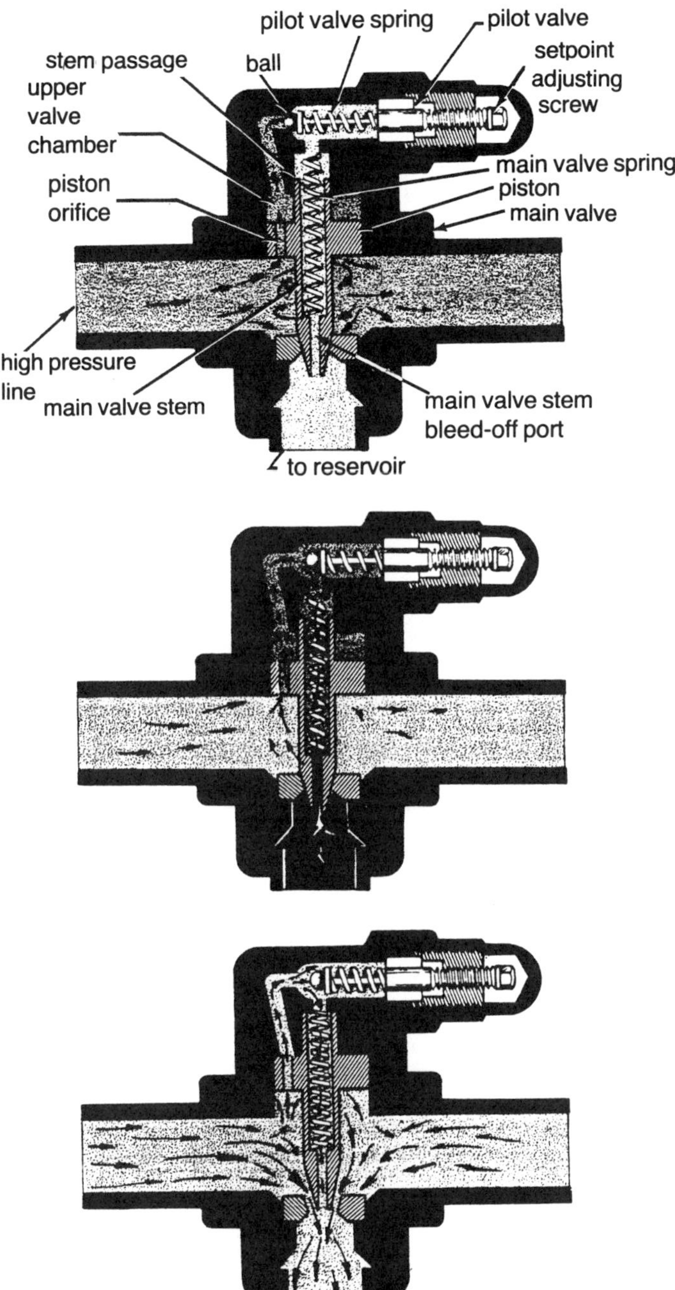

Fig. 6-2. Operation of a compound relief valve

the piston. The force of the oil acting on the underside of the piston will be able to lift the piston valve off its seat.

Even though both valves are open, the pressure differential across the control orifice permits oil to pass through. The upper chamber fills easily with oil because the lifting of the piston valve has greatly reduced the volume of the upper chamber. Despite restricted flow across the orifice, sufficient force is transferred to this area to keep the poppet valve open. Therefore, as long as the excessive pressure condition continues, the valve remains open.

When the flow rate, or excess load on the system, is reduced, the resulting pressure is reduced, in addition to the pressure transferred across the control orifice. The poppet valve closes with oil continuing to pass slowly across the control orifice.

As the control oil passes into the upper chamber, the oil pressure will be lower than the oil pressure below the piston. However, the total force above the piston is actually the oil pressure in the upper chamber plus the spring force, and acts to close off the piston valve.

There are two important points to understand about the closing of the valve. First, the speed at which the piston valve closes off is a result of the force differential existing across the piston. While the force above the piston is greater during the closing of the valve, the force below the piston resists its movement. Secondly, because of the relatively slow movement of the piston, the valve is not "slammed" onto its seat, and water hammer does not occur.

Sequence Valve

Similar in concept to the relief valve, the sequence valve is still another pressure control device (Fig. 6-3). The function of this device is to permit the complete operation of one segment of the system before a second operation is started. To comprehend how this valve operates, you must understand the pressure relationship of oil flow to the actuator during extension and at the end of its stroke.

During extension, the oil pressure of the relatively high flow rate to the lightly loaded actuator is relatively low when compared with the oil pressure once the actuator has stopped. For example, a simple hydraulic drill press is used. Here, the first actuator is used to clamp the workpiece in place. After the workpiece has been secured, the drill head will be extended hydraulically, as well as rotated (Fig. 6-4).

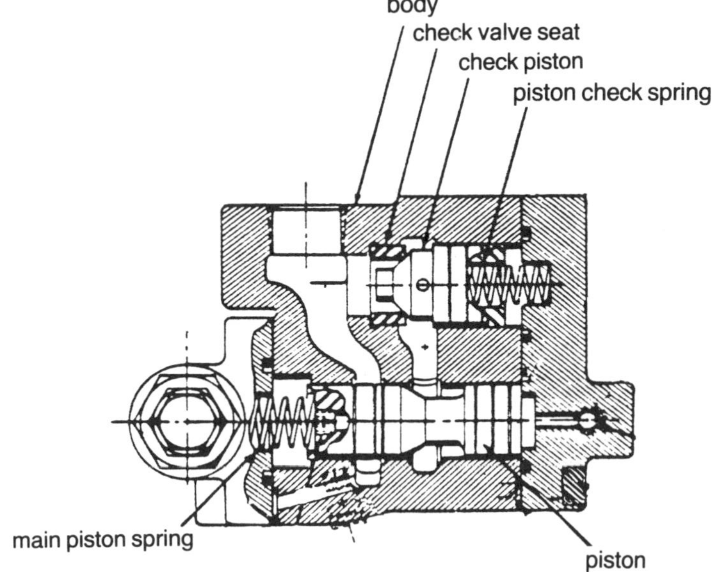

Fig. 6-3. Cross-sectional view of a sequence valve

Clamping the workpiece in place is fast, but it requires little effort for the system, since the initial resistance is low. The actuator, of course, stops once the workpiece has been secured. Since oil flow to the actuator can no longer continue, the pressure rises rapidly. The sequence valve, having similarities to the relief valve, opens at a prescribed setpoint. Upon opening, the sequence valve diverts the flow to the second actuator, an actuator used to extend the drill head.

At this point, the only difference between the relief and the sequence valve appears to be in the area of oil flow diversion after the valve has opened. If this were true, then why not use a relief valve? You do not do so primarily because there is no way for a relief valve to allow oil to return from the actuators during their retraction.

To visualize what would happen, you could install a relief valve in place of the sequence valve. During the initial operation of the actuators you will see that the actuators extend in sequential order. While attempting to retract both actuators, the oil returning from the second actuator flows to the area above the valve disk. However, with the valve seated, the return path is blocked, and retraction is prevented.

On the other hand, the sequence valve permits extension of the actuators. During retraction, oil is permitted to exhaust from both

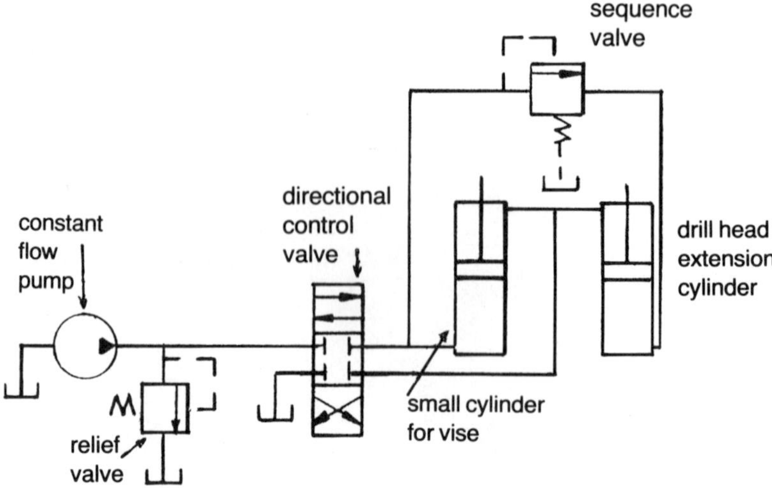

Fig. 6-4. Simple hydraulic schematic of a sequencing circuit

actuators and flow back to the sequence valve. Because of the internal design of the sequence valve, oil bypasses the valve disk, preventing hydraulic lock, and eventually returns to the sump.

Counterbalance Valve

Another relief type pressure control is that of the counterbalance valve (Fig. 6-5). Also referred to as a holding valve, its primary function is to prevent the stray movements of loads until required. Essentially, this valve is considered as a relief valve placed in parallel with a simple check valve.

Its operation permits the free flow of oil across the check valve to the actuator during extension to raise the load. When the actuator has been extended, the back flow of oil from the cap end is blocked by the relief valve. Because of gravity, the load exerts a downward force on the oil in the cap end of the actuator. In this condition, the oil is forced from the cap end and allows the actuator to drop.

For example, if a particular system has an adequately sized pump that can extend an actuator with a 10-square-inch piston area, to lift the 5,000-pound load, a pressure of 500 psi will be exerted at the cap end during extension. If the directional control valve were a full, open-centered type, oil would be able to circulate from the cap end to the rod end, and allow the load to drop.

To maintain the actuator's position, a counterbalance valve is installed in the line between the control valve and the actuator. By

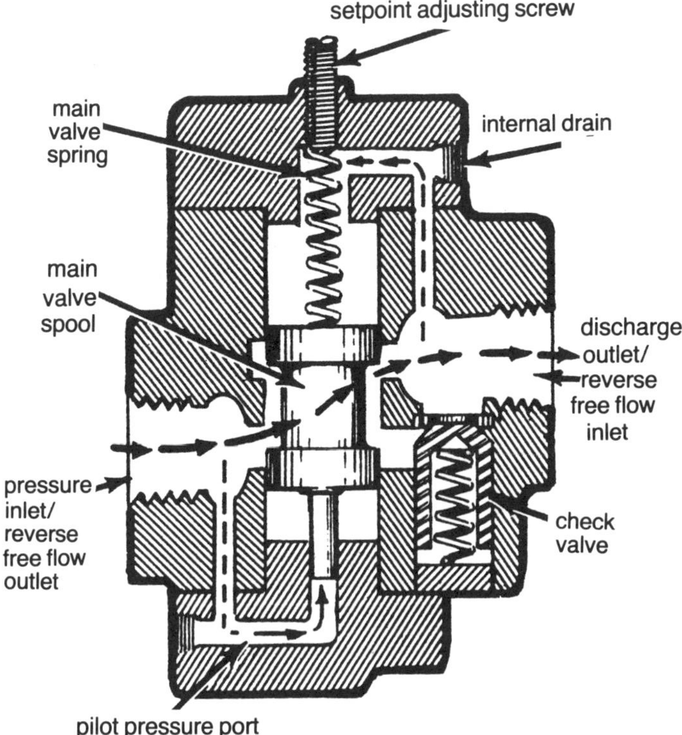

Fig. 6-5. Cross-sectional view of a counterbalance valve

setting the relief valve to open at a pressure slightly above 500 psi, the load remains in position. During retraction, oil is pumped to the rod end. Because of the force generated, oil is expelled from the cap end and is at a pressure above that of the relief valve (Fig. 6-5) pressure setting. As long as oil continues to flow to the rod end, the valve remains open to allow the actuator to retract. Once the oil flow has stopped, there is no longer a sufficient force applied to the oil leaving the cap end. The counterbalance valve then closes and hydraulically locks the actuator in place until the actuator is required to move.

Unloading Valve

The unloading valve is also similar in design and operation to the relief valve, differing only by its function (Fig. 6-6). This valve provides for the diversion (unloading) of the pump discharge to the service tank until the discharge to the system is required. Operation

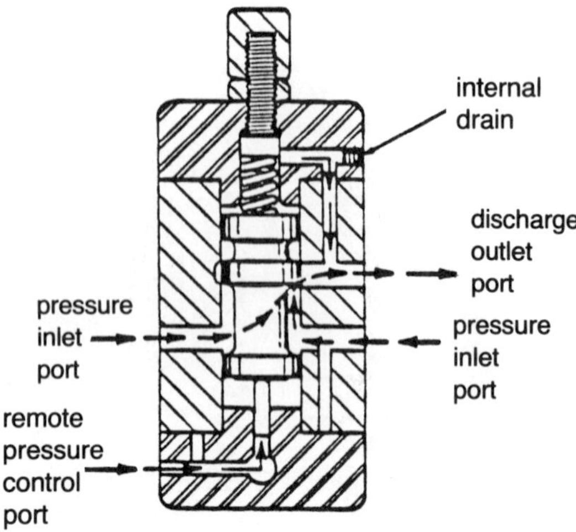

Fig. 6-6. Cross-sectional view of an unloading valve

of this valve includes the unloading of the discharge of one of two pumps operating in parallel, or the precharging of an accumulator to a predetermined limit.

In an unloading circuit, for example, the discharge from one pump element of a double pump unit constantly flows against a low load restriction. As the load is to be moved, the removal of the hydraulic lock on the load allows the discharge pressure to drop. The drop in pressure, in turn, allows the unloading valve to close, no longer diverting the discharge of the second pump element to the service tank. The flow rate to the system is now doubled to enable the actuator to move faster, but not increase the oil pressure. When the actuator is stopped, the pressure increase causes the unloading valve to open and to again divert the discharge of the second pump element to the service tank. Thus the unloading valve reacts to the operating pressure in the system to aid in the speed change as the actuator is repositioned.

Pressure-Reducing Valve

Of the six major categories of pressure control valves, the pressure-reducing valve is the only one which is normally open (Fig. 6-7). Its

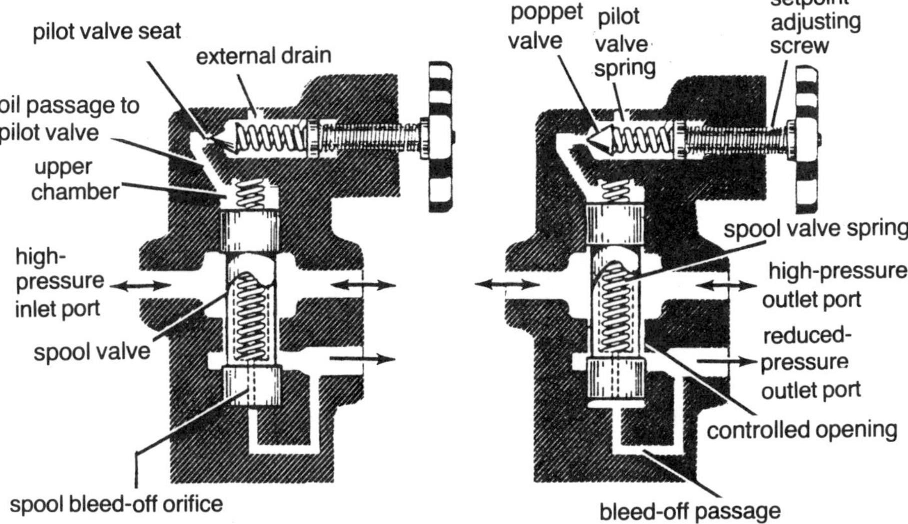

Fig. 6-7. Operational cross-sectional view of a compound reducing valve

primary function is to deliver a low oil flow rate to a secondary part of the system at a pressure below that of the main pump discharge.

As the valve is held in the open position by spring force, downstream pressure acts upon the valve assembly to close it. Again, you should realize that an increase in flow to the secondary load increases the downstream pressure of this valve. As the demand drops for the existing flow rate, the pressure rises and acts to close the valve. When the valve closes, the flow rate to the downstream side drops. A balance is established between the spring, trying to open the valve, and the downstream pressure, trying to close it. If the demand increases to require a higher flow rate, the resultant pressure drops, and the opposition to the spring is then lower. The valve is forced to open farther by the spring force increasing the flow rate and, consequently, the pressure until a balance is reestablished.

CHAPTER 7

FLOW CONTROL

In the previous chapters, considerable attention was given to the various aspects and effects of flow within the hydraulic system. Now it is important to discuss in detail the effects of flow rate and its control in relation to actuator speed.

Flow Control Circuits

Since linear actuation includes both extension and retraction, three metering circuits (Fig. 7-1) are used in hydraulic systems to precisely control actuator speed. They are discussed specifically as follows:

1. the metered-in circuit
2. the metered-out circuit
3. the bleed-off circuit

The *metered-in circuit* incorporates a flow control device installed in the system between the pump discharge and the actuator cap end to control the flow rate of oil to the actuator during extension. By restricting the flow to the actuator in this manner, the speed of extension can be infinitely maintained once the circuit has been properly set.

However, there are some problems with the *metered-in circuit.* With the flow rate downstream of the flow control device less than the flow rate from the pump, the pump will operate at normal, or at greater than normal, system pressure. This results in the motor drawing more electrical power than is actually necessary, and may cause the relief valve to open.

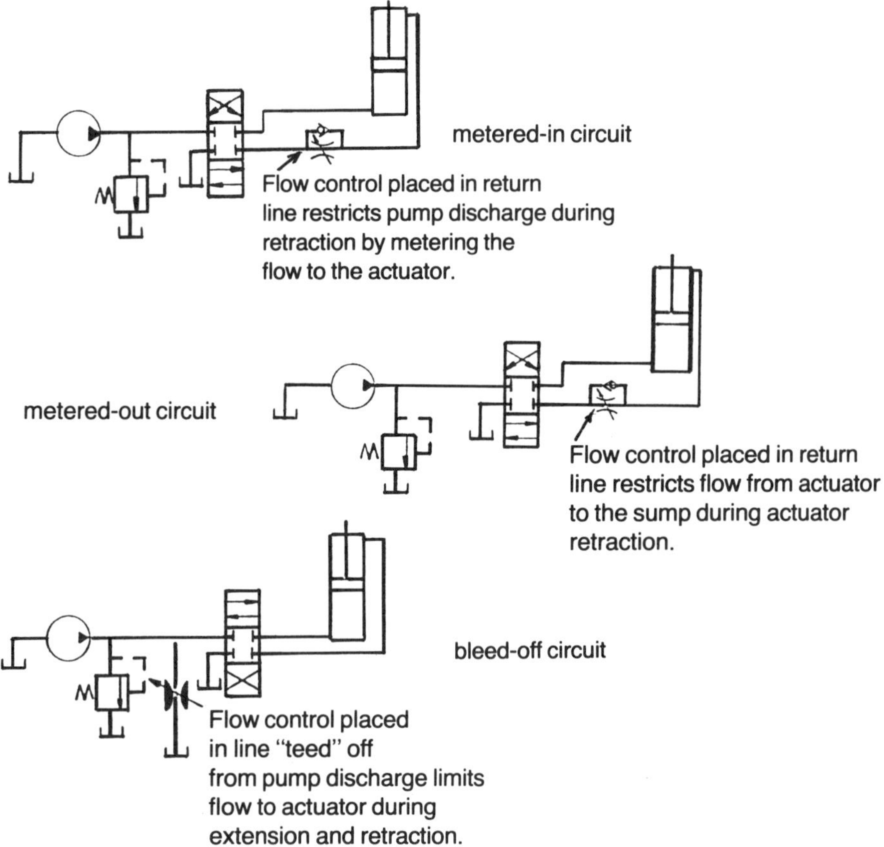

Fig. 7-1. Schematic representation of metered-in, metered-out, and bleed-off metering circuits

Another problem, considered to be more severe, occurs when the metered-in circuit, used by itself, allows the load to "run away." During retraction, pump discharge must flow across the flow control device. Once the actuator begins moving, oil is forced from the cap end at a rate greater than the oil flow to the rod end. The load, acting as a "prime mover," causes the piston to act as a "pump." The weight of the load produces a force that determines the flow rate leaving the actuator. The flow rate passing to the actuator from the pump, being less than the exhausting flow, allows the retraction to become uncontrolled. Therefore, caution should be exercised in the application and operation of this circuit.

The second circuit, the *metered-out circuit*, incorporates a flow control device installed between the cap end of the actuator and the service tank during retraction. The advantage of this circuit, over the metered-in, is that the oil flow leaving the actuator during retraction can be infinitely controlled to prevent the load from "running away." The only disadvantage of this circuit is that the pump prime mover does its work with greater power consumption. This is because the oil flow rate leaving the cap end of the actuator is less than the oil flow rate to the rod end, hence the pump discharge.

The last type of metering circuit, the *bleed-off*, solves the problem of excessive power consumption that was experienced in using the first two. In this circuit, the flow control device is "teed off" from the pump discharge. This permits a portion of the oil flow to the actuator to be diverted directly to the service tank. Although the system will not have to operate at maximum pressure conditions, actuator "runaway," as was the case with the metered-in circuit, exists as the major disadvantage of this circuit as well.

Needle Valve

In order for the circuits to be functional, a metering device must be incorporated. The simplest of these flow control devices is the variable orifice (*needle valve*) (Fig. 7-2). The needle valve may be fitted with a micrometer drum in order to determine precise valve opening and, therefore, precise oil flow rate. This device permits oil flow to be restricted in either direction.

Restrictor Valve

Where it may be more desirable to have restricted flow in one direction and unrestricted flow in the opposite direction, a restrictor valve is required (Fig. 7-3). This device incorporates a check valve in parallel with the needle valve. With a restrictor valve, free flow can occur across the check, while free flow in the opposite direction is blocked. As the oil flow is forced solely across the needle valve, restricted flow occurs in this direction.

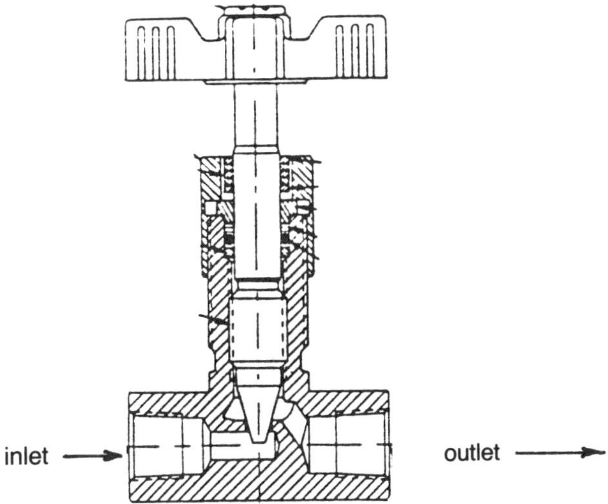

Fig. 7-2. Simple needle for regulating flow

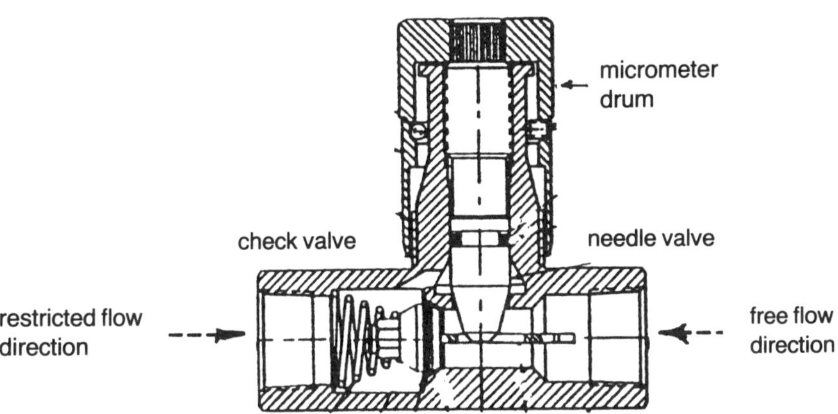

Fig. 7-3. Restrictor valve (flow control) permits free flow in one direction, but restricts flow in the opposite direction.

Temperature Compensation

Systems that are in continuous operation increase the system operating oil temperature. Since the temperature increase causes the oil to "thin out," oil flow across any restriction increases. This permits a change in the speed of actuation, which is undesirable. To rectify this condition a temperature compensating device will be added to the flow control device. Usually, this is a heat-sensitive rod which expands linearly as oil that is passing around the rod increases in temperature. With the temperature increase, proportional linear expansion of the rod results, and the restricting valve disk, connected to the rod, restricts flow.

Pressure Compensation

Another situation that can arise is the effect of the load on the system pressure as the load angle changes. The change in the angle produces a variable pressure range to the oil as it passes on to the flow control device. As the pressure increases, an increase in flow rate across the device occurs. The flow control device is equipped with a pressure-sensitive piston type controlled restriction, opposed by a compression spring (Fig. 7-4).

As the restricted oil flow to the inlet of this device increases in pressure, the piston moves to compress the spring. This causes the restricting valve to increase the restriction to flow, so that actuator speed can remain constant.

Deceleration Valve

Although the next device controls oil flow, it is not necessarily a part of the design considerations, as were the previous devices. The deceleration valve falls somewhere between the directional control and the flow control devices (Fig. 7-5). The deceleration valve is cam-operated and spring-returned. In the relaxed position, oil free flow is permitted across the valve. The cam-operated valve spool, in parallel with the check valve, is a tapered shank. Oil flow to the actuator, blocked by the check, must flow around the tapered shank valve. As the actuator approaches the end of its stroke, the valve cam is depressed by the cam actuator that is part of the piston rod. As the tapered shank moves farther into the flow port, the flow of oil to the actuator becomes progressively less. Therefore, the actuator speed proportionally decreases with the diminished flow rate.

Reversal of the actuator causes the oil, which is now blocked by the tapered shank, to choose the path of least resistance across the check valve. As the actuator continues its movement, the spring unseats the tapered shank, so that full exhaust flow results shortly after the actuator has begun to retract.

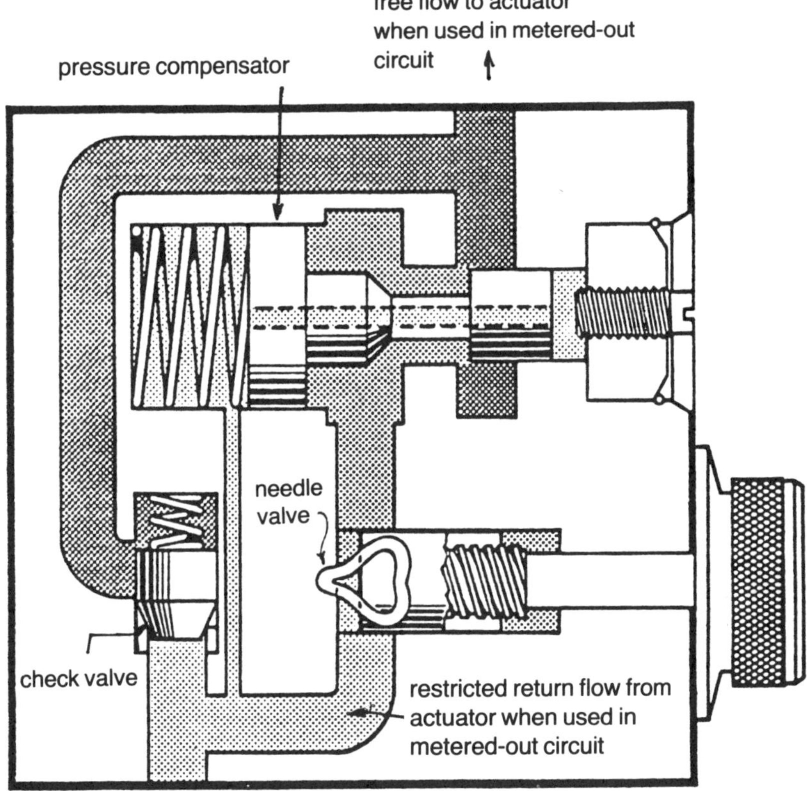

Fig. 7-4. Pressure compensated flow control valve

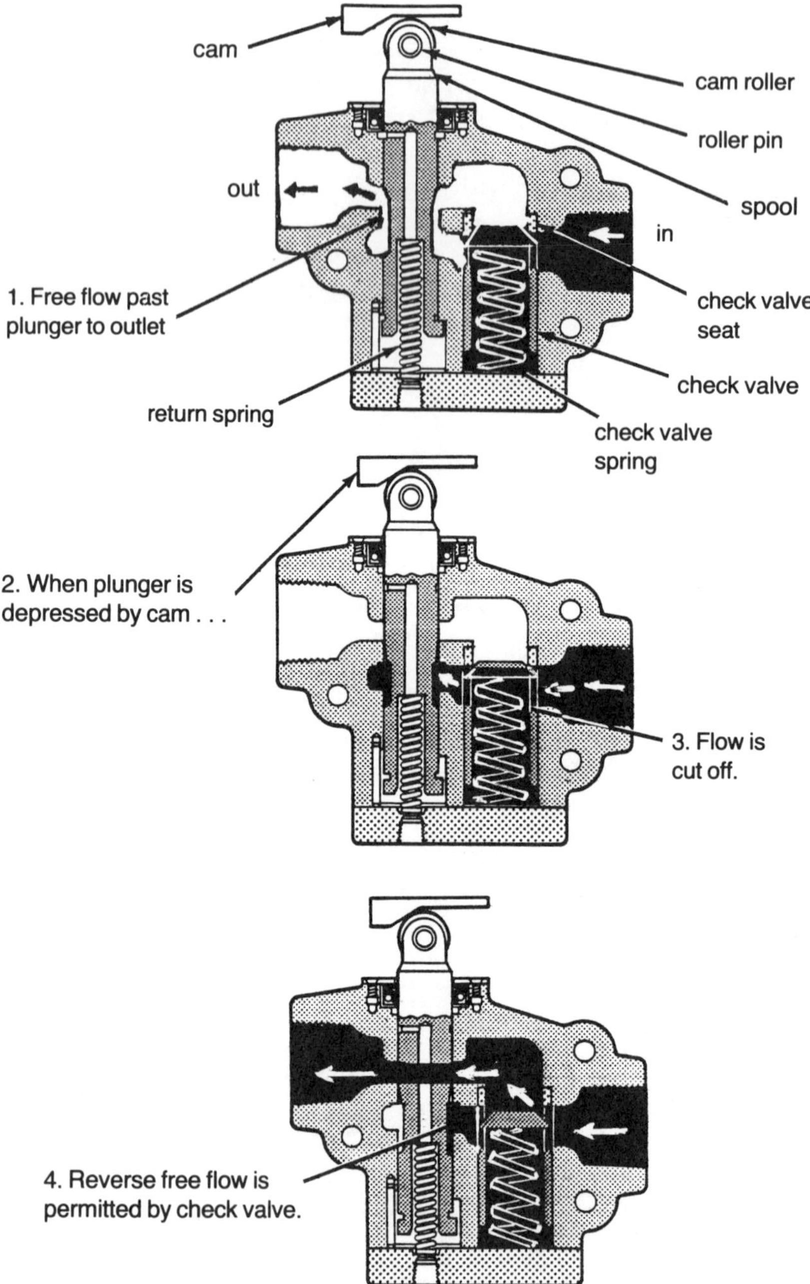

Fig. 7-5. Cam-actuated deceleration (flow control) valve

CHAPTER 8

SERVO CONTROLS

In the preceding three chapters the functions and operations of directional, pressure, and flow control valves were explained. Some hydraulic systems require the unique control that incorporates the combined functions of all three concepts. This is the servo control that, with one device, assists in the modulation of the system output.

The function of the servo control generally provides infinite positioning of another mechanical device, which in turn acts as a directional control. Equally important is the fact that the servo control acts as a force amplifier, or booster, capable of transforming small inputs into larger mechanical outputs. To simplify the discussion of the servo control, descriptions are limited to the output control of the tilting box of an axial piston pump, although it should be understood that other applications can be provided by different servos.

The Basic Servo Control

The servo control unit is attached to the controlled pump and is essentially a small, hydraulically manipulated actuator (servo piston). The displacement of the servo piston is adjusted by an infinitely variable directional valve with mechanical feedback existing between the servo piston and valve. This relationship permits the servo piston and the tilting box to maintain mutually corresponding positions, referred to as "follow-up" (Fig. 8-1). Typically, low-pressure oil flow is supplied by a small constant flow pump or charge pump, usually separate from the main circuit source. While the "charge" pump can be driven by its own prime mover, it has become a common

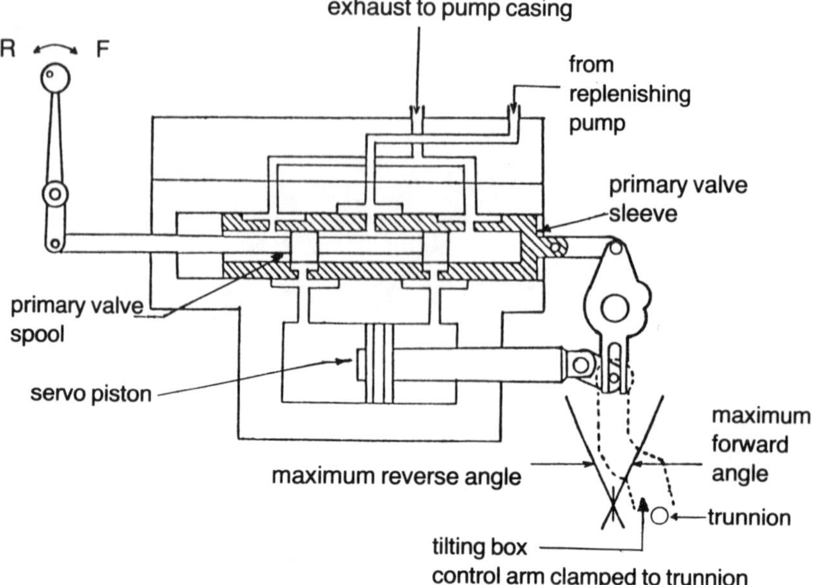

Fig. 8-1. Basic servo control

practice to devote one of the pump elements, in a combination pump unit, for this function. However, this should not be interpreted to mean that the flow from this pump cannot be used to fulfill more than one subsystem function, such as system replenishment.

The low-pressure oil flow is fed at a constant rate to the primary valve unit, composed of two main parts, an externally manipulated primary valve spool and a corresponding primary valve sleeve. As shown in Fig. 8-1, movement of the primary valve spool to the left permits low-pressure oil flow to pass across the primary valve unit and to the cap end of the servo piston. Simultaneously, the rod end of the servo piston is aligned to exhaust to the pump casing.

The result of the oil flow displaces the servo piston to the right. Through suitable linkage, i.e., the tilting box control arm, clamped to the trunnion, the servo unit begins to tilt the tilting box in a clockwise direction. As the tilting box forward angle increases, the follow-up cam, also linked to the servo piston rod, rotates in a counterclockwise direction. Rotation of the follow-up cam forces the primary valve sleeve to slide in the same direction as the spool, but lagging behind in its movement. Once the primary spool movement stops, the sleeve catches up. As the sleeve position is matched to that of the spool, oil flow to the servo piston is stopped. Further increase in the tilting box angle does not occur, as this action places the servo piston in hydraulic lock.

Ideally, with the servo piston hydraulically locked, the only way the pump tilting box angle can be changed is to reposition the primary spool. By moving the control lever to reversed position, with regard to neutral stroke, not only is the primary valve position changed, but the direction of the tilting box angle and the flow from the pump are also changed.

Aside from the desired position change, the servo always acts to maintain the original command position until it is required to be changed. Again, as the pump flow rate increases, regardless of the direction of flow, the resulting oil pressure reacts on the pump pistons, gradually forcing the tilting box toward neutral stroke. For example, despite the hydraulic lock that was placed on the servo piston, as described, oil can be squeezed from the cap end and passed to the rod end. As the tilting box angle "slips," the primary valve sleeve is physically shifted toward the right because the follow-up cam is forced to rotate clockwise by the movement of the tilting box.

As the sleeve is forced to the right, oil flow is reestablished to the cap end of the servo piston, since the primary valve spool position had not been changed. The servo piston is stroked toward the right by the renewed oil flow, causing the tilting box angle to be reestablished to its original position. Consequently, the primary valve sleeve is moved by the mechanical linkage to match the spool position, again blocking the oil flow to the servo piston.

Until the primary spool position changes, the servo control always works to maintain the designated flow rate and direction of flow from the main pump. By maintaining the tilting box angle, understand that for each position of the operating lever, there is one, and only one, flow rate and direction of flow from the main pump and it results from the condition of "follow-up."

As long as the flow from the variable stroke pump is directed to a constant load, the basic servo control unit works satisfactorily. However, certain systems are required to operate under varying, wide-range load conditions. These conditions cause the system to consume excessive power or to stall. To prevent this, a variation of the basic servo control can be incorporated.

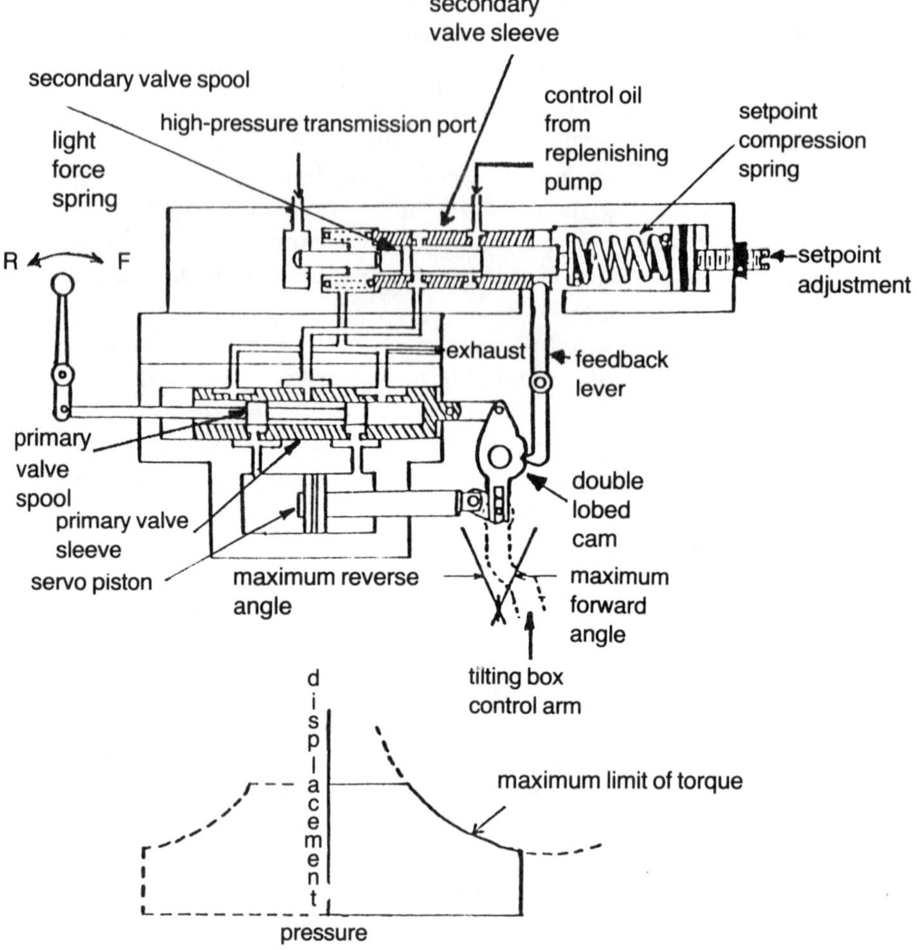

Fig. 8-2. Horsepower-torque limiter servo control

Horsepower Torque Limiter

This device (Fig. 8-2) is essentially the basic servo control. It is assembled with an additional two-part secondary valve in series to the primary valve unit. The secondary valve modulates the flow of control oil to the basic servo control.

Operation of this device occurs in the following manner. When the pump is in neutral stroke, the secondary valve spool is forced to the left by the indicated compression spring to its right. Movement of the secondary valve sleeve, not yet affected by the feedback lever as the sleeve position remains to the far right, is dictated by the force of the light coil spring acting from the left. The relative position of these two components allows control oil to pass freely to the primary valve. By moving the control lever, the tilting box angle is increased, as previously described. Now, one additional set of actions occurs, and they are initiated by the rotation of the double-lobed follow-up cam.

Extending from the double-lobed cam, to the right-hand end of the secondary valve sleeve, is the pivoted feedback lever. Regardless of the angle or the direction of tilt of the tilting box, the feedback lever rotates counterclockwise because of the shape of the cam. As the lever rotates, it forces the secondary valve sleeve toward the left to compress its coiled spring. This results in restriction of the flow of control oil to the primary valve because the ports of the sleeve are partially blocked by the lands of the secondary valve spool.

As the main pump flow rate to the load begins to increase, the system high side pressure must also increase. By the use of a double-check valve, oil pressure from the high side of the system, regardless of the direction of flow through the system, is exerted on the spindle at the left-hand end of the secondary valve spool. Under normal flow rate and pressure conditions, the valve spool shifts toward the right, against the setpoint compression spring. Shifting of the spool stops when balance is achieved between the setpoint compression spring force and the high side pressure. However, as high side pressure builds above the spring setpoint, the spool continues to move and further restricts the control oil flow.

If the strain on the system continues to increase, the increase in load will drive the high side pressure up to develop two actions, which occur simultaneously. First, the tilting box begins to slip gradually toward neutral stroke as a result of the pressure acting on the pump pistons. Second, the secondary valve spool is forced farther to the right, resulting in a complete blockage of control oil flow to the primary valve.

Remember, when only the basic servo control was used, slipping of the tilting box resulted in an upset, or unbalancing, of the primary valve spool and its sleeve. In turn, this permitted control oil to flow to the servo piston and to begin to renew the tilting box angle as it was orignally designated.

With flow to the primary valve now blocked by the secondary valve unit, the reestablishment of the original tilting box angle cannot occur. Also, with the tilting box angle decreased, the pump flow rate decreases. This means that the high side pressure will not be higher than before the decrease of the tilting box angle. If the high side pressure continues to increase, the tilting box angle continues to slip, as a reaction to the increase in pressure, and the control oil flow is still blocked by the secondary valve.

Despite the decrease in the pump discharge rate, the load currently on the system maintains the system's high pressure, yet when calculated, shows that the hydraulic horsepower has not changed, even though the load has increased. For example, if at normal load, the system pressure is 2,000 psi at a flow rate of 30 gpm, the hydraulic horsepower will be:

$$\text{hp} = \frac{\text{gpm} \times \text{psi}}{1{,}714} = \frac{30 \times 2{,}000}{1{,}714} = \frac{60{,}000}{1{,}714} = 35 \text{ hp}$$

If the load increase raises the system pressure to 2,100 psi, it is found that the flow rate will have to be reduced to 28.6 gpm in order to maintain the hydraulic horsepower setpoint at 35.

$$35 \text{ hp} = \frac{\text{gpm} \times \text{psi}}{1{,}714} \text{ or gpm} = \frac{1{,}714 \times 35}{2{,}100} = 28.6 \text{ gpm}$$

As the flow rate is required to be reduced, the tilting box slips to reduce pump piston stroke and produces the lower flow rate, maintaining the hydraulic horsepower at setpoint.

The indicated setpoint, as established by the variable force setpoint spring, opposes the secondary spool valve movement. As the high side pressure continues to build, because of the load increase, the tilting box continues to decrease its angle and, therefore, the flow rate.

However, if the flow rate is reduced excessively, the resultant pressure is also reduced. This upsets the balance previously established between the high side pressure and the setpoint spring. In turn, this allows the secondary spool to shift toward the left and permits control oil to flow toward the primary valve again.

Because of the slipping of the tilting box, the primary valve unit becomes unbalanced. Renewed control oil flow to the servo piston will shift it to reestablish the tilting box angle. The angle continues to increase until the increase in flow, resisted by the load, causes the pressure to rebuild. This, in turn, shifts the secondary valve to the right, again cutting off control oil flow to the primary valve. The servo piston is then prevented from developing any further increase in the tilting box angle. Therefore, by balancing and limiting the existing discharge rate versus the existing high side pressure, as established by the load, the required hydraulic horsepower will be achieved.

Electric Servo Control

Other types of servo controls may employ an electric signal to indirectly control the infinite adjustment of a valve spool. In Fig. 8-3, a solenoid is used to modulate the position of a reed to manipulate control oil flow. Notice that a high-pressure control oil supply is directed to two fixed orifices, in addition to the center of a hydraulically piloted, center-closed, three-position, spring-loaded directional control valve.

If the left-hand solenoid is energized, the reed is drawn to the left to block the bleed-off of control oil from the left nozzle. With the exception of the resistance created by the right-hand nozzle, the control oil bleeds rapidly from the right-hand control loop, reducing the pressure at the right end of the directional control valve. The control valve is shifted to the right by the high pressure exerted from the left, against the low-pressure end at the right. The directional valve is now aligned to permit oil flow to the left-hand end of the nondifferential linear actuator, simultaneously bleeding the right-hand end, permitting the actuator to shift toward the right.

Although it is not indicated on the diagram, a linear potentiometer is installed so that as the actuator changes its position, an electric potential changes in magnitude. Also, depending upon which direction the actuator moves, relative to midstroke, the polarity of the potentiometer output is changed.

Therefore, as the actuator moves, it eventually causes the potentiometer to develop an output that is of the same magnitude, but with opposite polarity of the original electrical input to the solenoid. The effect will cancel the electrical input and cause the reed to be recentered. The control oil pressure becomes equal on both sides of the directional control valve so that it is recentered by the centering springs, blocking any further movement of the actuator, with follow-up being achieved.

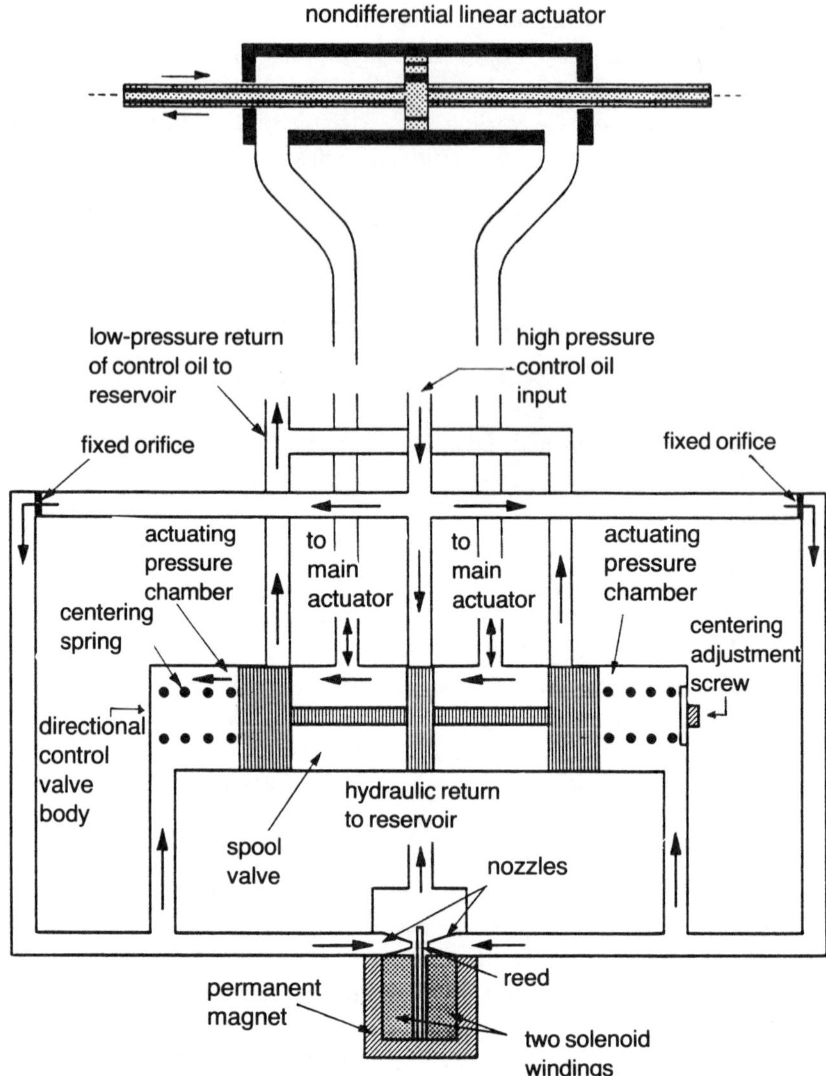

Fig. 8-3. Electric servo control valve with hydraulic pilot actuation

CHAPTER 9

HYDRAULIC PLUMBING

In this chapter you will learn how to connect the components used to assemble a hydraulic system. Four methods are typically used to conduct the oil from one point to another. These methods include piping, tubing, hoses, and manifolds.

Piping

Piping, to some extent, is a very general term that refers to a seamless steel conduit (pipe) which can be threaded or welded to make up the required connections. Because of its availability and relatively low cost, pipe was originally used. Today, it is not used as extensively, primarily because of its weight and lack of flexibility.

Over the years, various changes, from the standpoint of nomenclature, have been made in pipe sizing. In the past, the outside diameter of the pipe was a constant, with the size of the wall thickness changed to accommodate working pressures. This meant that the thicker the wall, the smaller the inside diameter. Consequently, the inside diameter was considered the pipe size. Today, the nominal pipe size refers only to the thread size used for connection.

Various pipe wall thicknesses are available, and are manufactured in terms of schedule numbers specified by the American National Standards Institute (ANSI). These numbers range from 10 to 160 (Fig. 9-1). Although the thicknesses cover a wide range, it is more typical for pipe schedules of 40 and 80 to be used in hydraulic systems.

To join sections of pipe, or to provide for bends in the piping, a variety of fittings may be used. It is a common practice for these

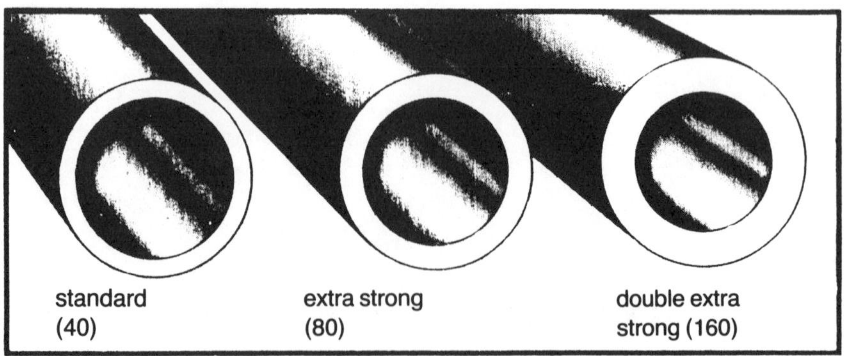

Fig. 9-1. Pipe sections showing relationship of "old" wall thickness and schedule numbers currently used

fittings to be threaded and screwed onto the pipe, although the fittings may be welded on for certain applications. The threads used on hydraulic piping differ significantly from those used in other common piping systems.

The American Standard pipe thread is tapered. When screwed together, the flanks of these threads engage before the roots and crests do (Fig. 9-2). This tends to create a problem when the joints are unscrewed; for when these joints are reassembled, the connections must be overtightened in order to prevent leakage.

In contrast, hydraulic pipe threads are straight, and are referred to as dry seal threads. With these threads, the roots and crests engage first, thus preventing spiral clearances from developing. With the flanks sealed by tape, such as teflon, leakage from disassembly is usually less of a problem.

Flanges, used as an alternative for connecting pipe joints, are costly and generally must be welded to the pipe. However, flanges are convenient when disassembling a portion of the system.

Although a typical raised seat flange can be used in conjunction with a flat oil-resistant gasket for sealing, a special flange for hydraulic systems is preferred (Fig. 9-3). This flange type, for connection to the pipe, can be of the threaded or welded socket type. It is significantly different from other flanges because it is manufactured with mating grooves. The grooves are fitted with an O-ring that provides for efficient sealing.

As you can surmise, piping requires more extensive work and costs more for installation. Flexible stainless steel tubing with thin

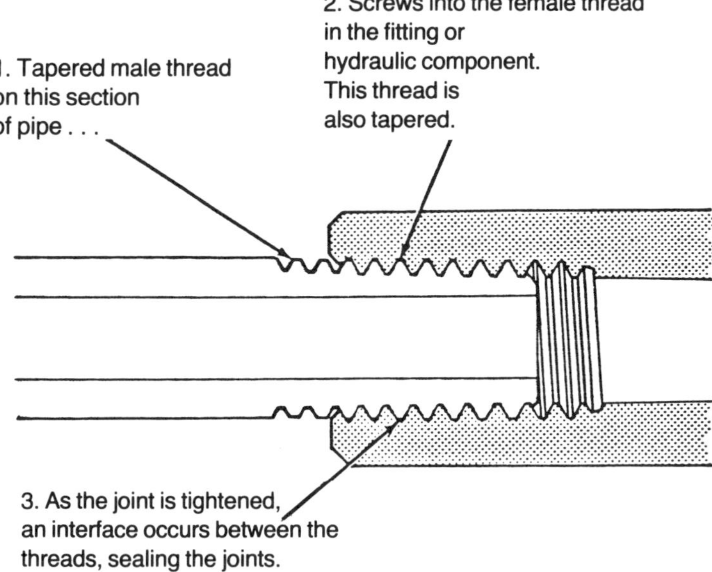

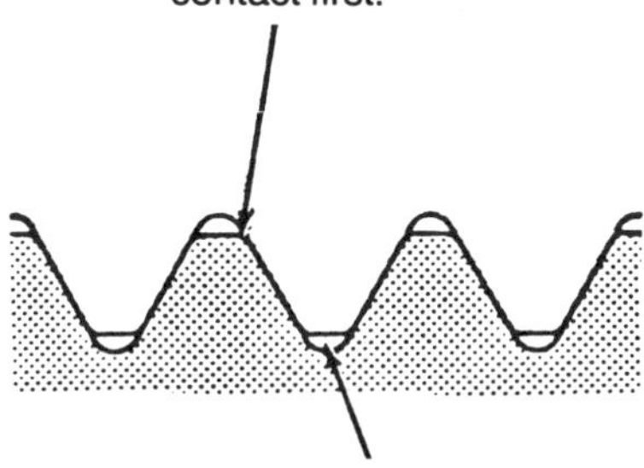

Fig. 9-2. Comparison of normal pipe thread to that of the dry seal thread used in hydraulics

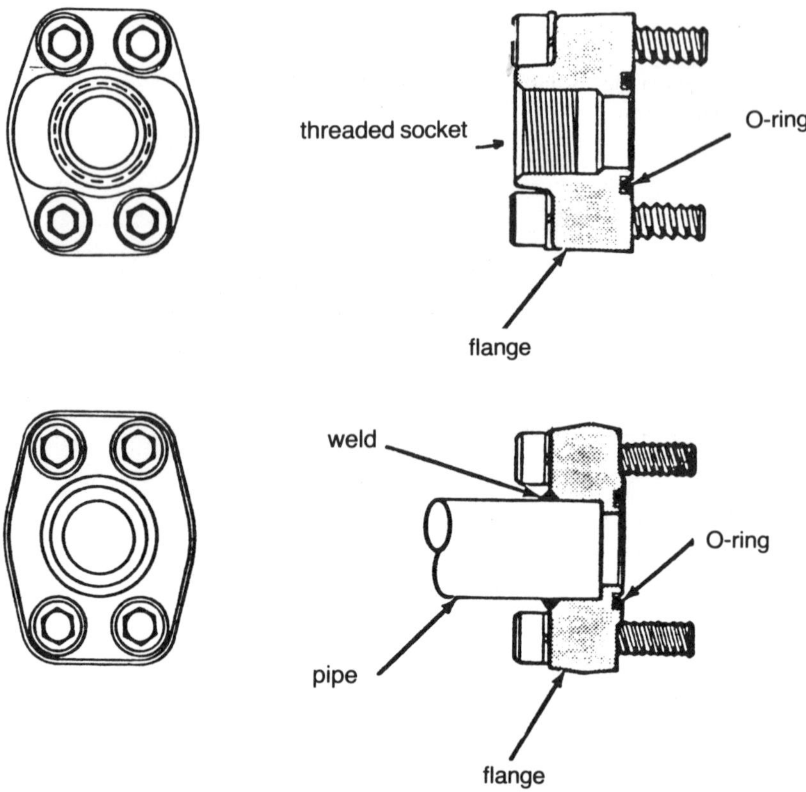

Fig. 9-3. Typical threaded and welded type sockets used in conjunction with hydraulic piping

wall construction offers a viable alternative with many advantages over seamless steel piping for modern systems.

Tubing

Despite the fact that seamless stainless steel tubing is more expensive than pipe, it is lighter and more flexible to accommodate turns in the system. One advantage of the seamless stainless steel tubing is that the only fittings in the system are those used to connect one length of tubing to another, or the system's components to the tubing. This means there is less likelihood of leaks because the numerous assembly joints of pipe are reduced. Special connectors, however, are necessary to join the tubing, such as the flare or compression fitting (Fig. 9-4).

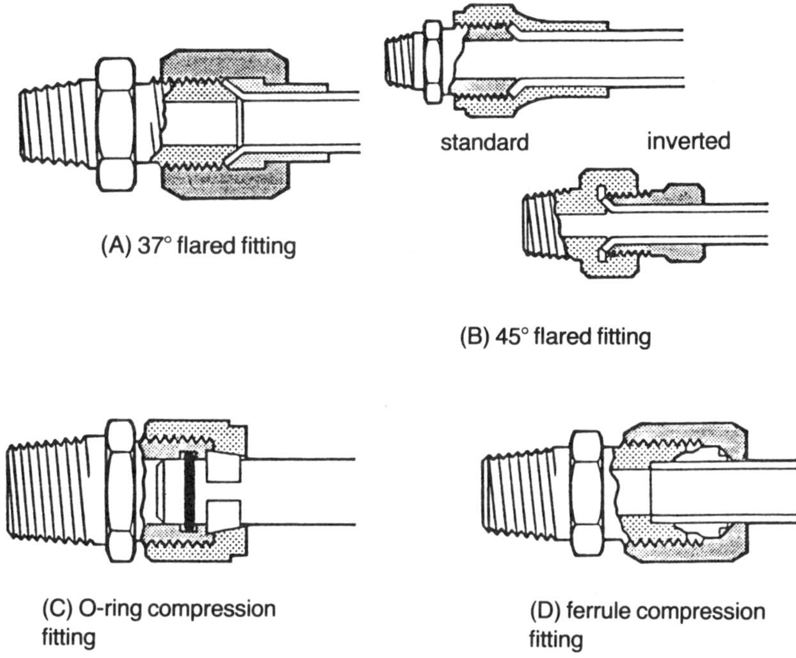

Fig. 9-4. Typical fittings used in conjunction with tubing used in hydraulic systems

Fittings for Tubing

Flared fittings require special flaring tools to flare or expand the tube end. When the female-threaded flare nut is screwed onto the male-threaded adapter, the tubing flare is compressed between the two halves to provide a static seal. The flare angles are generally 37° and 45° with respect to the tubing centerline, with the different angles being used for low- and high-pressure systems, respectively.

Compression fittings are more common in hydraulic systems, as special tools are not necessary for installation. Two common compression fittings used are the O-ring and the ferrule (Fig. 9-4C). The O-ring is composed of four parts: the female-threaded nut, the male-threaded adapter, a split-compression ring, and the O-ring seal. An O-ring groove, machined into the internal bore of the male adapter, is fitted with the O-ring. When the tube is inserted into the adapter bore, a high-pressure static seal is created by the O-ring. The split compression ring is compressed to the tube when the female-threaded nut is tightened to the male adapter. The interaction of the split compression ring and the nut clamps the tube in place without crimping the tubing.

High-pressure applications may cause the O-ring to extrude from its groove, causing it to leak, but additional tightening of the nut does not help to stem the leak. An alternative to this method of connection is found in the use of ferrule connectors.

The *ferrule fitting* uses a ferrule, or compression sleeve, providing both functions of sealing and holding the tubing in place within the fitting (Fig. 9-4D). As the ferrule is compressed between the female-threaded nut and the male adapter, it spreads linearly as it is forced to narrow its inside diameter. As a result, it develops a metal-to-metal contact with all surfaces in contact with the ferrule. While it is a less expensive method than the O-ring fitting, it tends to leak when used again after being disassembled. Also, improper installation, such as overtightening, can cause the tube to become crimped, which will disturb the laminar flow within the system.

Hoses

In other installations, where relative movement is required between sections of the system, flexible hoses are needed to conduct the flow (Fig. 9-5). Hydraulic hoses, fabricated of layers of various materials, contribute to the ability of the hose to conduct flow, withstand high pressures, resist chafing, yet remain flexible.

Since natural rubber will break down in the presence of oil, synthetic rubbers are used in hydraulic systems. Neoprene, or another synthetic, is generally used as the inner layer of the conductor. Because of the elastic nature of the material, the inner layer needs to be reinforced to withstand expansion or bursting. Usually, a loosely braided fabric or a stainless steel braid is used as the second or reinforcing layer. Even where stainless steel braid is used as the second layer, it must be protected from chafing. Another layer of synthetic rubber is used as the third layer to protect the reinforcing braid from environmental conditions. The three layers are usually sufficient for most systems that operate at 1,000 psi or less. However, to provide operating longevity for the system and safety to personnel, additional fourth and fifth layers are added by the application of a braid and synthetic rubber, respectively.

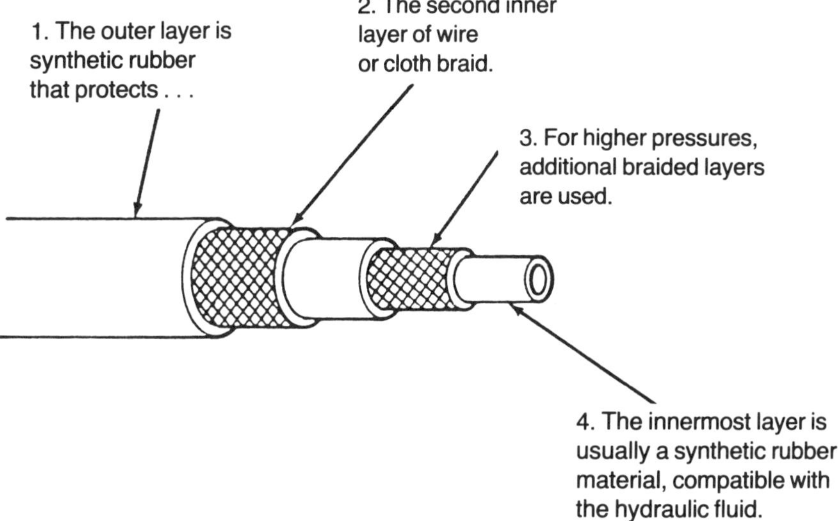

Fig. 9-5. Layered cutaway of multi-layered high-pressure hose

Regardless of the pressures of the system, or the construction materials used, the industry has developed standards in reference to the bursting of the conduits. As a rule, where operating pressures range from 0 to 1,000 psi, there should be a safety factor of 8 to 1; where the range is 1,000 psi to 2,500 psi, the safety factor should be 6 to 1; and above 2,500 psi, the safety factor is recommended to be 4 to 1. Therefore, the wall thickness of the tubing or hoses is sized, in part, according to the required factor of safety. The safety factor for the hoses is calculated as:

Factor of safety = bursting pressure/working pressure

Manifolds

The last method of channelling fluid flow from one point to another is through the use of the manifold. Although the term manifold is applied to several types of arrangements, reference here is made to flow passages formed in one or more plates stacked together. This eliminates the need for flexible conduit in an effort to provide a compact system (Fig. 9-6). Just as the function of a printed circuit board in electronics is to conduct current between components, the manifold serves a similar function in hydraulics. While the manifold helps to reduce the overall weight and size of a system, it is difficult to repair openings that develop between adjoining passages. Also, flexibility in the use of a manifold is limited if it is necessary to expand the functions of the system. Furthermore, if a mistake is made in laying out the passages, a new casting or manifold must be produced.

Installation of Tubing and Hose

The greatest problems that occur with the conduits during operation are usually attributed to improper installation. With any hydraulic system, contaminants result as a matter of poor operational procedures and internal physical damage of the components. When pipe and, to some extent, stainless steel tubing are stored, various forms of scale and oxidation develop. To prevent either from becoming scaled, the manufacturers coat the inside of these conduits with a light oil. Therefore, before installing the conduits, make sure that this oil, which is not compatible with the oil in the system, is removed. A petroleum solvent, such as trichloroethylene, is suitable for this process, known as degreasing.

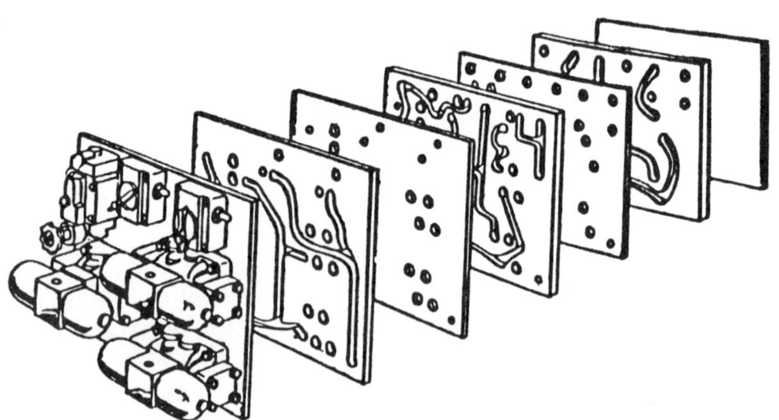

Fig. 9-6. Stacked hydraulic manifold, the "printed circuit" of hydraulics

Despite the manufacturer's efforts, scaling of the interior surfaces can still occur because the effort to coat the surfaces internally will not always be satisfactory. Where scale is suspected, a pickling process is recommended.

Pickling involves the use of a dilute acid solution passed through the conduit. After pickling, use a cold water rinse through the conduit, and rinse again with a neutralizing solution. Before using the degreased and pickled conduit, you should flush oil through the conduit to remove any traces of the solution, and to provide a compatible coating to temporarily inhibit the reoxidation of the internal surfaces.

Another problem occurs with tubing when it is installed between two ridged points. If these points are fairly close together, a straight run of tubing is not satisfactory (Fig. 9-7). To install a short straight run of tubing, you must perform operations that are not recommended, if not impossible. For example, "tube stretching" and over/undertightening of an elbow are poor practices. Instead, it is recommended that you bend an excess length of tubing into an expansion loop, so that linear flexibilty is provided.

Vibration presents an additional problem. Long runs of piping or tubing must be firmly supported by brackets or clamps to prevent them from sustaining damage caused by excessive vibration. As vibration of the system should always be considered to exist, copper tubing is not recommended. The copper becomes work-hardened and develops cracks at its joints because of vibration.

Even hoses must be properly installed to prevent damage—by avoiding twists, sharp bends, and stretching (Fig. 9-8). It is common practice for manufacturers to have a "lay line" as part of the hose.

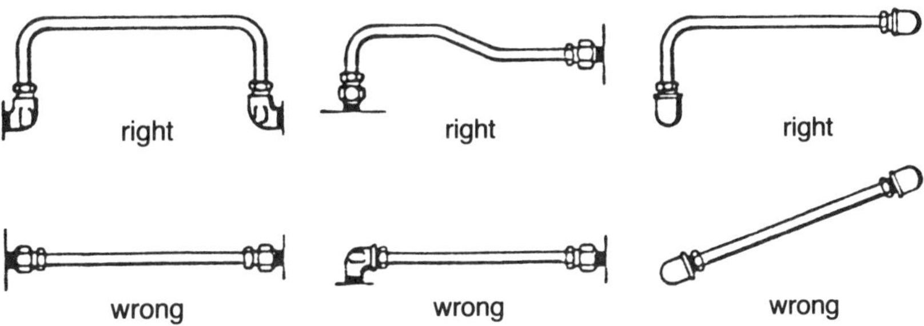

Fig. 9-7. Installation of steel tubing

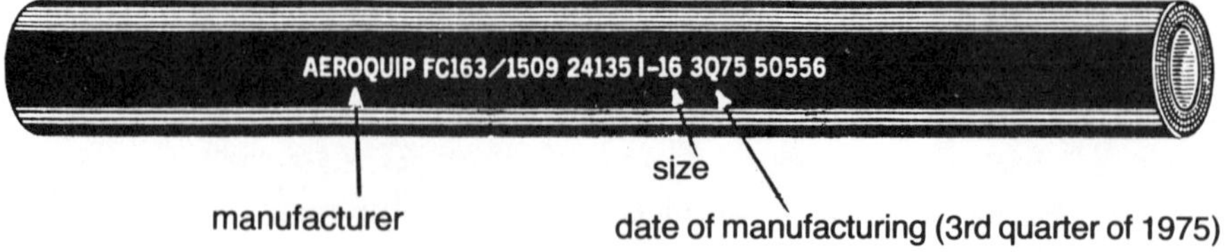

Fig. 9-8. Manufacturer's code number used as the hose lay line

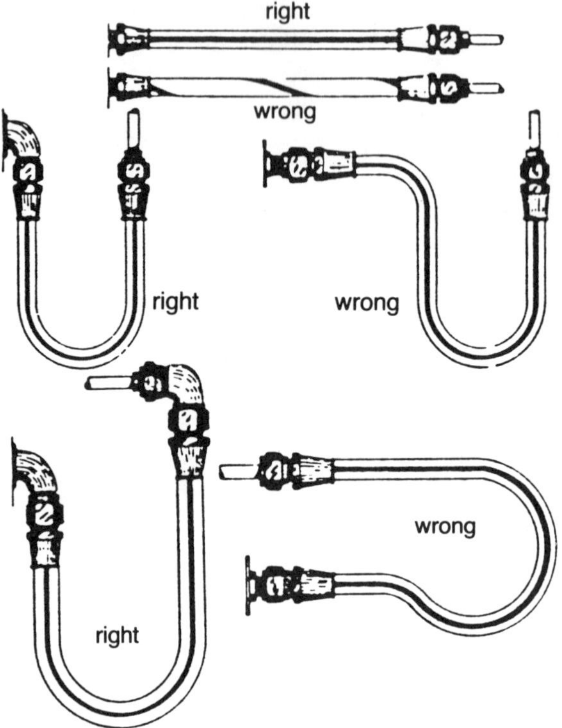

Fig. 9-9. Flexible hose installations

The lay line may be identified by a colored stripe or by the manufacturer's catalog number.* In any event, this line provides a guide to avoid twisting during installation and operation.

If twisting of the hose occurs, an internal restriction to flow develops. As oil under pressure attempts to pass the restriction, the hose expands in diameter prior to the restriction. In order for the hose to expand, it draws material elsewhere from the hose. Usually, the drawing comes from the direction of the flow, so that the material is thinned. Unfortunately, the thinning ultimately occurs where the hose is held in place by the fitting, allowing the hose to pull out of the fitting (Fig. 9-9). To avoid this condition, the hose must be suspended to form a U or a J with pipe fittings used to make any ninety-degree bends from the vertical where the hose is to be attached. Ordinarily, oil flow through a hose is opposed by sufficient friction for a natural restriction to develop. Unless additional slack is provided in the hose, it expands in diameter and contracts in length as it did when the hose was twisted.

*Although every manufacturer's catalog number varies as to content and meaning, two of the numerical groupings within this series tend to be standard, and include the manufacturing date and hose size. The manufacturing date is represented, for example, by: 3 Q 75. This means that the hose was produced in the third quarter of 1975. Elsewhere in the lay line, a number standing off by itself represents the hose inside diameter in sixteenths of an inch. Hence, "8" represents 8⁄16 or ½-inch inside diameter.

CHAPTER 10

FLUIDS, FILTERS, AND SEALS

Considerable attention has been focused on the components of the hydraulic system and their relationship to each other. But, it is important to realize that without a suitable hydraulic fluid, the system will not operate satisfactorily, or it will fail to operate altogether. Hydraulic fluids are the liquids that provide the required functions for operation and that maintain accepted properties and characteristics. Oils are generally used and may be either mineral oils with added compounds or synthetically produced products. In addition to their primary function of power transmission, hydraulic oils also provide lubrication, system cooling, and sealing.

Functions of Hydraulic Fluids

Since the transmission of power is dependent upon the ability of the system to allow the oil to move from one area to another, lubrication of the components is required to make this possible. Therefore, the internal resistance to flow, or viscosity, is of extreme importance and needs to be given considerable attention. Furthermore, if viscosity inhibits the oil from flowing freely, a considerable amount of power is consumed and wasted.

Lubrication of the system is necessary to prevent wear to those components that are subjected to rapid motion that produces friction. Consequently, continuous flow of any lubricant is essential. Hence, the hydraulic oil, as the power transfer fluid of the system, more than adequately satisfies this function.

Another function of the oil is to cool the components. This is also achieved by a continuous supply of the oil passing through the system. Heat (which is a result of friction developed by the components) and energy (which is not transformed to produce useful work) are absorbed and carried away by the oil.

Lastly, the hydraulic fluid acts as a sealant, where the oil adheres to the internal surfaces of the components in close tolerance with each other. In many systems, the major portion of internal sealing is a function of the viscosity of the oil in conjunction with the close clearances existing between the moving parts, such as the valve spool and its body.

Characteristics of Hydraulic Oils

For the system to function properly, the hydraulic fluids must possess certain important properties. Typical properties of these fluids include:

1. viscosity
2. viscosity index
3. pour point
4. demulsibility
5. flammability

Viscosity

In any fluid system, viscosity must be given the most consideration because it has a considerable bearing on the system's overall performance. To appreciate this, keep in mind that viscosity is the measurement of the internal resistance to flow. When you choose an oil because of its viscosity, you are attributing to it some of the basic physiochemical relationships associated with fluids.

For example, in the relationship of fluids, one characteristic distinguishing a gas from a liquid is the bonding attraction of their molecules. Under certain conditions, the thermal content of a liquid may be sufficient to permit a portion of the liquid to vaporize, whereas under typical room temperature conditions, gas molecules such as oxygen and nitrogen demonstrate poor quality bonding (because of their thermal content) and remain as gas. Thus, it is important to note that a liquid is a fluid composed of molecules that are highly attracted to each other or that have good cohesive qualities under existing pressure and temperature conditions, cohesion being the attraction between like substances.

The relatively high cohesive attraction of liquid molecules maintains them in close proximity to each other. As the molecules attempt to roll over each other during flow, the degree of cohesion creates the resistance to the movement of the molecules. Hence, the internal attraction of the molecules to each other gives the fluid its internal resistance to flow. The greater the internal resistance to flow, the greater the internal friction will be between the molecules and the greater will be the heat that is generated. In relation to solid surfaces that slide or roll, however, fluid friction is the least heat-producing form of friction.

On the other hand, the ability of the lubricant's molecules to maintain the bond prevents it from being squeezed from between two objects in relative motion to each other. It is desirable for high viscosity liquids to be used when the rate of relative motion is low. Conversely, when the rate of motion is high, a liquid with a high cohesive property does not readily "stick" to the surfaces in motion.

Instead, liquids that do tend to "stick" to surfaces, when subjected to a high rate of motion, are preferred. This natural ability, known as adhesion, is the attraction existing between dissimilar substances. Generally, a liquid with a high cohesive quality has a low adhesive quality, and vice versa.

Unfortunately, the conclusion may be made that a high adhesive quality oil is always preferred. Keep in mind that a low cohesive quality oil will be easily "squeezed" from between two objects that demonstrate high load characteristics. The more realistic conclusion is that a compromise must be attained with regard to choosing an oil based on its viscosity.

Of equal importance are liquids that possess a high cohesive property for proper sealing purposes. They produce the following traits within a hydraulic system:

1. high resistance to flow
2. increased power consumption from frictional losses
3. high operative temperatures from friction losses
4. increased pressure drop from high internal resistance
5. slow or sluggish operation from the inability to maintain required flow rates
6. difficulty in separating air from the oil in reservoir

On the other hand, if the adhesive quality is high, low viscosity exists, and the result is:

1. an increase in internal leakage despite the existence of the components' close clearances
2. a decrease in pump efficiency, allowing slower operation of the actuators, as the oil flow rate diminishes
3. higher operating temperatures developing from excessive internal slippage
4. high power consumption, as the system works longer to produce the required amount of work
5. excessive wear of the components, as the oil film used to separate the moving surfaces is easily reduced

Although relatively low viscosity oils are preferred for hydraulic systems, any choice of an oil, with regard to its viscosity, will be nothing more than a compromise. To choose the proper oil, you must first determine its viscosity.

The most common method to determine viscosity is to establish the time required for a standard quantity of oil, at a specific temperature, to pass through an orifice of a known cross-sectional area. The viscosity classification system used in the United States for hydraulic oils is most commonly that of the Saybolt Seconds Universal (SSU). With this system, oil is placed in a device known as a viscosimeter, and is heated and held at a specific temperature (Fig. 10-1). The number of seconds the oil takes to pass through the orifice is assigned as its SSU number. For example, if the oil in question were to take 150 seconds to drain from the viscosimeter, the oil viscosity will be 150 SSU at the tested temperature.

Although the test temperature must be maintained throughout the determination process, the viscosity measurement can be made at any desired temperature. Therefore, graphs are developed for the interpolation of viscosity for anticipated operating temperatures. This is important, since the operating temperature has a direct effect on the operating viscosity; i.e., the higher the operating temperature, the lower the viscosity. Considering that temperature variations have an overwhelming effect upon the change in viscosity, it is desirable to have an oil that changes viscosity very little over a wide operating temperature range.

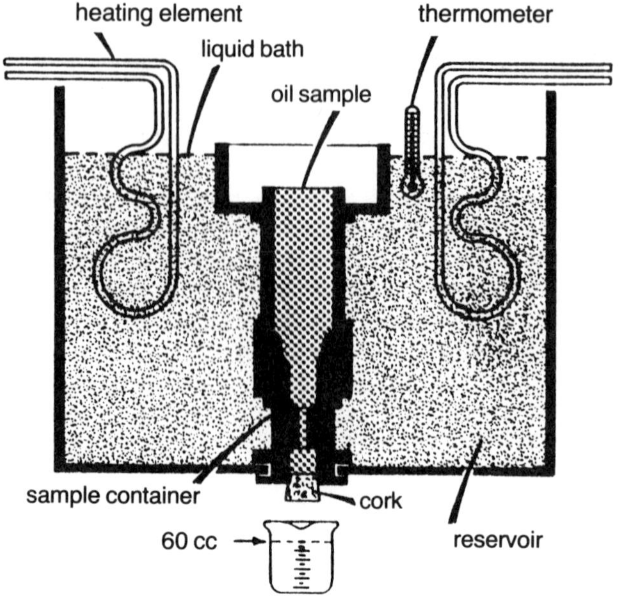

Fig. 10-1. Viscosimeter

Viscosity Index

The viscosity index is an arbitrary system developed to indicate the resistance of an oil to change its viscosity relative to temperature changes. Originally, the viscosity index had an established range value of 0 to 100. More recently, the range was increased to include numbers higher than 100, as performance additives and synthetic oils have improved this concept. Therefore, the higher the viscosity index number, the lower will be the expected change in viscosity, over a wide temperature operating range. Consequently, an oil with a high viscosity index number is desirable for a hydraulic system.

It is worthwhile to note at this point that although viscosity varies inversely as temperature changes, viscosity increases as pressure increases. With pressure conditions remaining constant, an increase in temperature will cause the viscosity to decrease. However, when a liquid in motion is exposed to *extreme* pressure conditions, even though the temperature increases as well, the viscosity will rise.

Although they are usually considered to be incompressible under atmospheric conditions, liquids under elevated pressures will experience a volumetric reduction by ½ of 1 percent per 1,000 psi. Therefore, at 3,000 psi, the volume of the oil will be reduced by nearly 1.5 percent. As this volumetric reduction requires the "space" between the liquid molecules to be reduced, the molecules are no longer able to "roll over" each other as freely as when they were not under compression. Hence, greater internal resistance to flow, or higher viscosity, results.

Pour Point

Normally, hydraulic systems operate at relatively constant temperatures. However, since a system is directly exposed to ambient conditions which may make for depressed temperature conditions, the oil in the system should possess a low pour point.

The pour point of an oil is the lowest temperature at which it continues to pour. The rule of thumb for pour point is 20°F below the lowest expected operating ambient temperature. It should be noted that there is no direct correlation between pour point and viscosity. The pour point is based primarily upon the crude oil from which it was produced, although its performance can be improved by the use of additives.

Demulsibility

Another important operating property of oil is its ability to separate freely from water to avoid forming an emulsion, a quality known as demulsibility. Ordinarily, oil and water do not readily mix, except where agitation and/or heat are present. Hydraulic systems, however, possess the potential condition for oil and water to form harmful emulsions. Since moisture enters the system through the service tank vent, additives are mixed with the oils to improve their ability to separate.

While water in the system promotes the oxidation of steel components, it is equally important to realize that water helps to form acids. When emulsions develop, and are subjected to heat and agitation in the presence of anhydrides, acidification of the oil develops. For example, carbon dioxide (freely associated with the atmosphere), in the presence of water and oil emulsions, provides the catalyst for acidification, i.e., carbonic acid.

The bonding attraction of the oil molecules, in the presence of water and heat, particularly the hydrocarbon-based oils, results in the rearrangement of the hydrogen molecules into hydroxyl ions and a modified hydrocarbon chain. Hydroxyl ions readily bond with simple inert compounds, such as the carbon dioxide, to form carbonic acid. As acidity increases in quantity, the percentage of oil emulsions increases, producing a detrimental and debilitating cycle.

With the percentage of the acid increasing, the viscosity of the oil increases because the "bulkier" molecules remain when the hydroxyl ions break off to form the acid. Consequently, damage to the system becomes a greater problem. Not only will the acids directly corrode components, but gums and varnishes form and will be deposited on the internal surfaces. Therefore, oxidizing resistants are added to the oil to help prevent these potential problems.

Flammability

Despite the precautions used to prevent external leakage, oil deposits will inevitably collect outside the system. When this condition exists, a potential fire hazard is present. Flammability of the oil is required to be high, not only to prevent this hazard, but also to prevent spontaneous combustion in the normal operation of the system.

Types of Hydraulic Oils

Having considered the various properties and characteristics of the hydraulic fluids, it will be beneficial to briefly identify some of the fluids used in hydraulic systems. Basically, these fluids fall into two broad categories—petroleum-based and fire-resistant.

Petroleum-Based

Petroleum-based hydraulic oils are by far the most widely used. Their operating characteristics depend upon the following factors:

1. the type of crude oil from which they were refined
2. the degree and method by which they were refined
3. the additives used to improve their operating characteristics

In general, for shipboard use, petroleum-derived oils possess excellent lubricity. Depending upon the sources of crude oil, they retain characteristics such as high demulsibility and high viscosity index, and are more oxidation resistant at high temperatures than are other liquids. Oil naturally prevents oxidation of metals, as well as dissipates heat easily. It is easily kept clean by filtration and settling. Where certain operational properties are lacking, these oils are improved by the refining process, and/or the incorporation of additives.

The greatest disadvantage of these fluids is their flammability. While flammability requirements for shipboard use of these oils is generally satisfactory, other industries require higher flammability levels.

Fire-Resistant

Three basic types of fire-resistant fluids are used when flammability is a problem:

1. water-glycol solutions
2. water-oil emulsions
3. synthetically produced fluids

Water-glycol fluids are typically composed of three major components:

1. 35 percent to 40 percent water—to provide flammability resistance
2. synthetically produced glycols
3. a water soluble thickener to improve viscosity

Because of the nature of water glycol solutions, they must contain additives to prevent foaming, rust, and corrosion, as well as additives to improve lubrication.

As long as high speeds and high loads are avoided, water-glycol solutions generally display good wear-resistant characteristics. However, these fluids must be measured continually for water content. Evaporation losses require the make-up of water to maintain proper viscosity. Evaporation also leads to the loss of certain additives that prolong the life of the fluid and the hydraulic components. In addition, certain metals, such as zinc, chromium, and magnesium, as well as paints and enamels, react unfavorably with these liquids.

Lastly, operating temperatures must remain low in order to avoid separation of the compounds.

Water-oil emulsions are the least expensive of the fire-resistant fluids. Like the water-glycol fluids, they also depend on the water content to produce their fire-resistant property. In addition to water and oil, the emulsions contain emulsifiers, stabilizers, and other additives to hold the two liquids in a homogenous solution.

Based on their relative percentage of water, these emulsions are regarded as oil-in-water or water-in-oil emulsions. The former contain tiny droplets of specially refined oil dispersed in water. The water, considered as the *continuous phase,* creates the characteristics of this fluid; and it is found to behave more like water, rather than other types of hydraulic fluids. This fluid is, therefore, highly fire-retardant, low in viscosity, and provides excellent cooling capabilities. Additives are obviously required to improve lubrication and to protect against rust.

The water-in-oil emulsion, on the other hand, has tiny droplets of water dispersed in the oil, the continuous phase. Therefore, like oil, these fluids have excellent lubricity and body. In addition to its good fire-retardant capability, it has cooling ability, because of the dispersed water. Both rust and anti-foaming inhibitors need to be added to the solutions to improve their overall operating characteristics.

Although these emulsions are compatible with most seals and metals, precautions must be taken to prevent freezing and thawing, as separation of these fluids will result. Also, these emulsions have a greater affinity for contaminants, and require closer attention than straight mineral oils with regard to filtration and maintenance.

The third type of fire-resistant fluid is represented by the laboratory synthesized chemicals, which are less flammable than the petroleum-based oils. Typical of these synthetics are: phosphate esters, chlorinated (halogenated) hydrocarbons, or a mixture of both of these plus other minerals.

Synthetic fluids work well at both high temperatures and pressures, as they contain no water or other volatile materials. However, they do not work well under low temperature conditions, and they have extremely poor viscosity index ratings, ranging from 80 to as low as -400. Consequently, these fluids are limited to use in systems where the anticipated operating temperatures are not expected to vary, and the temperature of operation is not expected to drop below that of normal room temperature.

Another problem with synthetic fluids is that they are not compatible with typically accepted seal materials, such as Buna-N. Coupled with the fact that these fluids are the most expensive to produce, the operating cost of the system is escalated by the use of specialized seal materials.

Maintenance of Hydraulic Oils

Regardless of the type of hydraulic fluid used, they all have one factor in common. The cleaner the fluid, the longer it lasts, and the more effective it is in performing its designated functions. To help maintain the cleanliness of the oil in these systems, any process of filtering, straining, settling, centrifuging, or combination of these are used.

In attempting to differentiate between filters and strainers, certain problems occur as a result of "accepted misuse," rather than the inability to define the terms properly. A filter is a device whose primary function is the retention, by some porous medium, of fine, insoluble contaminants. Strainers, on the other hand, have the ability to remove particles generally coarser than those particles removed by filters.

Filters are typically categorized as being of the absorbent or adsorbent types. Absorbent filters perform their job by "soaking up" the contaminants into the porous filter medium, just as a sponge absorbs water. A wide range of porous materials have been used, including paper, wood pulp, cotton, yarn, and cellulose.

Adsorbent filters, on the other hand, remove contaminants by having them "cling" or adhere to the porous material. Materials such as charcoal or fuller's earth have been used for this type of filter. However, adsorbent filters have the ability to remove oil additives and thus are not generally used in hydraulic systems.

Filter elements are additionally identified as being surface or depth type (Fig. 10-2). The surface type element, the most common, is constructed of closely woven fabric, compressed fiber material, or treated paper so that the pores permit fluid flow through the element.

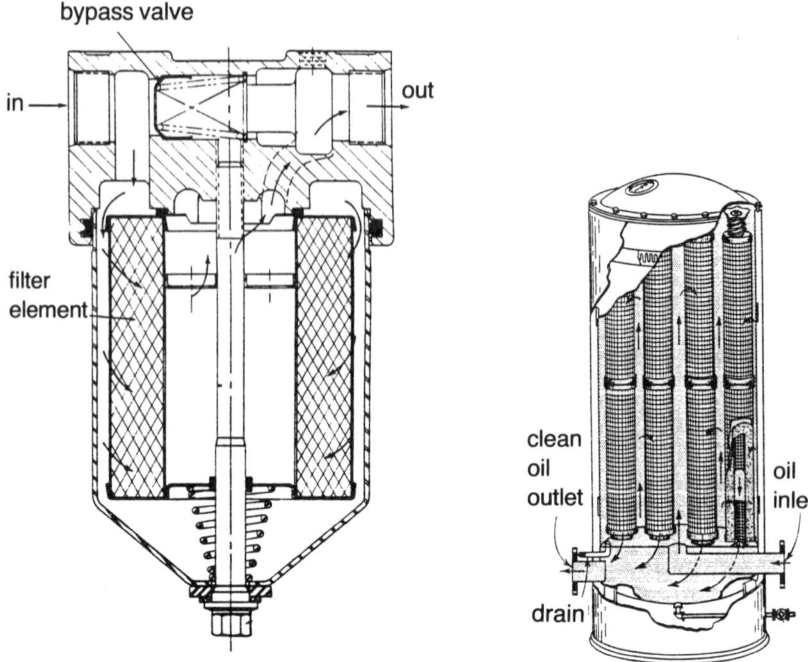

Fig. 10-2. Typical surface and depth type filters

The size of the contaminant that can be removed is indicated by the filter nominal or absolute rating. The nominal rating is an indication of the smallest size particle that can be effectively removed by the filter. Thus, a 10-micron rating means that 98 percent of the particles of a 10-micron diameter (1 micron equals .000039 of an inch) will be removed. The absolute rating for the same filter would be slightly higher, such as a 25-micron rating, where 100 percent of the particles 25 microns or larger will be extracted from the filtered liquid.

A depth-type filter is composed of layers of fabric or fibers, which provide many tortuous paths to the fluid flow. The pores, or passages, vary in size, where the degree of filtration depends upon the flow rate through the filter. Increasing the flow rate through the filter dislodges trapped particles. Therefore, this type of filter is limited to low-flow, low-pressure-drop conditions.

In addition, filters are also designated as full flow. As the filter element is gradually saturated, flow across the element becomes proportionally limited or blocked. A spring-loaded bypass valve is incorporated and opens to permit oil flow to pass around the element. This allows operation of the system to remain unaffected by the loss or reduction of flow. To aid the operator in knowing when the element becomes saturated, requiring changing or cleaning, a mechanical indicator is provided. The indicator changes its position because of the increased pressure drop across the filter. Therefore, the position change of the internal mechanism externally changes a "flag," or rotates an internal colored drum, which notifies the operator.

Remember that strainers remove only coarse particles. Usually, they are constructed of a wire mesh, or are a perforated, thin-gauge sheet metal. Because of the size of the openings, only those particles observable to the naked eye are removed. The greatest advantage of the strainer occurs under low-flow, low-pressure conditions where a relatively low pressure drop is desirable. For this reason, strainers are used exclusively on the pump inlet where coarse debris is prevented from entering and damaging the pump. Since this permits fine insoluble contaminants to be discharged to the system, discharge filters are required to complement the strainers for proper fluid decontamination.

Ordinarily, the heavier coarse metal particles settle out and collect on the bottom of the sump. Normal design considerations prevent these particles from being re-entrained by the oil flow as it passes through the sump on its way to the pump inlet. The strainer complements the sump design in order to remove these errant particles by prudent placement of magnets. Ideally, coarse metal particles should never be able to pass into the pump. Magnets are either a part of the strainer device, or the sump itself.

Regardless of the hydraulic oil used, constant replacement of these fluids is extremely expensive. Therefore, a good maintenance program is essential to prevent needless replacement. Where extremely large quantities of hydraulic oil are used, purification through centrifuging is more practical. Although centrifuging is the quickest and most effective means of removing contaminants, the first three methods will be satisfactory for most hydraulic systems.

Sealing the Hydraulic System

Just as the type of oil and the methods of keeping the oil clean are essential for proper operation of the system, keeping the oil in the system, or within the designated areas of the system, is equally important. The proper seal provides this important function, and is encompassed by a vast array of types and applications. Poor sealing permits internal or external leakage and also results in inefficiency, power loss, or, simply, "housekeeping" problems.

As noted previously, hydraulic system components are often designed and built with close operating clearances in which a small amount of internal leakage is permitted. In certain instances constant internal leakage is provided to allow moving components to be lubricated. In addition, certain hydraulic controls have designed internal leakage provided to prevent hunting (or oscillating) of valve spools and pistons.

Internal leakage does not represent a loss of fluid from the system, since the fluid finds its way back to the sump. However, as components begin to wear, and these clearances become greater, more fluid is able to bypass the components. Consequently, the work normally provided by the system drops off, and in certain cases, excess heat is generated.

External leakage is more obvious. Aside from the potential hazards, external leakage becomes expensive because the lost fluid cannot be reclaimed. The principal cause of external leakage is improper installation. While joints may leak as a result of improper assembly, vibrations and shock cause them to become loose. Failure to connect drain lines, excessive operating pressures, and fluid contamination also contribute to external leakage.

Proper sealing is required to maintain operating pressure, and to prevent fluid loss and the entrance of contaminants. Various methods and types of seals are used, depending upon whether the seal is to be positive or nonpositive; and whether its application is static or dynamic.

Positive seals, such as gaskets used to seal flanges, prevent the most minute amount of leakage. On the other hand, nonpositive seals allow a small amount of internal leakage. An example of the latter type is the clearance of a valve spool in its bore, where the lubricating oil film seals the "gap" (Fig. 10-3).

Static seals are devices compressed between two rigidly connected parts. While some shifting of the seal occurs as pressure alternately increases and relaxes, the joined components do not move relative to each other. Dynamic seals are installed between components requiring them to move relative to each other. At least one component rubs against the seal, so that it is subjected to wear.

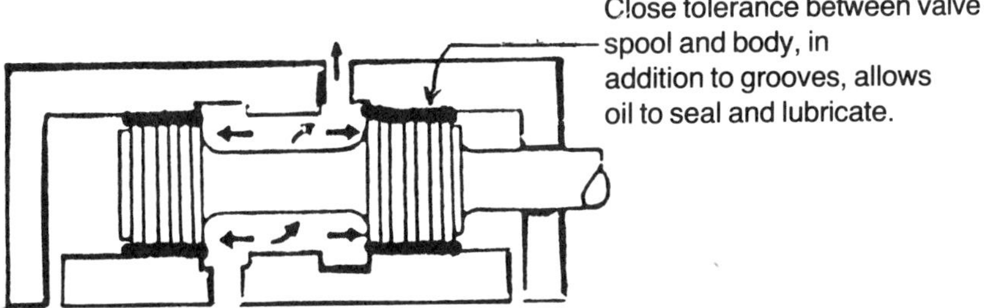

Fig. 10-3. Viscosity of oil instrumental in sealing spool valve

O-Rings

The most common static seal used in hydraulic systems is the O-ring, a molded synthetic rubber seal with a rounded cross-sectional area. Generally, it is installed in an annular groove machined in one of the mating parts. When the mating parts are assembled, the top and bottom surfaces of the ring are lightly compressed, developing a static seal under low-pressure conditions. As pressure on the ring increases it is forced against the side of the annulus, away from the source of pressure. In this manner the O-ring increases its seal at the top and bottom contact areas because of the change in its shape (Fig. 10-4). Since the seal is pressure actuated, as it is compressed and the applied pressure continues to increase, its sealing ability increases.

Despite the O-ring's excellent static sealing ability, its use with devices that move an appreciable linear distance is impractical. Under certain conditions, drag will cause the pliable material to slip in between the clearance of the two mating surfaces. This results in the "pinching off" of a small portion of the ring, distorting the shape of the outer surface to allow leakage. Consequently, O-rings are mainly suitable for static sealing or limited motion devices, such as valve spools.

Backup Rings

Again, O-rings extrude easily under extremely high pressure and excessive linear motion. Despite this drawback, a backup ring can be placed in the annular groove with the O-ring (Fig. 10-5). Usually made of nylon, the backup ring is installed on the low-pressure side of the O-ring in direct contact with its mating surface. The stiffer

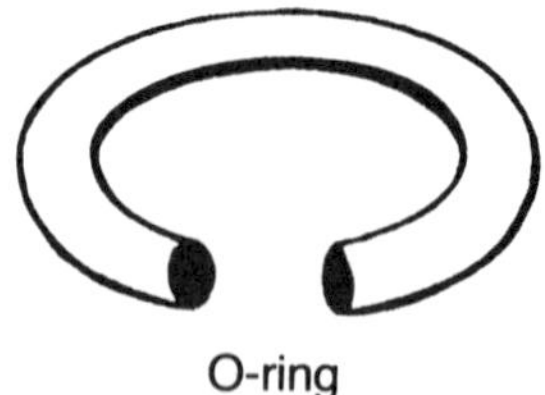

Fig. 10-4. Cross-sectional view of O-ring

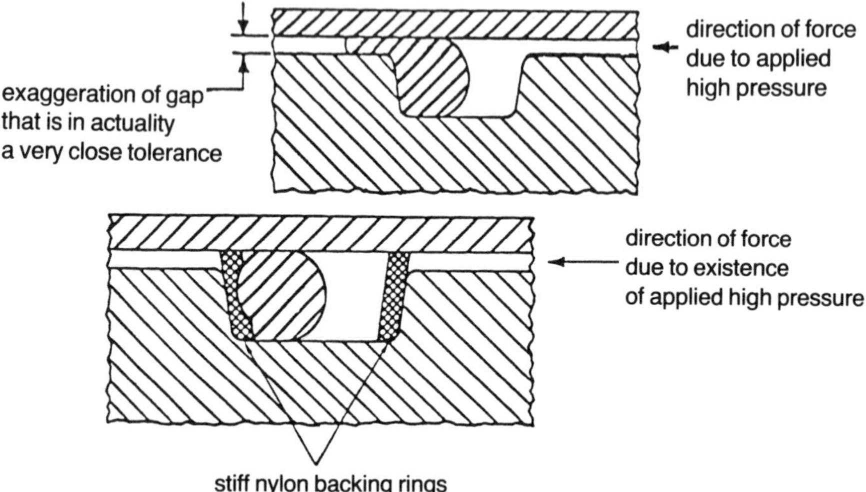

Fig. 10-5. Results and remedies of high pressure exposure upon O-rings

backup ring prevents the O-ring from extruding and from being pinched when exposed to high pressure.

If high pressure is applied in either direction, such as a double-acting piston, it might seem reasonable to use the backup rings. This has proved to be satisfactory; however, there is a tendency for them to "cock" in the annulus or to allow the O-ring to roll.

Therefore, on some reciprocating pistons, a T-ring, also made of synthetic rubber, is preferred (Fig. 10-6). On either side of the tail of the "T," a softer sealing ring is installed, usually with a rectangular cross-sectional area. As pressure builds on either side of the "T," the tail is able to inhibit the seal extrusion, regardless of the direction of linear motion.

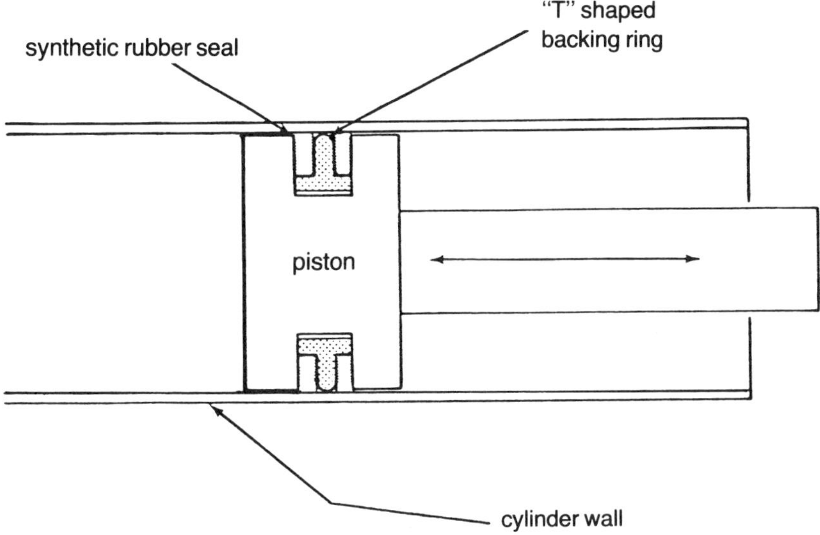

Fig. 10-6. "T"-shaped nylon backing ring used to reinforce synthetic rubber seals on small high-pressure actuators

Piston Seals

Another method of sealing the piston is with the use of cup seals (Fig. 10-7). Primarily used on low-pressure cylinders, the cups fit snugly in the cylinder and are held firmly to a multipiece piston. While oil under pressure forces the cup sides to press securely against the cylinder wall, a substantial amount of seal surface area is subjected to wear.

As an alternative solution, pistons used for extremely high-pressure applications are provided with automotive type metal rings (Fig. 10-8). Since these rings are split, to facilitate installation in the ring groove, one lone ring is unsatisfactory for sealing. Consequently, four or five rings are used to seal the high-pressure side from the low-pressure side. Because of the nature of the rings, small amounts of internal leakage are not uncommon, and are usually expected to be in the range of 1 to 5 cubic inches per minute.

Elastomers have become more prevalent as seal materials. U- or V-shaped elastomer compression seals are widely used for both

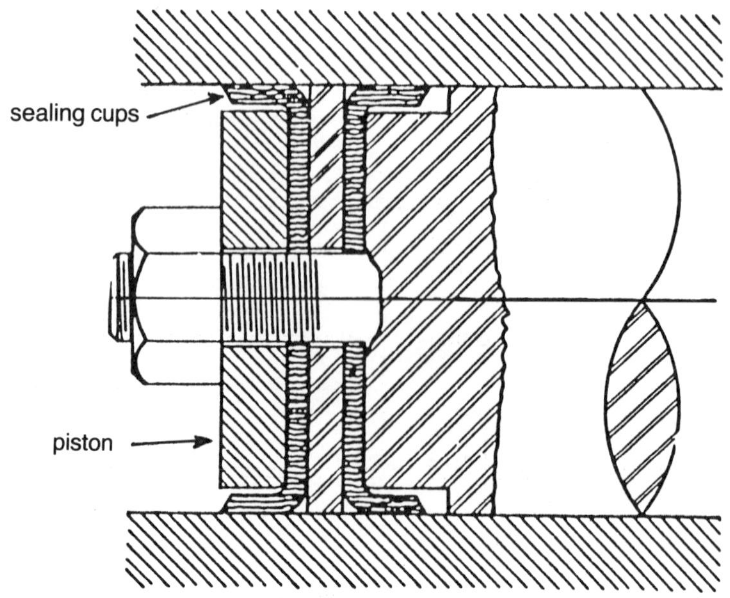

Fig. 10-7. Cup type seal for low-pressure linear actuator piston

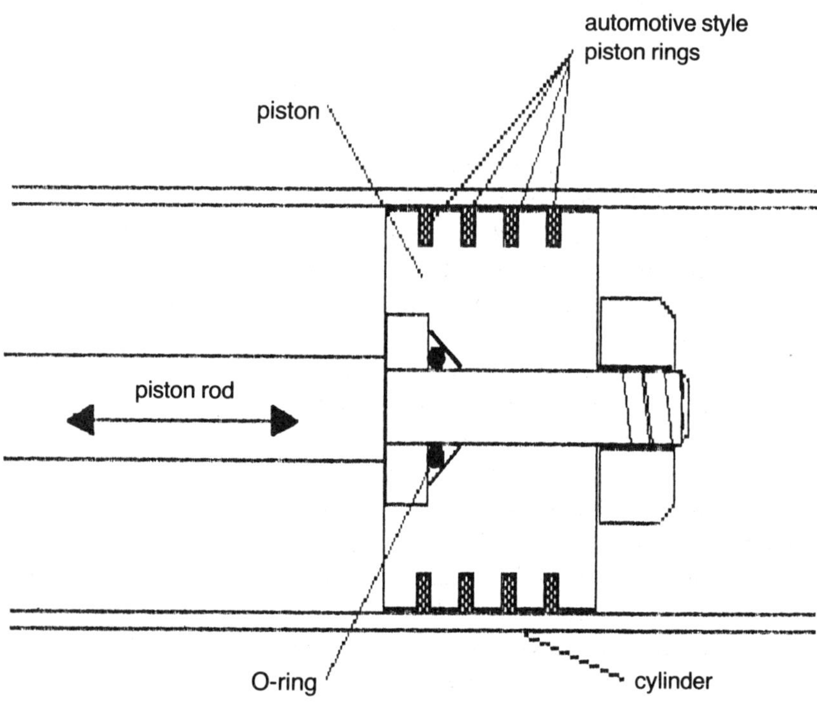

Fig. 10-8. Linear actuator with automotive type piston rings

the piston and the rod end seals of linear actuators. These multi-ring seals are also referred to as self-adjusting because of the manner in which they are assembled and the way they react to pressure increases (Fig. 10-9). The innermost, or male ring, is flat on the pressure side and shaped to mate with the inner surfaces of the subsequent adjoining U- or V-ring. There are as many as six intermediate rings between the inner male ring and the outer female ring. The rings are held in place in the stuffing box by the gland ring that is either bolted or screwed to the cylinder. As the internal pressure increases, the ring stack is compressed with the intermediate rings becoming somewhat flattened. As the rings "flatten out," they expand radially (perpendicular to the cylinder axis) to increase their seal capability.

Rotating Shaft Seals

Rotating shafts, such as pumps and motors, are sealed with "lip" seals or mechanical seals (Fig. 10-10). O-rings are impractical for this application, as they will be "grabbed" by the shaft during rotation. This allows the ring to be thinned in one area, and permits leakage. Instead, lip seals composed of synthetic rubber collars are placed around the shaft and are held in place by a housing within the casing. The seal lip extends inward, held to the shaft by a retaining spring, in order to seal the shaft under low-pressure conditions. As the internal pressure increases, the seal is forced to "hug" the shaft to prevent external leakage.

Pumps and motors, operating in higher-pressure ranges, are more suitably sealed by mechanical devices. Mechanical seals are generally set up in two stages (Fig. 10-11). The primary or dynamic seal is composed of two rings. The stationary steel ring, held firmly in place, is forced to maintain contact with a carbon ring secured to the rotating shaft. Because of the nature of these materials, the mating surfaces become highly polished. This reduces friction with the full contact area maintained during rotation. The secondary or static seal is usually an O-ring fitted around each of the primary seal rings to prevent oil from leaking around the outer edges. With the use of a coiled spring, sufficient linear force is developed to keep the rings in contact under all operating phases.

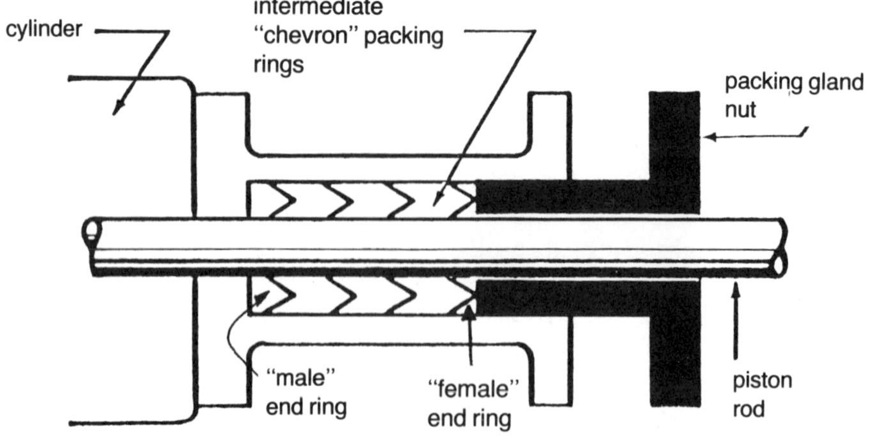

Fig. 10-9. Self-adjusting, compressive "chevron" type packing

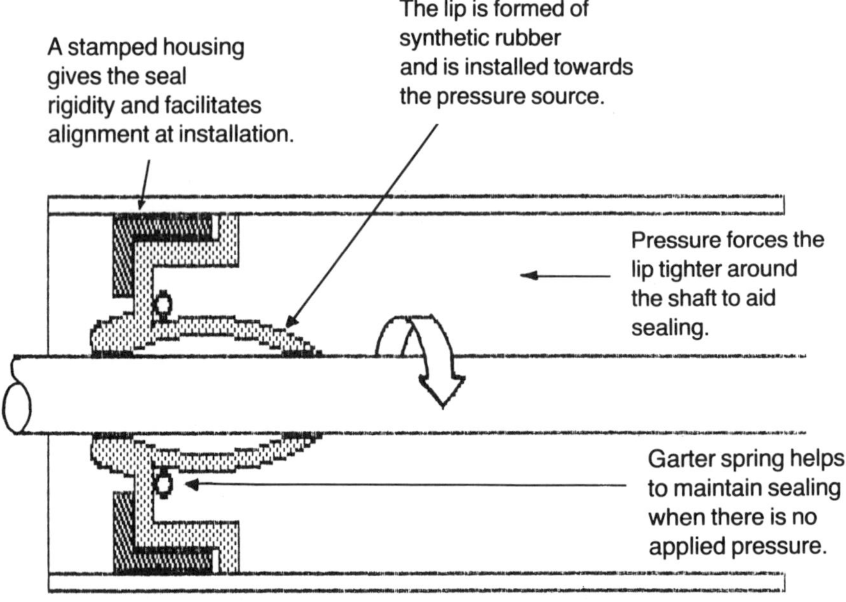

Fig. 10-10. Lipseal used on low-pressure rotating pump and motor shafts

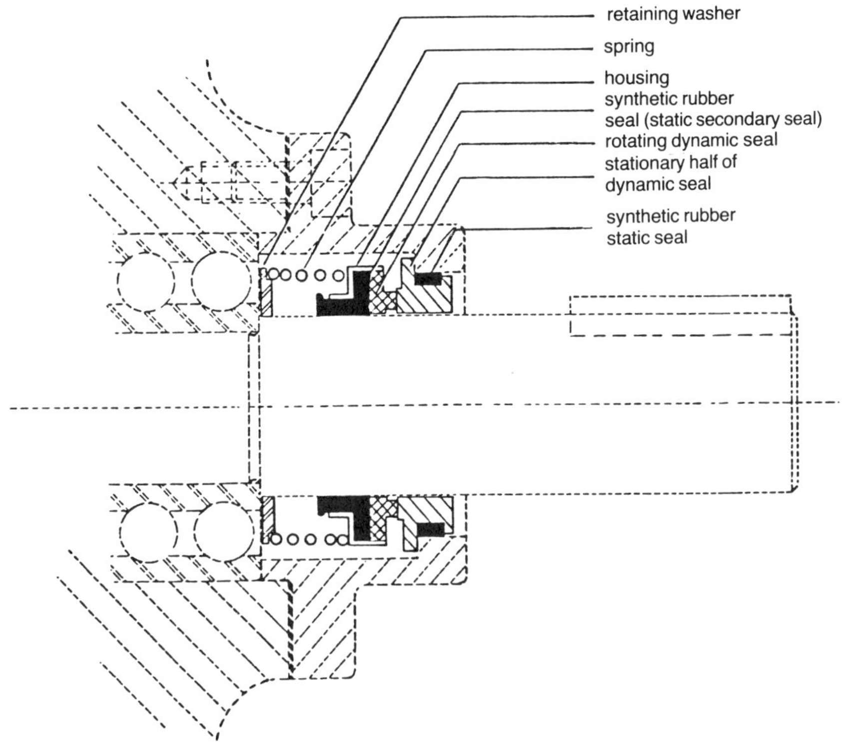

Fig. 10-11. Mechanical seal for high-pressure pump and motor shafts

Seal Materials

With the exception of steel piston rings and the primary segment of the mechanical seal, seals are made of flexible elastomers. In the past, materials such as leather, cork, or impregnated fiber materials were used. They all possessed intrinsic drawbacks of either swelling or developing particle breakoff. As advances in the production of elastomer products have occurred since World War II, materials such as Buna-N, silicone, neoprene, and fluoroplastics have increased in popularity.

Buna-N (nitrile) is a compound that is moderately tough, wears well, and is inexpensive. It maintains its shape and sealing ability reasonably well over a wide temperature range of −40° to 230° Fahrenheit.

Silicone, another elastomer, has a much wider operating range than Buna-N. It has become a very popular material for rotating shaft seals that operate in conditions ranging from very cold to very hot. It retains its shape and sealing abilities in temperatures as low as −60° Fahrenheit, and as high as 500° Fahrenheit. However, at elevated temperatures, it tends to absorb oil and to swell. When this occurs, it also tends to tear and abrade easily, making it unsatisfactory for most reciprocating devices.

Neoprene, the earliest elastomer used, is still widely used today. However, it becomes vulcanized or cooked at temperatures above 150° Fahrenheit. A durable material, nonetheless, it is well suited for low temperature operating conditions that use petroleum-based fluids.

Fluoroplastics are synthesized materials combining fluorine with an elastomer or plastic. Various brand names exist for similar materials, such as Teflon, Kel-F, and Viton-A, with Teflon being the best known. Nylon is yet another synthetic material with similar properties. Often this material is used in combination with elastomers as backup rings and as sealing materials in limited application. Teflon is very popular as a pipe joint sealing material, although it is available in other usable forms. It is compatible with most hydraulic fluids and has a high resistance to heat (500° Fahrenheit).

Teflon's greatest disadvantage is its lack of elasticity, i.e., it does not readily return to its original shape. Consequently, attempts to reuse the Teflon seal will show that it does not prevent leaks it had originally sealed.

CHAPTER 11

STORAGE OF HYDRAULIC OILS

The many aspects of hydraulic oils required for a system and the need to keep them free of contaminants are of obvious concern and importance as you have seen in the last chapter. However, the inability to maintain an adequate supply of oil causes the system to fail just as easily as if the wrong or contaminated oil were used.

In order for the hydraulic oil to be maintained and adequately supplied, it must be stored properly. There are three types of oil storage: for continuous normal use, for emergency and short duration, and for long-term replenishing.

Service Tanks

Storage of oil during normal continuous use is performed by the service tank (also known as the sump or reservoir) (Fig. 11-1). Efficient design of the service tank also provides:

1. a means to allow entrapped air to escape from the oil
2. an area for solid contaminants to settle out
3. a means for heat to be dissipated from the oil
4. a convenient mounting base for the power unit

As time is an important consideration in the design of the service tank, certain physical concepts need to be considered. As a rule of thumb, the tank should have sufficient volume to hold a quantity of oil two to three times the flow rate of the system for one minute. In other words, if the pump develops a flow rate of five gpm, the reservoir should hold ten to fifteen gallons. During the period of

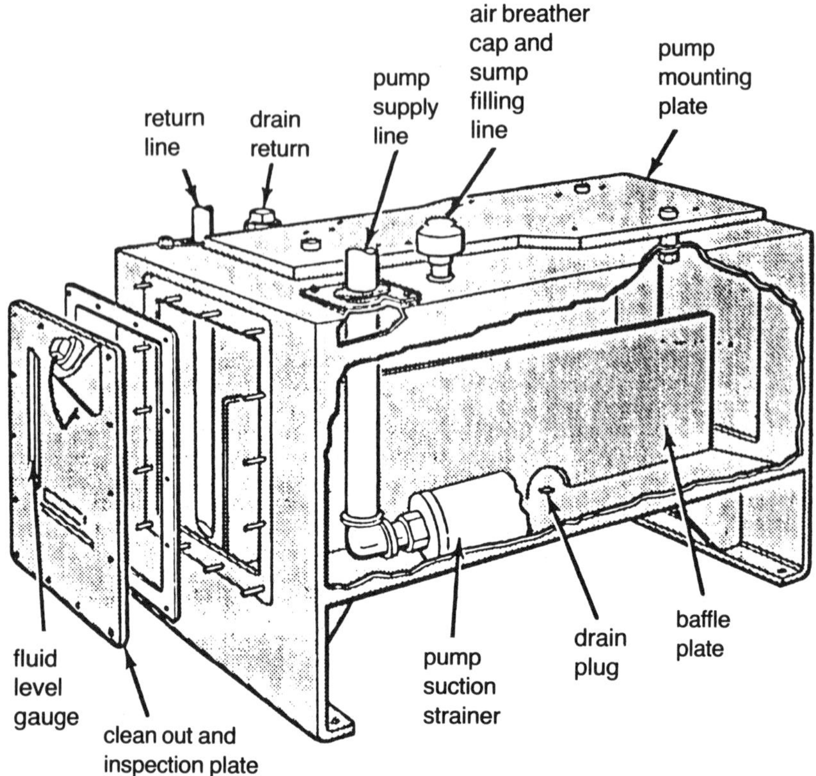

Fig. 11-1. Typical arrangement of a hydraulic reservoir

storage, it is important for air, solid contaminants, and heat to be dissipated from the oil. Therefore, the design of the reservoir should permit two to three complete changes of the oil to occur before the original quantity passes through the system a second time.

To facilitate this, the physical shape and internal design of the tank are extremely important. Since physical limitations are placed on the tank by its installation location, considerations as to height, width, and depth comprise the general guidelines. The height of the tank is recommended to be no greater than the width, whereas the tank length should not be less than twice the width. The height/ width relationship allows sufficient depth of the oil to avoid placing the pump in a position that would demand an excessive suction lift. The length of the tank is important to provide sufficient distance for the oil to travel in order for time and gravity to help settle out solids. Generally, this is accomplished by having the oil reenter the sump in an area diagonal to the pump suction.

In certain instances, the installation limitations shorten the length of the tank and require the installation of internal baffles. One advantage of the baffles is that they limit the free surface effect on the oil (surging). Most important, however, is the extension of the distance the oil travels from the time it reenters the tank until it reenters the pump suction.

Another plus to the time extension of oil passage to the pump suction is the release of entrapped air. By having the return line located below the normal oil level, foaming of the oil will be avoided. Otherwise, the oil impinging on the surface causes the pump to starve or to cavitate as the oil foams.

Time is important in allowing contaminants to settle out of the oil, but once they have dropped out of suspension, they must not return to it. Consequently, the bottom of the tank is sloped, or dished, to allow the contaminants to gravitate to and collect in one area. As the contaminants gravitate away from the suction, they are prevented from being picked up. This also provides for easy removal of the sludge during the periodic cleaning and inspection of the tank.

It is important that the pump suction line be kept as short as possible. Yet, it must be kept fully submerged and away from the area where sludge has accumulated. Excessive suction line heights and/or lengths develop sufficient pressure drops, because of increased frictional losses, to lead to pump cavitation. Since the pump is usually mounted on top of the tank, these errors can be easily avoided.

Atmospheric pressure exerted on the oil within the tank is necessary to produce a pressure differential to force the oil into the pump inlet. To facilitate the atmospheric pressure to act upon the stored liquid, a vent must be installed. Dust will enter the tank with the exchange of air because of the constant heating and cooling of the oil during normal operation. To limit the entrance of dust, a vent breather/filter cap combination is employed. This device, packed with a noncorrosive filament, allows air to pass, but traps dust within its fibrous passages. The breather cap, fitted with a dipstick to measure sump level, is used as a convenient means of capping off the filling tube.

Other design considerations of the tank include a drain plug, clean-out cover, and sight glass. It stands to reason that the drain plug must be placed at the lowest point of the sump. This allows for accumulated water to be drawn off, and the tank can be easily drained of its contents when it is to be opened.

For thorough internal inspection, the clean-out cover is provided to allow the tank to be cleaned of accumulated sludge, and for examination of the tank sides to determine the condition of the internal protective coating.

The protective coating is used to prevent the steel sides from becoming oxidized, as this would add to the contamination of the stored oil. Despite the aspect of oxidation, steel is desired over nonferrous metals, as these materials can affect the quality and longevity of the oil.

The sight glass provides a quick reference of the available oil supply in the tank. It must be of sufficient length to show minimum and maximum acceptable tank levels. The normal level of the retained oil should therefore occur at mid-position of the glass.

Accumulators

All shipboard hydraulic systems utilize vented service tanks, although various aerospace systems require the use of pressurized reservoirs. While only a minority of hydraulic systems employ the pressurized reservoir, there is a definite need for oil to be maintained under pressure in vented systems by devices known as accumulators.

The function of the accumulator is twofold. First, it maintains a limited quantity of oil under pressure for short-duration emergency use. Second, it absorbs shock waves in systems that would not be handled by the "popping" of the relief valves.

Accumulator design is primarily of three types: weight-loaded, spring-loaded, and gas-charged.

The weight-loaded accumulator is simply oil within a cylinder that is acted upon by a piston designed to support a set of weights (Fig. 11-2A). The force of the weights, exerted over the surface area of the piston, results in the pressure being applied to the oil. When pressure in the system drops momentarily, the oil is forced into the system to maintain the required operating pressure. While the ability of this design is excellent for absorbing system shocks, it has certain inherent limitations which prevent it from being used extensively.

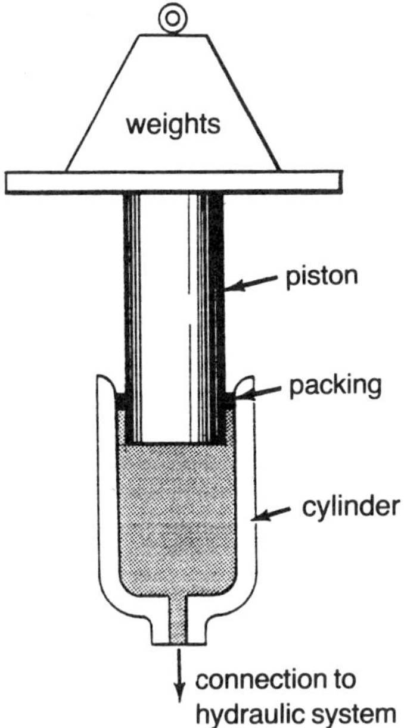

Fig. 11-2A. Weight-loaded accumulator

Although this type of accumulator maintains consistent exertion of pressure on the oil throughout its voiding cycle, the quantity of oil stored is limited. If the system requires a substantial quantity of oil in order to stroke the actuator during an emergency, the accumulator size must be increased. As the accumulator volume is increased, the size of the weights that produce the desired output pressure need to be increased. Consequently, the overall size and weight of the unit may no longer be satisfactory. In addition, as the amount of weight dictates the accumulator output pressure, the amount of weight must be changed when it is necessary to reset the working pressure of the system.

One method used to attain the advantage of the weight-loaded accumulator is to exchange the set of weights for an adjustable compression spring (Fig. 11-2B). With this variable spring force capability, any system changes can be accommodated.

However, since its design is similar to that of the weight-loaded type, the quantity of oil reserve remains limited. Also, as oil is forced from the cylinder, the spring expands, and the resultant pressure

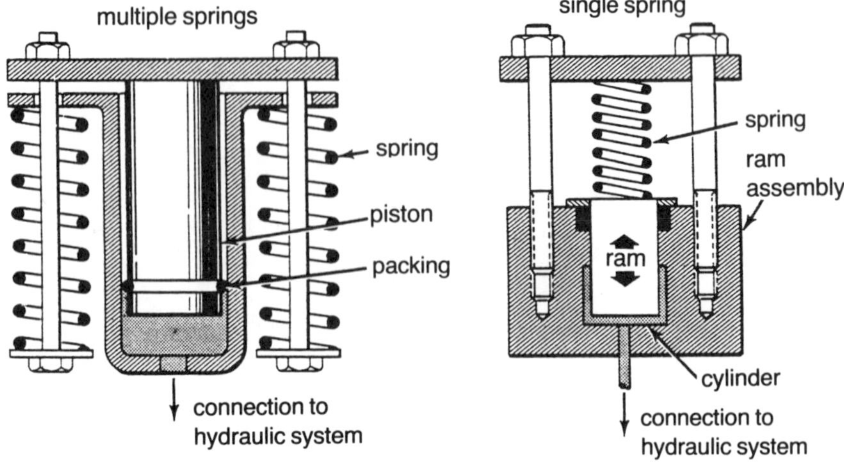

Fig. 11-2B. Spring-loaded hydraulic accumulators

continues to drop off. Therefore, the prime advantage of the spring-loaded accumulator is to provide shock absorption for the system.

Although both types of accumulators are simple in design, and are relatively inexpensive, their inherent disadvantages may limit their application. Various systems require a substantial reserve of oil to be maintained under pressure for emergency operation. It is obvious that neither of the previous designs provides this function.

The gas-charged accumulator, however, can be made sufficiently large without substantially increasing the weight of the unit (Fig. 11-2C). As one-half to three-quarters of the total volume of the accumulator chamber will be filled with oil, the remainder is occupied by the pressurized gas. Thus, the amount of stored oil can be properly maintained for one operating cycle of the system. Despite this favorable advantage, there are disadvantages of this type that also limit its use.

For the accumulator to be charged, a supply of clean dry inert gas, such as nitrogen, must be kept on hand. A bladder or bag is preferred to separate the gas from the stored oil to prevent direct gas absorption by the oil. If compressed air were inadvertently used, and the bladder were to leak, an explosion would be possible. In addition, as oil is forced from the accumulator the gas expands, reducing the applied force to the trapped oil.

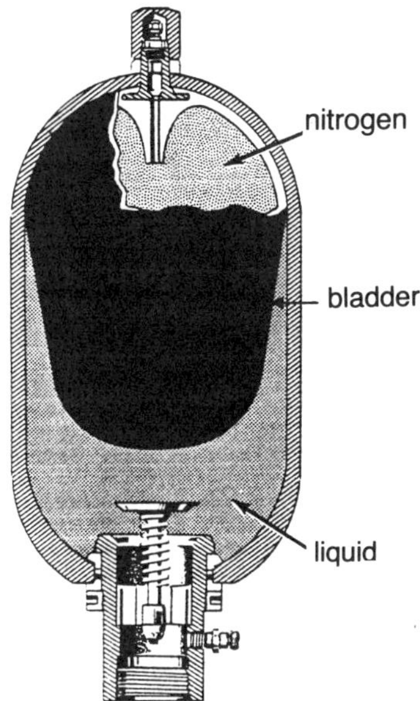

Fig. 11-2C. Gas-charged accumulator

As ambient temperature changes occur, the volume of gas is affected; hence a change in available oil volume and charge pressure results. For example, as ambient temperature increases, the gas expands and increases the pressure in the accumulator. As compensation, the oil is forced from the accumulator chamber until a pressure balance is achieved, but with a lesser volume of oil available. Conversely, as ambient temperature drops, the gas volume contracts. Despite more oil entering the chamber to reestablish gas pressure, the existing volume of the stored gas, to force oil into the system, is less than designed. Therefore, the system is only partially able to cycle the system under emergency conditions.

Regardless of the accumulator type, when repairs are to be carried out on these systems, special attention from the standpoint of safety must be exercised. Weight- or spring-loaded accumulators need only have the weights removed or the spring force relaxed to remove their effects from the system. Simple observation of these devices allows operating personnel to know whether or not a potential danger exists before repairs are attempted.

Gas-charged accumulators present an additional problem while effecting repairs on a hydraulic system. Although it is costly to bleed off the gas charge, it must be done to ensure safety. Most of these accumulators are provided with a sectionalizing valve to segregate them from the system. If this is not provided, either the oil must be bled off the system to release the pressure, or the gas bled from the accumulator. After repairs are made, the system and accumulator must be carefully and properly recharged.

Bulk Storage

Oil must also be stored to make up for normally expected losses, and to provide for losses caused by damaged seals or piping joint leaks.

The proper bulk storage of oil is just as important to the system as is preventive maintenance. Improper storage, like improper operation of the system, results in contamination and deterioration of the oil. By following some simple guidelines, clean oil for immediate use will be easily attained.

Oil is available in various quantities, from quart containers to large-capacity delivery trucks. Most of your concern is the one-quart, five-gallon, and fifty-five-gallon containers. Here, the first rule is to keep these containers as free from dirt and debris as possible. Keeping the containers covered, or on their sides, keeps dirt from collecting around the areas through which oil is poured into the system.

Also, by storing the containers on their side, moisture that would rust container tops cannot collect. In addition, when oil is to be added to the system, water cannot be inadvertently poured into the system with the oil when stored in this manner. As plastic or fiberboard containers are being more widely used, some of the problems encountered with metal containers have been alleviated. However, as with many technological advances, other problems arise. Regardless of the container used, it must be stored where it will not be susceptible to physical damage, as the contents may either be lost or contaminated through penetration of the container. By keeping the containers properly stored, sealed, and clean, good quality oil will always be available when needed.

PART II

Applied Hydraulics: Shipboard Systems

CHAPTER 12

THE SHAFT ALLEY WATERTIGHT DOOR

The function of the shaft alley watertight door is to segregate the machinery space from the shaft alley during emergency conditions. The design of the door makes a watertight barrier, and is also constructed to be "flametight" and controlled by an independent hydraulic system. The flexibility of operation of this system during emergencies is vastly improved over older mechanical methods. With this system the door can be closed:

1. from the navigation bridge
2. from the engine room central console
3. automatically, when carbon dioxide is released into the machinery space
4. from a commonly travelled area of the house
5. locally, by manual or electric pump operation

In general, the hydraulic system (see Fig. 12-1) includes the required pumps, pressure-actuated control valve stack, linear actuator, and suitable electric controls. As each system is designed to meet the needs of an individual ship, the following description of operation of the shaft alley watertight door provides only an overview of those systems currently utilized.

As shown in the schematic, there are two manually operated reversible pumps provided. One each is located on the machinery space and shaft alley sides of the door for local manual operation. A reversible, electric, motor-driven pump is also located in the vicinity of the door on the machinery space side. This pump can be operated remotely from the navigation bridge and central console, but only for closing. Note also that another unidirectional pump is

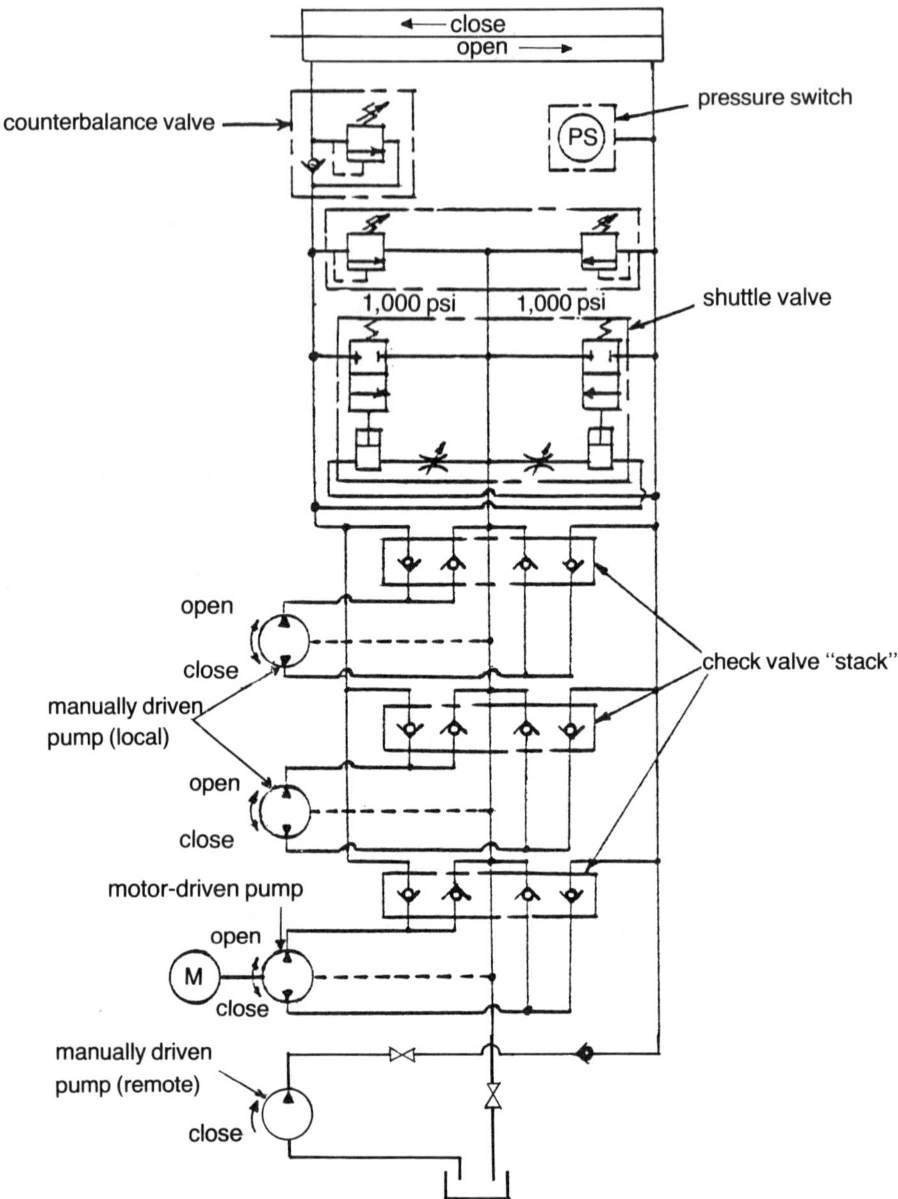

Fig. 12-1. Hydraulic schematic for watertight door

provided, located outside of the machinery space for remote closing, if the main power aboard ship is lost and the machinery space evacuated. All of the pumps are piped to a two-gallon head tank provided for surge and expansion, as well as for replenishing.

Since discharge from these pumps passes through the pressure-actuated control valve stack for either opening or closing, it is immaterial whether the door is installed horizontally or vertically. In either installation, a linear actuator of suitable bore and stroke is used to control the movement of the door.

Now, consider the sequence for opening the door. As oil is discharged from any of the three locally installed pumps, it passes across the appropriate circuit selector valve (check valve) to the left side of the circuit. As oil flows to the rod end of the actuator, high side pressure increases. Simultaneously, the pressure increase strokes the two-position shuttle valve (indicated in the return side of the diagram). Shifting of this valve permits oil to pass, at a restricted rate, from the cap end of the actuator to the indicated central return line.

As the actuator is stroked to open the door, a greater quantity of oil is displaced from the cap end than is necessary to fill the rod end (return side). To accommodate the displaced oil, a head tank is provided and is always open to the return line. The fixed height of the tank above the system results in a minimum static pressure being maintained on the return side. This also ensures that replenishing oil is always available to the pumps when the tank level is properly maintained.

When the door is closing, the smaller quantity of oil forced from the rod end develops a pressure on the return side which is lower than that during the opening operation. And, since the oil in the head tank is available to replenish the system as necessary, a greater quantity of oil is required to close the door than was necessary to open it.

Tracing the oil flow required to open the door is relatively simple. The sequence of events for closing the door, however, is somewhat involved, particularly for a door installed vertically. Note that in the line just before the rod end of the actuator, a counterbalance valve is indicated and is installed in systems where there is a vertical movement of the door.

As pump discharge commences, and the cap end pressure rises, the resulting force is transferred across the piston to develop static oil pressure on the rod end. The rise in static pressure eventually forces the relief valve segment of the counterbalance valve to open. Since the pressurized flow to the cap end forces the left side shuttle valve to open, oil flow across the counterbalance valve is permitted to pass to the return side of the circuit.

When the door reaches the end of its travel, and the matching tapered portions between the door and the frame come into contact, resistance to movement of the door increases. This action causes resistance to the extension of the actuator to increase, which in turn resists the existing flow rate of oil, and develops a further rise in the high side pressure. The pressure switch (indicated on the right side of the circuit near the cap end of the actuator) reacts to the pressure increase, opening the circuit to shut down the motor-driven pump. The door is now tightly closed.

While this operation is relatively simple, there are conditions regarding the counterbalance valve, shuttle valve, and pressure switch that need further explanation. As noted, the counterbalance valve is used to maintain the position of a vertical door until it is necessary for the door to be lowered. Otherwise, this valve unit is not essential for a horizontal door installation.

The function of the check valve segment is to permit free flow to open the door, while the relief valve segment remains closed in order to maintain the raised position of the door. To keep this position, the relief valve segment setpoint is slightly higher than that of the static pressure resulting from the gravitational load of the door.

The primary function of the shuttle valve is to restrict the flow of oil passing to the return side of the system. Since these valves are shifted by pilot pressure, from the existing high side, a bleed-off orifice is provided for each valve. The purpose of each variable orifice is to establish sufficient back pressure to shift the valve. While adjustments to the orifice are usually not necessary, consider what would occur if they were improperly adjusted.

If the orifices are opened too wide, sufficient back pressure is not able to develop to shift the shuttle valve. Without the valve being shifted, oil return from the actuator is blocked, and the door is hydraulically locked in that position. On the other hand, if the orifice is closed off, the shuttle valve actuator is unable to bleed off when the door stops moving. Once oil flow commences in the opposite direction, oil is able to flow directly to the return side without moving the door, because high side pressure is not generated.

The pressure switch, as pointed out, is used to ensure that the door is tightly closed, regardless of which electrically operated remote station is employed. It is automatically reset as pressure is gradually bled off across the shuttle valve bleed-off orifice from the pressure switch side of the circuit.

In addition to the pressure switch there are two mechanically actuated limit switches (not indicated on the hydraulic schematic, Fig. 12-1). The LSC (limit switch-closing), when opened through the mechanical action of the door at the end of its travel, opens the red indicator light circuit, extinguishing that lamp at each remote location.

Conversely, the LSO (limit switch-opening), when similarly actuated by the door at the end of its travel, opens both the green indicator light and motor circuits. Otherwise, the pump will short-cycle as the oil pressure continually bleeds off and rebuilds on the high side. The red indicator light remains lit to indicate that the door is closed. Anytime the door is traveling between its fully opened and its fully closed position, the limit switches permit both of the indicator lights to be lit.

CHAPTER 13

THE HYDRAULIC CRANE

The hydraulic circuit of the crane consists of a power unit supplying oil to one of three individually controlled subcircuits: slewing, topping, and winch (Fig. 13-1). The slewing circuit controls the rotation of the entire cab unit and the swinging of the boom. The lower end of the boom, being pivoted to the cab for vertical movement only, has the angle of the boom controlled by the topping circuit. The winch circuit is considered simply as the hydraulic motor rotating a cable drum. As the motor/drum rotates, the cable is hauled in or paid out to hoist or lower various loads.

The hydraulic pump is a constant flow device, producing a 34-gpm flow at 1,800 psi when driven at a rated rpm. The pump is provided with a 75-gallon, atmospherically vented reservoir located aft of the crane cab.

Located in the cab in a manifold arrangement are three, three-positioned, spring-loaded, open-centered, six-way directional control valves, along with the manifold pressure gauge. Refer to the accompanying hydraulic schematic to note the graphic presentation of the three directional valves (Fig. 13-1). As long as all three valves are centered, a continuous flow from the pump occurs across the valves and back to the sump. When one of the valves is shifted to energize a subcircuit, oil discharge from the pump is completely diverted to that circuit. As a result, continuous flow to the sump through the other directional valves is blocked. Consequently, energizing more than one subcircuit at a time cannot be done. This prevents any of the subcircuits from being starved of oil flow during its required operation.

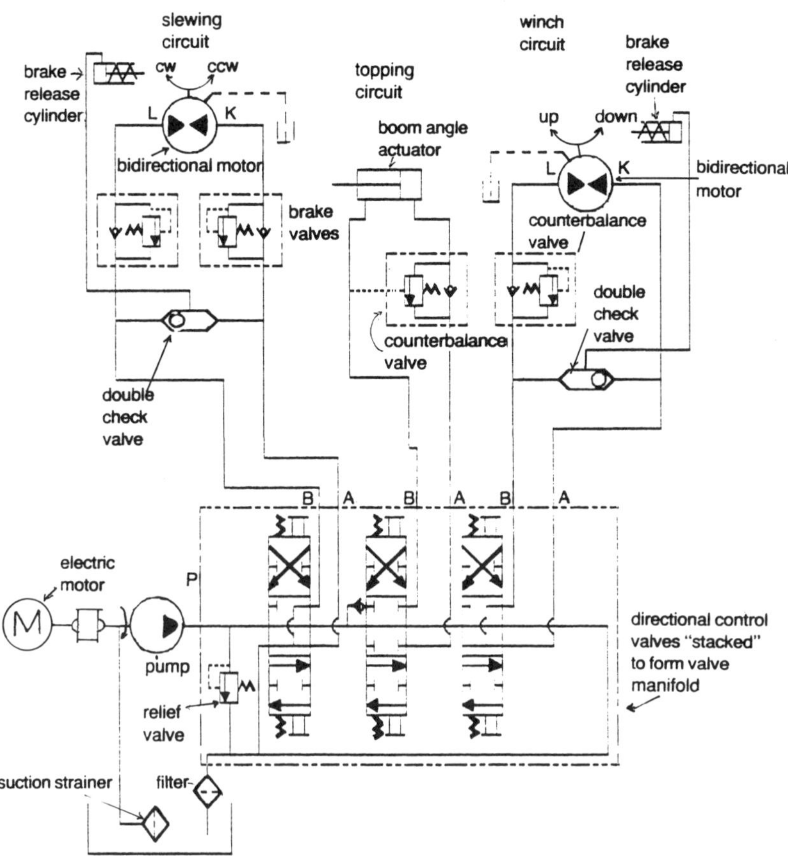

Fig. 13-1. Hydraulic crane schematic

Slewing

The body of the crane is pivoted about its center. The indicated bidirectional hydraulic motor rotates a spur gear, meshing with a circular internal spur gear rack. With this arrangement, the body can be rotated a full 360° in either direction, and it is accomplished in the following manner.

As the slewing directional control valve is moved into its operating position, oil from the pump is diverted to one side of the fixed displacement axial piston motor, via the check valve of the counterbalance valve. As high-pressure flow is maintained to one side of the motor, a high-pressure tap simultaneously forces the ball of the double check valve to shift toward the low-pressure end. This action permits high-pressure oil to actuate the brake release cylinder. When the brake release cylinder is actuated, sufficient force is developed to shift the piston to release the brake fitted to the hydraulic motor shaft. A spring resets the brake if oil pressure is lost to the system. This also occurs if the directional valve is recentered to permit the oil pressure to bleed off from the cylinder and across the double check valve to the sump.

As the oil flows to the motor, with the brake being released, the motor pistons are forced to recede from the valve plate, as a result of the high-pressure oil flow and the permanently angled motor swash plate. As the pistons continue to rotate past the vertical centerline, they move toward the valve plate, and force oil into the exhaust side of the circuit. Initially, the oil flow from the motor is blocked by the counterbalance check valve. However, as oil continues to exhaust from the motor, the pressure rises and overcomes the closing force of the counterbalance relief valve spring. The higher the flow rate permitted to the motor, the higher the flow rate exhausting from the motor. The pressure must increase, forcing the spring-loaded valve to open wider. Once the oil has exited the counterbalance valve, it returns to the sump by way of the directional valve.

When the directional valve is recentered, the oil flow to the motor stops. Motor rotation is slowed proportionally as the valve is recentered, and immediately stops when the valve is in its centered position. This action is a result of:

1. high-pressure oil flow to the motor being stopped
2. instantaneous drop of the motor exhaust side pressure
3. spring force rapidly closing the counterbalance valve
4. draining off oil to the brake release cylinder, allowing the brake to be set on the motor shaft

Topping

The control of the boom angle relative to the horizon is maintained by a nine-inch-diameter linear actuator with a sixty-two-inch stroke.

The boom is raised by modulating oil flow to the cap end of the actuator to extend the cylinder. As oil passes across the directional control valve and the counterbalance check valve, oil returns unrestricted from the rod end and back across the directional valve to the sump.

In order to lower the boom, the directional valve aligns the pump discharge through port B to the rod end of the cylinder. The counterbalance valve is installed in the return line when the boom is lowered. Its installation is unusual in that the relief valve segment is opened by high side oil pressure when the boom is being lowered, unlike similar counterbalance valves.

Also, unlike other circuits employing counterbalance valves, the pressure in this return line can vary as the angle of the boom is changed. Therefore, a single valve setpoint, related to return line upstream pressure, is either too low or too high.

If the setpoint is too low, the boom drops when raising a load. This is a result of the pressure at the cap end of the actuator varying over a wide range as the boom angle is changed.

On the other hand, if the setpoint is too high, the boom cannot be lowered because return pressure is insufficient to open the relief valve segment.

Therefore, the actuating line is tapped off the resulting high side when the boom is lowered. As oil pressure builds on the high-pressure side, the spring force holding the counterbalance relief valve closed is overcome. This arrangement permits one opening setpoint to be used because high pressure occurs only in that line when the boom is to be lowered. Until oil flow is established to the rod end, the counterbalance valve prevents the boom from being lowered prematurely, regardless of the boom angle.

Winch

Understanding the first two circuits makes it easy to understand the winch circuit, in that:

1. A hydraulic motor is used to rotate a winch drum, for paying out and retrieving the winch cable.
2. A mechanical brake is employed, similar to that used in the slewing circuit.

3. A counterbalance valve is employed in the circuit to prevent normally slung loads from dropping prematurely.

The winch directional control valve, when shifted, aligns the pump discharge via port B, to the L side of the motor and across the counterbalance check valve. The motor rotates to retrieve the cable in reaction to the high-pressure oil flow. Oil leaving the motor returns to the sump, unimpeded, by way of the A port in the directional control valve.

Simultaneously, high-pressure oil shifts the ball in the double check valve to allow high-pressure oil to actuate the brake release cylinder. Having overcome the opposing spring force, the brake shoes are released from the motor shaft. Once the directional valve is recentered to stop the rotation of the motor/winch drum, oil drains from the brake release cylinder. The spring retracts the cylinder and sets the brake on the motor shaft.

Once again, the counterbalance relief valve is set to open at a relatively high pressure. This is because the load, acted upon by gravity, attempts to unwind the cable from the drum, which causes the hydraulic motor to rotate and act as a pump. The hydraulic lock provided by the counterbalance valve prevents oil from being forced from the L side of the motor during any condition other than controlled lowering.

Once oil flow is provided to the K side of the motor, by shifting the directional control valve, oil exhausting from the motor is sufficiently pressurized to overcome the spring force holding the counterbalance valve closed. As the pilot line pressure increases and opens the valve, oil exhausts from the motor and returns to the sump, but only after it has passed through the counterbalance valve and the B port of the directional control valve.

CHAPTER 14

THE ANCHOR WINDLASS

The anchor windlass serves to raise and lower the ship's port and starboard anchors. The entire unit comprises two wildcat assemblies, two power units, two gear reducers, and two sets of power controls. Since both units are functionally similar, only one unit is discussed.

This unit is designed to raise and lower a 23,100-pound anchor, including 170 fathoms of 3⅟16-inch chain, at a rate of 5 fathoms per minute from a depth of 30 fathoms. The windlass assembly consists of an electric-driven pump-hydraulic motor unit, with a hydraulically released caliper disk brake, gear reducer, clutch, and vertical drive shaft, all located on the main deck. Mounted on the forecastle deck, above the power unit, are the wildcat, band brake, anchor windlass control stand, chain stopper, and deck pipe to guide the chain to the locker below.

Although reference is made to auxiliary electrical circuits and mechanical devices, this discussion deals primarily with the hydraulic circuits. The hydraulic schematic (Fig. 14-1) shows the main axial piston variable stroke pump, necessary controls, suitable piping, and the fixed displacement axial piston motor. There are also two subcircuits composing the replenishing pump circuit and the hydromechanical brake circuit.

Each main pump develops a maximum flow of 165 gpm at 1,154 psi to the motor via the path of the manually shifted transfer valve. Note that the transfer valve permits the following operations when shifted to any of its detented positions:

1. starboard side pump to line up to starboard side motor
2. port side pump to line up to port side motor

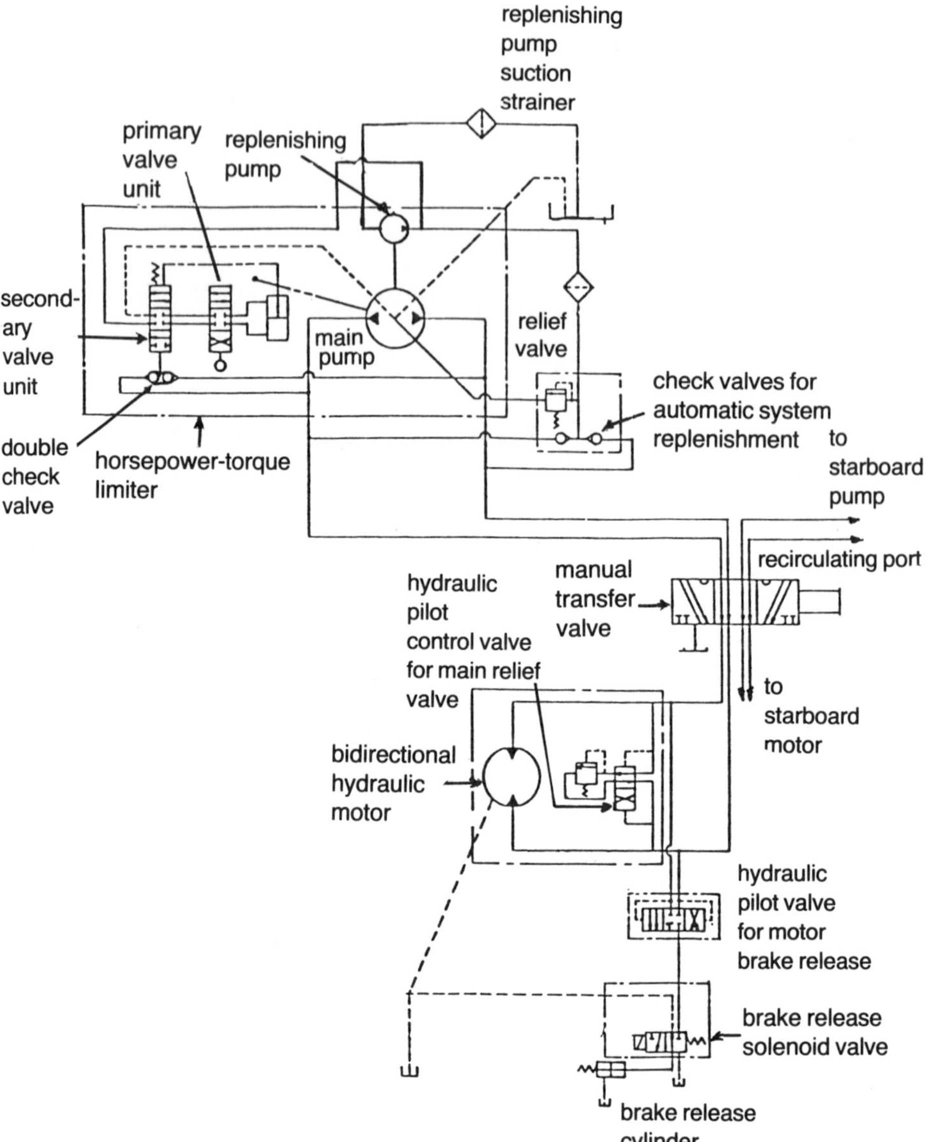

Fig. 14-1. Anchor windlass

3. starboard side pump to cross over to starboard side motor
4. port side pump to line up to starboard side motor
5. oil to be recirculated through either pump to allow for cold weather warm-up

Note: *One main pump will not be able to drive both motors simultaneously.*

The hydraulic motor rotates at a speed directly proportional to the flow rate of the variable stroke pump. Since the motor drives the gear reducer, which in turn drives the wildcat, both speed and direction of rotation of the anchor windlass depend upon the angle of the main pump tilting box. The tilting box angle is established by the use of a horsepower-torque limiter (speed control device), and is controlled by a 12-inch handwheel from the forecastle deck.

The horsepower limiter (Fig. 14-2) is a two-stage servo valve. The primary stage is modulated by the forecastle deck handwheel

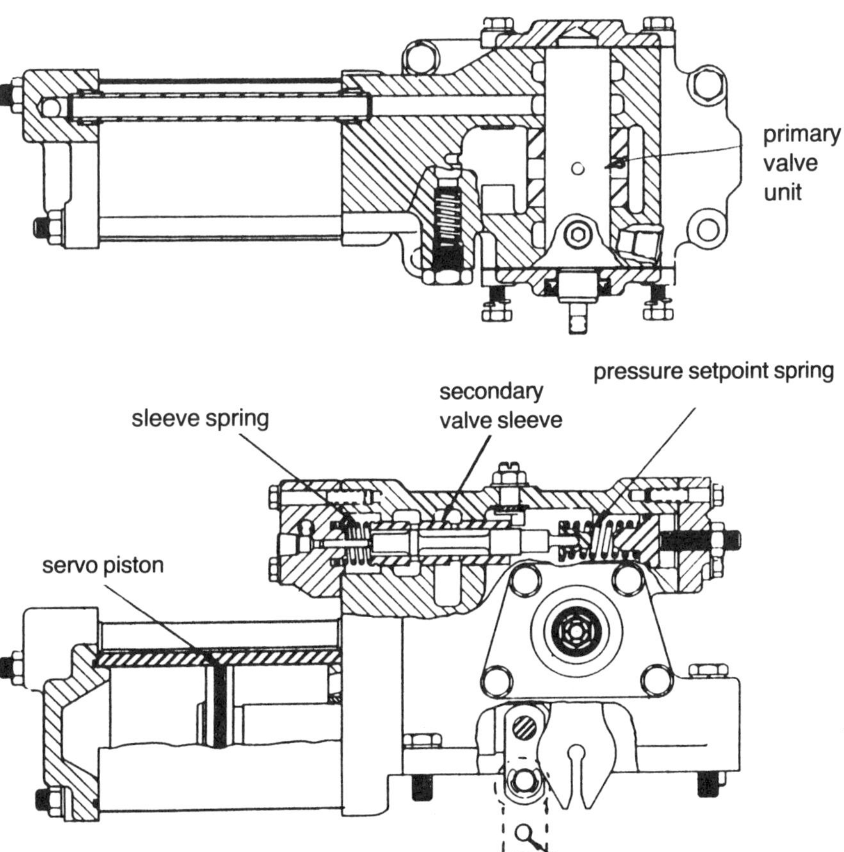

Fig. 14-2. Horsepower-torque limiter for anchor windlass

to control the tilting box angle. The secondary valve reacts to high-pressure conditions that develop at the pump discharge. The secondary valve not only stops the tilting box angle from increasing, but permits the reduction in the tilting box angle if excessive loading of the system develops. This is done to prevent the pump from being needlessly overdriven by the operator.

In order to rotate the hydraulic motor, the handwheel is rotated counterclockwise. This action also causes the valve spool to be rotated counterclockwise. Oil flow delivered by the replenishing pump, via the secondary valve unit, is permitted to flow to the cap end of the servo piston, forcing the servo piston to shift. As the servo piston moves, it forces the tilting box to tilt toward the front of the pump, placing it on stroke. When placed on "stroke," the mechanical linkage forces the double-lobed cam to rotate counterclockwise. In response to cam rotation, the primary valve sleeve also rotates counterclockwise, although initially it lags behind the movement of the primary valve spool.

Once the primary valve spool is stabilized in position, the primary valve sleeve catches up and covers the spool ports. At this point, the hydraulic lock is placed on the servo piston as oil is no longer permitted to flow to the servo piston. This interaction develops a follow-up between the control handwheel and the tilting box angle/pump flow rate. By maintaining the original handwheel position, the tilting box remains in that position until a new input is provided.

The secondary valve of the horsepower-torque limiter reacts to excessive pressures in the system. The excessive pressure conditions generated on the high-pressure side of the pump/motor unit are a result of the load exceeding setpoint conditions. Referring to Fig. 14-2, you see that the secondary valve is represented by the upper spool valve/sliding sleeve arrangement. Located at the right-hand end is an adjustable compression spring that is used to set the maximum high side operating pressure of the system.

To appreciate the interaction of the secondary valve unit, recall that the double-lobed cam rotates as the tilting box changes its angle. In response, the feedback lever is forced to rotate counterclockwise. Furthermore, the angle, or direction of tilt, rotates counterclockwise as a result of the cam design. Therefore, the feedback lever always shifts the secondary valve sleeve to the left and against the constant force spring whenever the pump is placed on stroke.

If the high side pressure does not rise above setpoint, the secondary spool valve barely shifts as the pump is placed on stroke. Oil flow from the replenishing pump is still able to flow toward the primary valve unit, although it is at a somewhat restricted rate. This is a result of the flow through the ports of the secondary sleeve being only partially blocked.

Regardless of which side of the motor is pressurized, high-pressure oil is always present at the left-hand end of the secondary spool valve because of the use of the double check valves. As the load on the windlass increases, resistance to hydraulic motor rotation increases, as does the high side pressure since flow across the motor is restricted. With the high side pressure always acting on the left-hand end of the secondary spool valve, the spool shifts toward the right against the compression of the adjustable setpoint spring. As the spool valve shifts, flow from the replenishing pump is further restricted, or blocked off, as the pressure continues to increase.

You should surmise that if the secondary valve blocks the oil flow to the servo piston before the tilting box achieves its commanded angle, a further increase will not occur. This also means that the system cannot be overdriven as a result of the secondary valve action, and that high side pressure will stabilize at that level.

You should also realize that as the high side pressure increases there is a reactive force developed on the pump piston's tilting box. This force is sufficient to begin to decrease the stroke angle. Normally, without a secondary valve, if the tilting box angle decreases, the balance of the primary valve is upset and permits oil flow again to the servo piston. As long as the secondary valve permits oil to flow to the primary valve unit, the servo piston is repositioned to correct for the diminished stroke angle.

With the system pressure rising, in response to the increasing load, the replenishing pump oil flow is blocked by the secondary valve, and the stroke angle decreases. The result is diminished oil flow to the main system, as long as the high side pressure remains at or above the setpoint. Therefore, the pressure and hydraulic horsepower are not able to rise above the predetermined limits established by the valve.

Referring again to Fig. 14-1, note that the fluid flow rate to the motor can be varied to control the direction of rotation and speed. The figure also indicates the unique arrangement of a single relief valve at the motor set to the lift at 3,000 psi. Regardless of which oil line is serving as the high-pressure supply, the relief valve is always aligned for service. This is accomplished by the use of the hydraulically piloted, two-position, four-way valve. When the high side pressure is piloted to one end, the valve shifts, permitting the high-pressure fluid to pass to the relief valve inlet. Exceeding the setpoint of the relief valve allows the oil to be dumped to the low-pressure side of the main circuit via the piloted control valve.

Aside from oil flow to the hydraulic motor, necessary for rotation, the hydromechanical brake must be released as well. The brake circuit comprises a:

1. three-position, hydraulically piloted, directional valve
2. two-position solenoid valve
3. brake-release cylinder controlling a disk caliper brake-mounted around the motor shaft

When high-pressure oil is supplied to the motor inlet, the hydraulically piloted valve is shifted. Once the valve shifts, only low-pressure (return side) oil flows to the brake solenoid valve. Oil is available at the brake-release cylinder, via the solenoid valve, only when power is available to the electric motor. Once the solenoid valve is shifted, oil from the low-pressure side strokes the brake-release cylinder to release the brake. If an electric power failure occurs, the solenoid valve is deenergized and allows the oil in the cylinder to drain off to the sump. The cylinder spring automatically resets the brake.

References have been made to the replenishing pump oil flow, but not in sufficient detail. The replenishing pump is a constant flow unit, integral with the main pump casing, and is driven off the shaft of the main pump. Aside from the oil flow provided to the horsepower-torque limiter, the replenishing pump automatically provides makeup oil to the main circuit on a demand basis.

Referring again to Fig. 14-1, note that the replenishing pump discharge can be traced to two individual check valves. Each check valve is fitted to the main flow lines, between the pump/motor combination. Since the return flow from the motor while rotating is limited in volume, the oil pressure on the return side is substantially lower than on the high side. As internal leaks occur within the system to provide pump lubrication, the amount of oil returning to the main pump, at this instance, is insufficient to maintain a sustained normal return side pressure. When the return side pressure drops below that of the replenishing pump pressure, the pressure differential permits the check valve to open to recharge the main circuit. As oil is replenished to the return side, the lowering pressure differential allows the check valve to close off.

The actual operation of the anchor windlass is then relatively simple. First, to start the windlass, place the main pump in neutral stroke. This allows the contacts of the electric interlock switch to be closed, to permit power to be supplied to the electric motor. The brake solenoid valve is energized after the momentary contact start button has been depressed. Once the main pump is stroked, the brake around the shaft of the hydraulic motor is hydraulically released, as described earlier.

While gravity actually drops the anchor, the power unit must be in operation to haul in the chain in order to remove the devil's claw that locks the chain in place. For lowering the anchor, the procedure is as follows:

1. Start hydraulic unit.
2. Engage clutch (lever located at windlass on weather deck).
3. Slack off brake band with 20-inch control wheel.
4. Place pump on stroke to haul up anchor chain to remove strain on the claw.
5. Lift devil's claw out of the way.
6. Reset band brake.
7. Declutch windlass from power unit.
8. Disengage chain stopper.
9. Release tension on band brake as necessary to control lowering of anchor.

CHAPTER 15

THE CONSTANT-TENSION MOORING WINCH

All large, oceangoing vessels are equipped with mooring winches whose primary function is to haul in and pay out the vessel's mooring lines when docking and undocking. As tides rise and fall, or as cargo is loaded and discharged, the mooring lines must have their slack and strain changed by the crew using the mooring winches. Besides being inconvenient, this practice requires the deployment of men needed to fulfill other duties. In addition, as dock time for ships has diminished, because of containerization and other "fast turnaround" concepts, the necessity of changing line tension arises more frequently. The constant-tension mooring winch does what other mooring winches cannot do, automatically, during tidal changes and cargo operations.

The constant-tension mooring winch comprises a mechanical speed-reduction gear, the warping heads, and the hydraulic power unit and its circuitry. The power unit consists of remotely operated, self-contained hydraulic controls, the hydraulic pump/motor combination, and the associated speed/tension control devices, replenishing pump circuit, and mechanical brake.

Deck Control Operation

The remotely operated, self-contained hydraulic controls located on deck are divided into two separate circuits. One set is used to control the hydraulic motor speed, while the other is used to control the mooring line tension, within the range of 10,000 to 30,000 foot-pounds.

Referring to Fig. 15-1, note the upper left-hand schematic representation of the tension control circuit. This unit includes the two masters (#18), one located at each of the port-starboard control stations. These are connected by suitable piping to the tension control master unit (#19), fitted with a filling-bleeding manifold, and are physically located at the power units. Immediately to the right of the pumping unit and control valves are the two speed control masters (#18), also provided at the port-starboard control stations. Through suitable piping these are connected to the speed control slave unit (#21), also fitted with the filling-bleeding manifold and located at the power unit.

Physically, the only difference between the two control circuits appears in the slave control handles. The tension-control lever is longer than that of the speed-control lever. The slaves and masters are essentially small pistons which can be infinitely adjusted within their respective cylinders.

By moving the control lever, the slave piston is forced to slide through its cylinder. This action exerts force on the hydraulic oil trapped between the slave and master cylinders, which in turn transmits this movement. Because of the piping arrangement between the slave and master units, the master piston moves in the same direction as the slave piston. As you can see in Fig. 15-1, the movement of the tension-control master controls the amount of spring compression applied to the tension-control valve. The compression of this spring opposes the movement of the hydraulically piloted valve spool. The speed master, when positioned by its slave, physically shifts the speed control valve spool, which in turn regulates the replenishing pump oil flow to the pump stroke control servo piston.

Since the speed-tension control circuits are physically the same, filling and bleeding of air for these circuits are accomplished in the same manner. Referring to Fig. 15-2, note the arrangement of the slave, master, and filling-bleeding manifold. Normally, valve B of the slave and valve A of the master are closed, with valve D of the filling-bleeding manifold fully open, with valve C and the suction check valve normally closed. During the filling-bleeding operation, valve A is backed off two turns, allowing oil to bypass the slave piston. Valve C is opened, and a suitable hose is connected to the manifold and inserted into the oil supply. Valve D is now completely

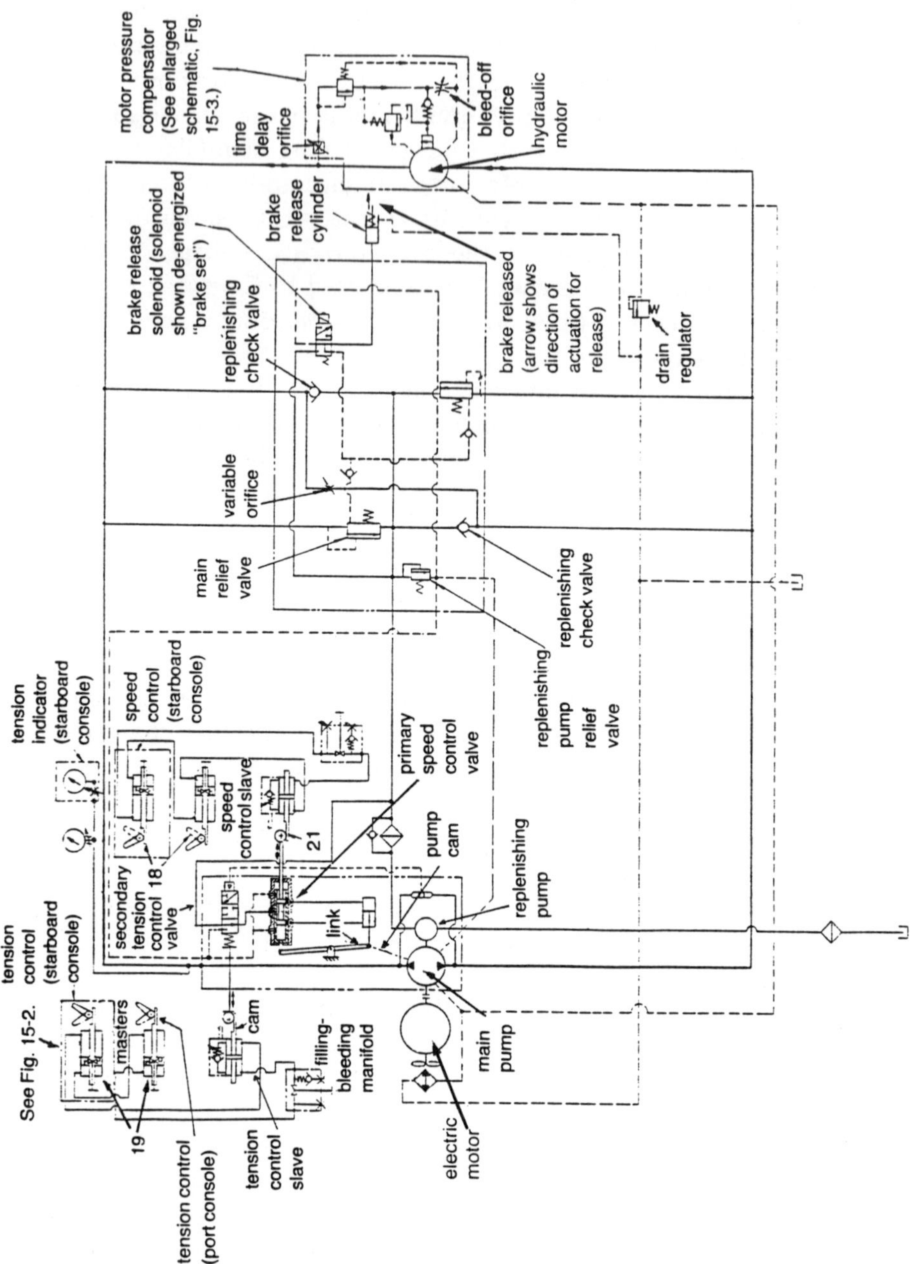

Fig. 15-1. Hydraulic schematic for constant tension mooring winch

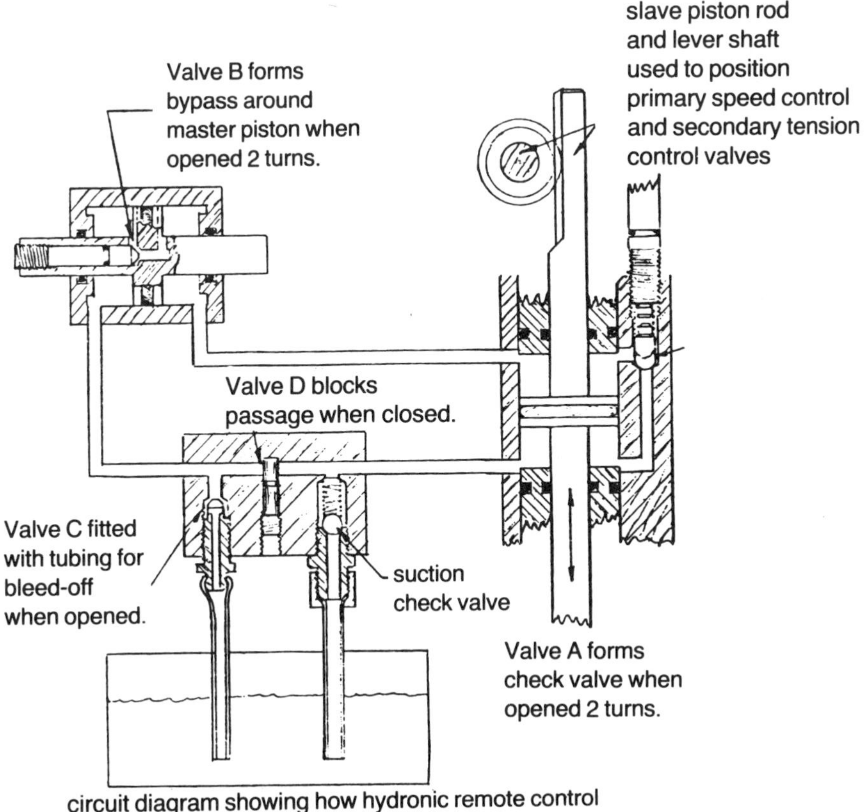

Fig. 15-2. Diagrammatic schematic of speed/tension remote controls

closed, and the suction check valve is opened when it is connected to the oil supply.

By manipulating the master control cylinder lever manually, the master piston reciprocates. As the piston of the master is forced to move up, check valve A closes. This develops a pressure lower than atmospheric under the piston. Atmospheric pressure acting on the oil in the portable reservoir forces oil to open the manifold suction check valve and to flow into the lower portion of the master cylinder. As the master piston is moved in the opposite direction, the oil previously drawn into the cylinder is pressurized, forcing the suction check valve to close and check valve A to open. Oil is forced toward the slave. Any oil and air in the slave cylinder passes through the piston and on toward the filling-bleeding manifold. With valve D closed, the oil and entrained air flow through valve C and into the supply reservoir. Continuing to stroke the master several times fills the system and bleeds out the air simultaneously.

After filling and bleeding the system, the control handles must be aligned with the correct position of the slave-master cylinders and the control valves. Then valves A, B, and C are closed, and the plugs secured in the filling-bleeding manifold, with valve D being reopened.

As you ready the closed loop remote control circuits, keep in mind that these circuits control only the positioning of the two control valves, which in turn control the main pump flow rate and direction of oil flow. By controlling the main pump flow rate and direction of oil flow, the hydraulic motor speed and direction of motor rotation are controlled.

Hydraulic Operation of the Winch

Although primary control over system operation is derived from the main pump, you should realize that the motor is constructed with a limited, but variable position tilting box. This is done so that high speed/low torque operation is available when the system is required to handle minor loads; higher load conditions require low speed/high torque operation controlled by the motor pressure compensator.

Normally, the fixed flow rate from a pump to a fixed displacement motor results in constant motor-rotating speed. With a fixed displacement axial piston motor, the piston stroke is relatively short. Hence, a relatively short length of time is required to fill each cylinder. This also means that reciprocation of the pistons occurs rapidly with a high output rotating speed.

An axial piston variable stroke motor that is equipped with a tilting box can increase the angle automatically with the use of a pressure compensator. As the tilting box angle of the motor increases, the piston stroke and the volume of each cylinder increase. And, as the length of time to complete the stroke increases, the speed of rotation decreases. Furthermore, as the speed decreases, the available torque from the motor increases. Therefore, it is desirable for the load increase to be handled automatically by the motor. (See also the discussion in Chapter 3.)

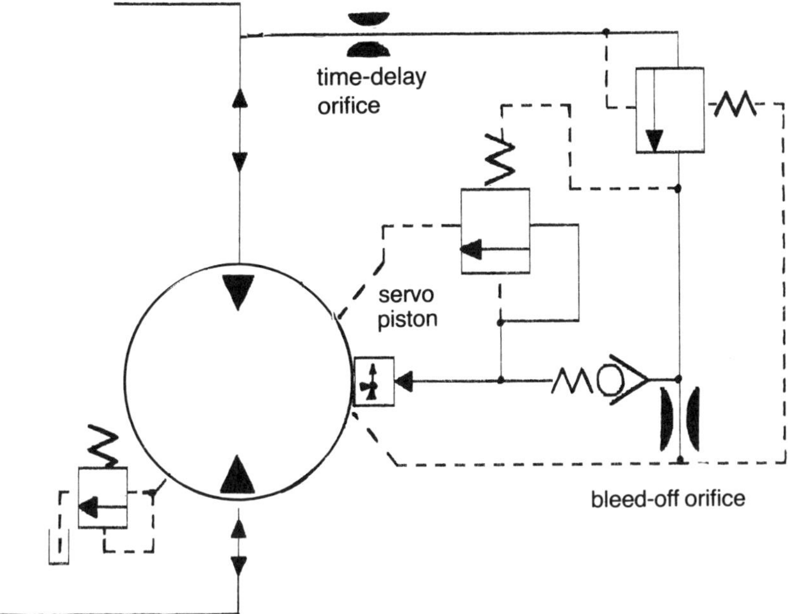

Fig. 15-3. Enlarged schematic of constant tension mooring winch compensating circuit

Consider that the automatic compensating device, indicated in the schematic (Fig. 15-3), is simply a small, linear actuator positioned to increase the tilting box angle of the motor, as high-pressure oil forces the compensating actuator to extend. You will note that the indicated mechanical enclosure around the motor contains the pressure compensator, which consists of two variable orifices, one to act as a time delay, and the other to maintain back pressure at the outlet of the pressure-control valve. A check valve opens to permit oil to flow toward the servo piston that controls the tilting box angle. A relief device is provided to bleed off the compensator piston oil pressure as the load on the motor decreases.

Immediately after the mooring line is made fast to the pier the line is slack. Initially, the motor speed will be high because the only load on the system is the mooring line. As the line breaks the surface of the water, a momentary high load, accompanied by high pressure surge occurs, caused by the line breaking surface tension with the water. Normally, the increase in pressure would force the pressure compensator to increase the tilting box angle. However, since this condition is only temporary, a time-delay orifice, placed in the actuating line to the compensator pressure controlled valve, allows only a sustained load on the mooring line to transfer a sustained increase in pressure to actuate the compensator.

As slack in the line is gradually reduced, resistance to rotation of the motor increases. Pressure in the high side increases as flow rate across the motor drops proportionally. Once the pressure is sustained, and is sufficient to open the pressure control valve, back pressure at the valve outlet is maintained by the variable bleed-off orifice. It is important to realize that the bleed-off orifice allows the hydrostatic pressure developed between these two points to be dissipated once the pressure control valve closes.

Hydrostatic pressure to the compensating actuator is transmitted across the check valve, as previously described, and forces the rotational speed to slow in response to the increase in piston stroke, causing the tilting box angle to increase. This, of course, provides the desired increase in torque to handle the higher load.

Once the motor is stopped by stroking the main pump to neutral stroke, or by diminishing the load on the system, the pressure control valve closes. Until this happens, pressure at the pressure-actuated valve outlet is maintained to the sensing line side of the relief valve and aids the spring to fulfill its function. This relationship keeps the relief valve closed as long as the pressure control valve is open. Once the pressure control valve closes, hydrostatic pressure bleeds off the spring side, and a greater force to open the relief valve is now present. Hydrostatic pressure acting on the compensator actuator is bled off, allowing the motor tilting box to return to its original shallow angle.

The remainder of the system's operation is understood by following the functions of the replenishing pump. Since it is an integral part of the main pump casing, the replenishing pump is also driven by the main motor, discharging oil flow to three distinct areas. First, the oil flow passes directly to the tension control valve, and, depending upon the operating conditions, is used to stroke the pump tilting box control servo piston, by way of the speed control servo valve. Second, the oil flow is traced to two check valves, each one able to permit oil to flow to one side of the main circuit but only when that is functioning as the return side of the system. The replenishing pump then supplies low-pressure oil to release the brake.

During normal operation, the return side pressure is above that of the replenishing pump discharge pressure. As leaks occur in the system, the lack of oil causes the return side pressure to drop below that of the replenishing pump, allowing the appropriate check valve to open and admit oil to the system. The replenishing oil flow continues until the differential pressure across the check valve no longer exists. In order for the replenishing oil flow to release the system's brake, power must be available to the main motor. By depressing the main brake release push button (Fig. 15-4), the brake solenoid is energized to allow oil to flow to the brake release cylinder. Once the solenoid is energized, the replenishing pump pressure is maintained to keep the brake released. If the brake does not release with this procedure, an emergency brake release push button can be depressed to energize the solenoid.

The significant difference between these two methods of brake release is that the normal brake release switch is a momentary contact type, allowing the circuit to remain energized until the brake reset button is depressed, or power is lost to the electric motor. The emergency brake release, on the other hand, must be continuously depressed until the winch operation has been secured.

In order to haul the mooring lines in and make them fast, the motor speed and direction have to be controlled. This mode of control is accomplished by the servo valve (speed control circuit), which is used to manipulate the replenishing pump flow to the control servo piston.

When the speed control lever, on either port or starboard control station, is vertical, the main pump is in neutral stroke. As the lever is moved in either direction, a corresponding movement is remotely transferred to the speed control master. The position of the servo valve spool shifts proportionally to the amount of change in the control lever position. Oil flow from the replenishing pump, via the tension control valve, flows to either the rod or cap end of the servo piston, depending upon the initial direction of movement of the speed control lever. As the servo piston moves through its cylinder, an external arm, attached to the pump tilting box, is repositioned through suitable linkage. The length of the pump's piston stroke is changed by the movement of the tilting box. The cam, which is also part of this linkage, rotates as well. As the cam rotates, it forces the sleeve around the primary valve spool to move in the same direction, but lagging behind the movement of the spool.

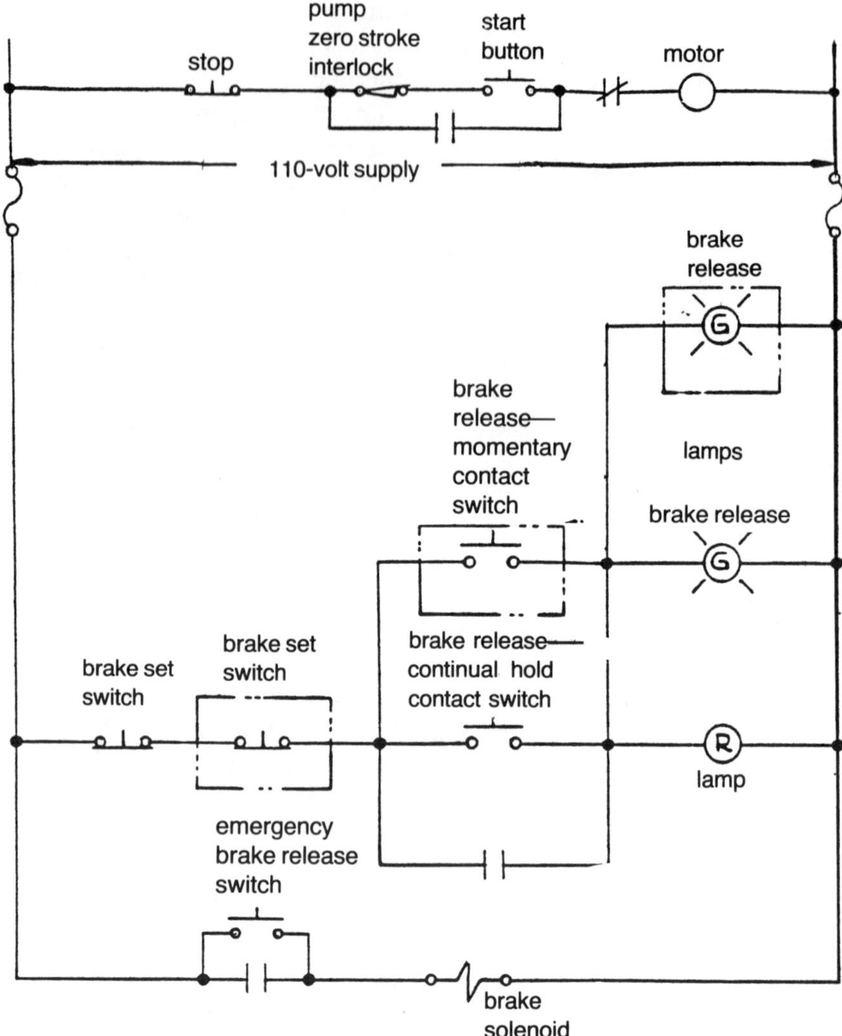

Fig. 15-4. Electrical diagram for constant tension mooring winch starter control and brake release circuits

Once the primary spool valve has achieved its position, through the action of the operator, the primary valve sleeve eventually "catches up" and blocks any further oil flow to the servo piston. The culmination of this action hydraulically locks the servo piston and the tilting box in place until a new command is initiated.

A "follow-up" is achieved with the primary servo valve to ensure for each position of the speed control handle that there is one, and only one, corresponding position of the tilting box. This also means that a specific angle of the tilting box develops a specific flow rate to the hydraulic motor, resulting in a specific motor speed. If it were not for the follow-up, the tilting box would continue to move to maximum stroke, regardless of the speed control handle position.

Tension Control

Once the ship is secure alongside the pier, the mooring winch power unit is kept in constant operation to maintain proper tension (initiated by positioning the tension control handle) on the mooring lines. Depending upon the final position of the handle, the mooring line tension is maintained within the range of 10,000 to 30,000 foot-pounds.

By pulling the control handle all the way back, the slave piston shifts to its full travel, with similar response from the master piston to develop maximum compression of the tension control force spring. Compression of the spring (indicated at the left-hand end of the tension control valve graphic symbol) opposes the hydraulic pressure piloted from the high-pressure side of the circuit.

Maximum tension control valve spring compression is set during the hauling in of the mooring line. Replenishing pump oil is permitted to flow across the indicated left-hand valve envelope to the primary speed control valve. Once the ship is secure alongside the pier, the amount of spring compression is reduced. Although the operator is not directly aware of the valve envelope position, the tension control is set so that the tension control valve is shifted to its center envelope.

With the tension control valve in this position, the replenishing pump oil flow to the primary valve is blocked. At this time, the primary valve and servo piston are hydraulically locked in their last designated position (the main pump is at a shallow stroke angle). As the ship changes its position relative to the pier, the line tension also changes.

Keep in mind that the final positioning of the tension control handle resulted in the tension control valve being placed in a centered position. Again, this is because the compression of the tensioning spring is balanced against the main circuit high side pressure. As tension on the mooring lines increases, there is an increase in the existing high side pressure. This occurs as the mooring line pulls on the hydraulic motor in a direction opposite to the direction toward which the main pump oil flow is attempting to rotate the motor in order to maintain tension. In turn, the hydraulic pilot pressure, acting on the tension control valve, begins to shift the valve spool against the compression spring. Compression of the spring increases as the valve element shifts in the direction of the spring. As the tension control valve shifts into the right-hand envelope, oil is permitted to escape across the primary valve from the servo piston. The bleed-off will continue as long as the primary valve spool and sleeve are not matched. At this point, the follow-up control provided by the primary valve, the servo piston, and tilting box movement normally returns everything to original position.

However, the replenishing pump supply is more than just blocked. In addition, any upset in the balance of the primary valve spool and its sleeve at this time permits oil to bleed off the servo piston. This occurs as a result of the tilting box being forced back toward neutral stroke because of the increase in pressure on the high side and the mechanical interrelationship of the servo piston, valve sleeve, and tilting box. Oil can bleed off from the servo piston, via the primary valve, across the tension control valve, to the main pump casing, on to the oil cooler, and, finally, to the sump. The tilting box begins to "slip" towards its neutral stroke. The pump displacement is reduced (the flow rate), as is the high side pressure. The motor, no longer receiving the former flow rate, to maintain pressure, slips, allowing some of the mooring line to pay out.

The motor "slipping" is caused by a reduction in oil flow rate, hence the resultant pressure reduction. Normally, a small quantity of oil from the high side continually bypasses the motor to the low side via the variable orifice (see Fig. 15-1). The orifice also permits oil to continually recirculate from the high to the low side, even though the motor is not rotating. This prevents cavitation and overheating of the main pump from occurring because of a lack of oil flow across the main pump when the motor is holding the lines tight, and is not rotating.

If the motor has slipped, and the oil flow rate has dropped off, the tension control valve begins to shift. The shift is to the right as the spring expands because of the lowering high side pressure at the pilot. Initially, this prevents further bleed-off of oil from the servo piston and again hydraulically locks the tilting box into place, but at a lower flow rate. When pressure begins rebuilding on the high side, the motor is prevented from slipping further. If the flow rate and, consequently, the high side pressure are too low after this correction, excessive slack develops in the mooring line.

The pilot pressure is now sufficiently low to allow the tension control valve to shift into the left-hand envelope. Replenishing pump discharge flows across the tension control valve to the servo piston via the primary valve.

This is all possible since the last follow-up relationship does not exist at this point. Remember, the tilting box having slipped upset the primary valve balance. Even though the primary valve imbalance existed, the position of the tension valve prevented oil flow to the servo piston that would have reestablished the balance and tilting box angle. Now that the replenishing pump discharge is able to flow again to the servo piston, a shift occurs to rebalance the system.

Consequently, this set of actions begins to restore the pump to its original displacement. As this eventually results in the rebuilding of high side pressure in addition to the hydraulic pilot pressure, the tension control valve is forced to return to its centered position. When the tension control valve is recentered, oil flow to the primary valve is again blocked. This condition holds true even if the primary servo valve has not regained its follow-up position. The tilting box merely stops at the angle it achieved when the oil flow was cut off at tension control setpoint.

CHAPTER 16

THE HYDRAULIC UNITIZED STEERING GEAR

The unitized steering gear is an electrohydraulic unit employing an electric motor to drive three hydraulic pumps simultaneously. These pumps supply oil, at various flow rates and pressures, to enable and to control movement of the steering gear. When compared with older steering gears, two conditions stand out. First, the changeover of the power units from a remote location is accomplished in one step. Second, all components are organized into a relatively small area, hence the terms *unitized* or *compact.*

Referring to the main schematic in Fig. 16-1, three pumps are shown for both the port and starboard units. The top pump symbol represents that of the main variable stroke pump. Its function is to control the supply and direction of oil flow to the steering gear rams, and thus to control the rudder angle. To control the direction of flow and flow rate, the main pump stroke is hydraulically controlled by the discharge from the servo pump. The replenishing pump provides a constant discharge that automatically supplies the main circuit, and controls the position of the main circuit unloading and distributor valves.

The sole function of the main pump is to supply oil at a controlled flow rate to position the steering gear rams. The following discussion will describe the complex service of the replenishing and servo pump circuits. By tracing the flow from the discharge of the replenishing pump (middle pump on main schematic of Fig. 16-1), you see that the flow divides. Part of it is fed to each inlet of two check valves. The outlet of each check valve is connected to the main circuit piping on each side of the variable stroke pump piped to the steering gear rams. During the movement of the rams, one of the two main conduits constitutes the *low*-pressure return side. If oil is lost from the main

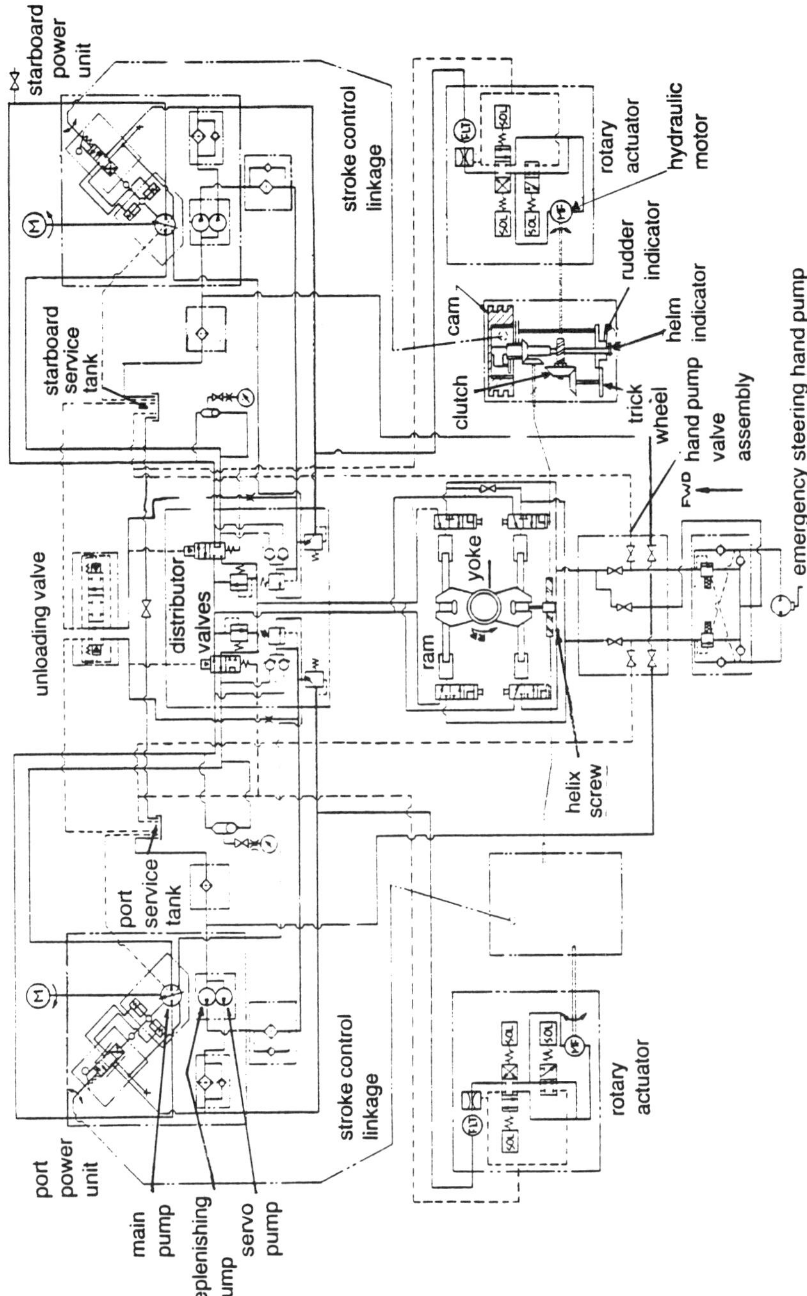

Fig. 16-1. Main hydraulic schematic for unitized steering gear

circuit, the pressure in the return side will be below that of the replenishing pump pressure. The pressurized oil is then able to force open the return side check valve and continues to flow to the system as long as sufficient pressure differential exists across the check valves.

Tracing the second branch shows flow to pass through a fixed orifice, toward the top center of Fig. 16-2, to the unloading valve. The unloading valve is a three-position, two-way, spring-centered, hydraulically piloted, priority valve. As a priority valve, the main function of the unloading valve is to determine which of the two power unit distributor valves is to be shifted. The shifting of the unloading valve determines which power unit is to be aligned to the steering gear rams.

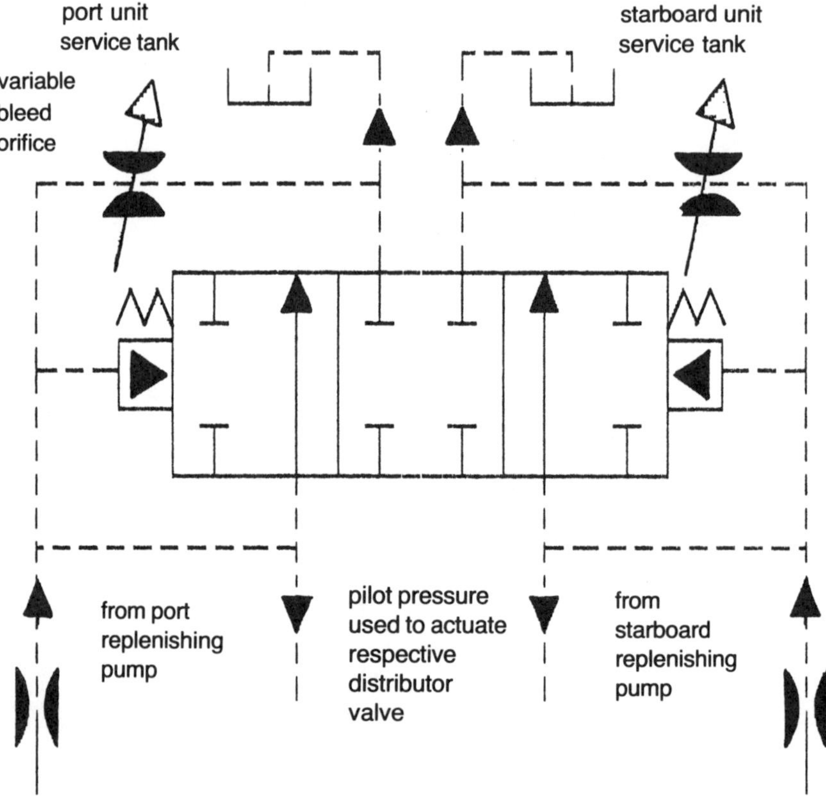

Fig. 16-2. Unloading valve schematic in centered position

As indicated on the main schematic (Fig. 16-1), the port power unit is aligned to the steering gear. This is accomplished by starting the port power unit electric motor that drives the three hydraulic pumps. When oil flow is established from the replenishing pump to the unloading valve, the flow is blocked from flowing directly across the valve. An internal port of the unloading valve channels the replenishing pump discharge toward the left-hand end. As this end becomes pressurized, the spool shifts in the opposite direction. Although the spool has shifted, it still blocks the flow from the port side replenishing pump. The shift, however, permits the free flow of oil to the sump across the unloading valve if the starboard unit is started later. The port unit replenishing oil flow continues to bleed across the needle valve, located on the pressurized left side, to the port side service tank (sump). This ensures that the springs recenter the valve spool so that it is not hydraulically locked in its shifted position should the port side power unit be shut down or fail.

With the port unit replenishing pump flow blocked by this valve, back pressure is developed and transmitted through the pilot line to the port unit distributor valve. With pilot pressure established to this distributor valve, the offset spool is shifted against the valve spring used to hold the spool in its downward, closed position. When shifted, the distributor valve aligns the port side main pump to the steering gear rams.

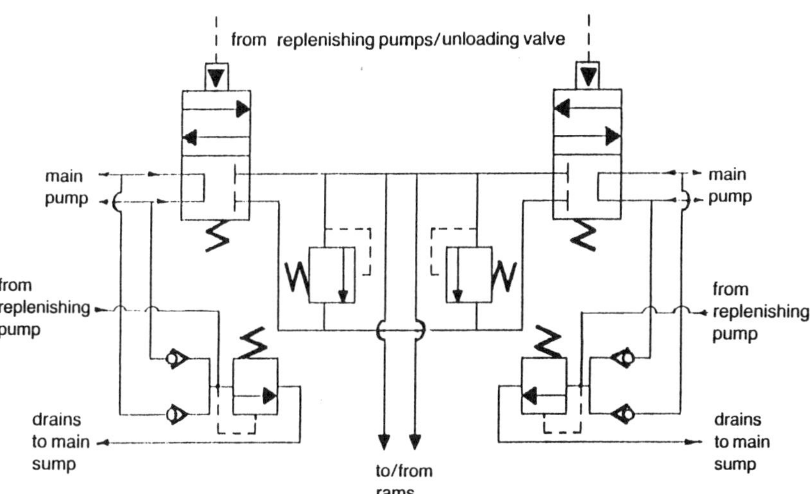

Fig. 16-3. Schematic arrangement of distributor valves

The distributor valve provides three other functions. One of these functions is to set up a recirculating path from one side of the standby pump to the other while the main unit is on the line. As previously described, another function is to provide a path for the replenishing oil to enter the main circuit. Lastly, the distributor valve places a hydraulic lock on the rams when both power units are secured for any reason.

Note the cross-sectional drawing (Fig. 16-4) of the distributor valve. The upper piston area of the spool, when closed (not shifted by hydraulic pilot pressure), blocks any oil flow attempting to return from the rams. Also, note the oil line connection from the other side of the rams and how it is related to the valve body port. Next, locate the pump connection between the two lower valve spool piston areas. If oil is forced toward the distributor valve through this line, the hydraulic forces are equal, but acting in opposite directions. Therefore, oil flow is blocked, since the valve is not shifted, with the rams and rudder hydraulically locked in place, as no flow across the distributor valve can occur.

As previously stated, the oil flow from the servo pump is directed to the stroke control actuators to hydraulically control the stroke of the main pump via the servo control valve (see Fig. 16-5). The actual flow is accomplished in the following manner.

The tilting box of the variable displacement main pump varies the length of pump piston stroke to accomplish its main objective, and tilts back and forth, on pivot points, provided by trunnions. One

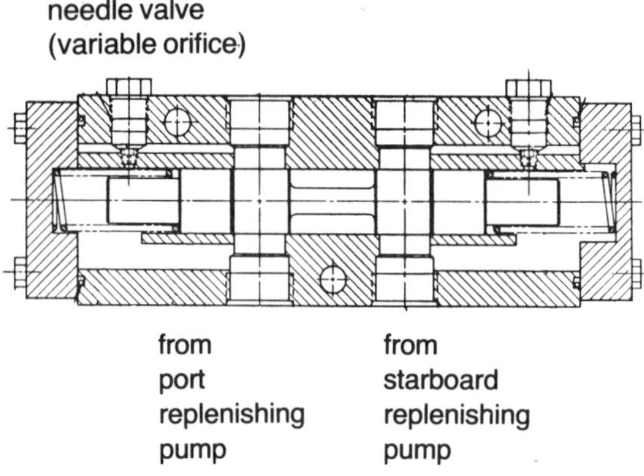

Fig. 16-4A. Cross section of unloading valve

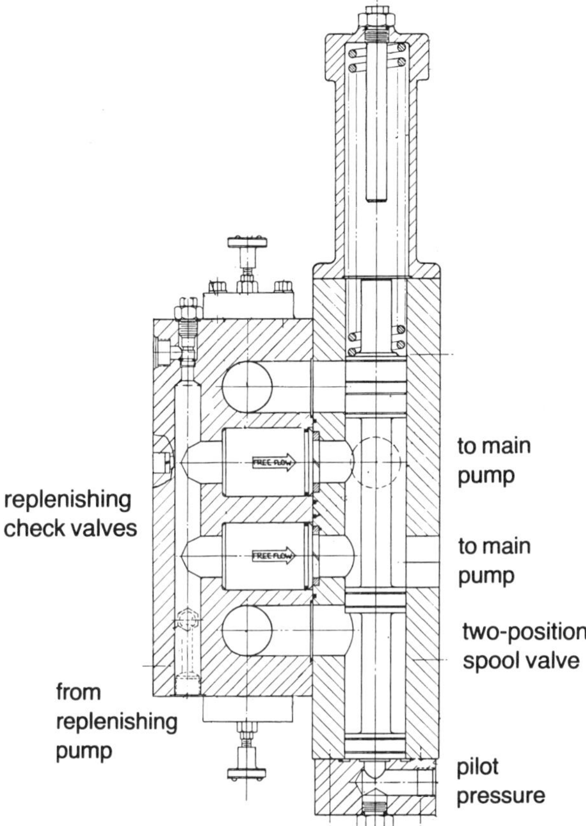

Fig. 16-4B. Cross section of distributor valve

trunnion extends through the casing for installation of a horizontal control lever and is acted upon by two single-acting actuators. As the single-acting actuators extend and retract, the end of the lever moves vertically to change the angle of tilt. This causes the pump pistons to change their length of stroke, and the pump to change its flow rate. By controlling the servo valve position, pump displacement and rudder movement are regulated, and oil flow is modulated to stroke the single-acting actuators.

The servo valve is controlled by the action of two inputs: one from the rotary actuator, while the other is initiated by the ram movement of the helix screw, via the follow-up differential gear. The rotary actuator (Fig. 16-6) consists of: a fixed displacement, bidi-

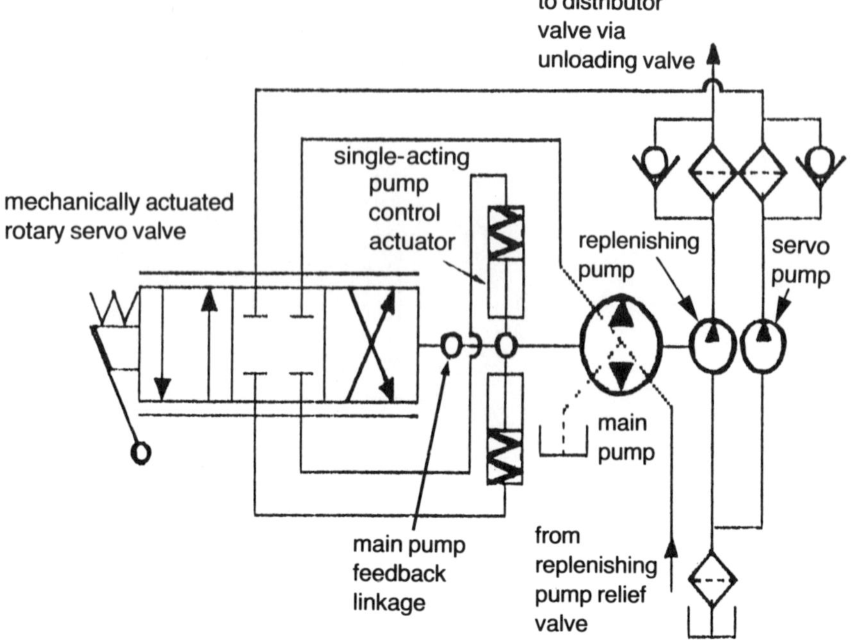

Fig. 16-5. Power unit and control circuit hydraulic schematic

rectional hydraulic motor; rotary potentiometer; a three-position, four-way, center-closed, double-solenoid-actuated directional valve; an offset two-position, three-way, solenoid valve; variable flow control; and oil filter.

Oil is fed at a constant rate to the flow control and filter, then onto the double-solenoid valve. Shifting of the double-solenoid valve controls the direction of flow to the hydraulic motor and, therefore, its direction of rotation. This is achieved by remotely unbalancing an electronic bridge circuit. Although somewhat complicated, the unbalancing is provided by turning the steering wheel of the electronic steering stand located on the navigation bridge.

When the rudder is to be swung, one of the double solenoids of the rotary actuator unit is energized to shift the valve spool in one direction. Oil passes to one side of the hydraulic motor, resulting in its rotation. As the hydraulic motor rotates, it drives the rotary potentiometer, and the uniquely shaped cam, through the gear arrangement in the follow-up unit.

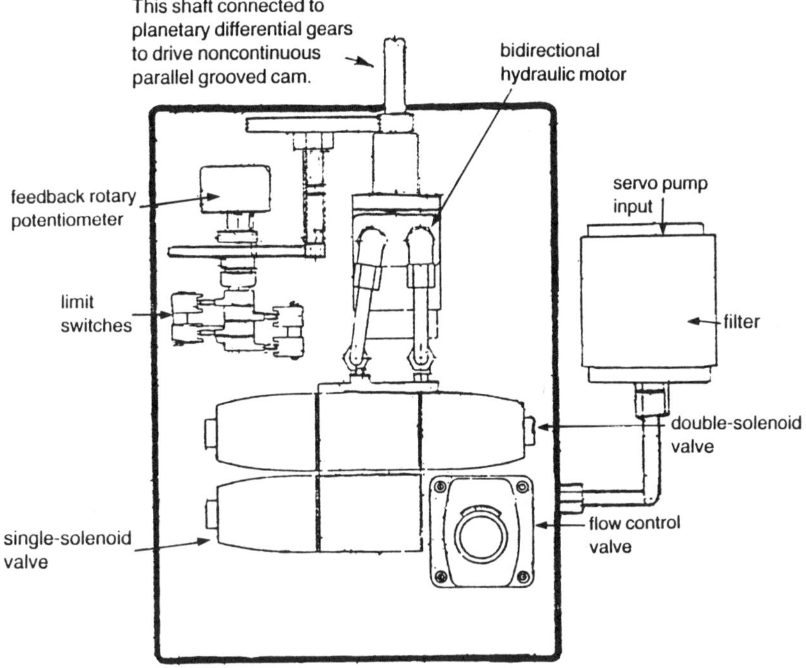

Fig. 16-6. Physical layout of rotary actuator (courtesy Sperry)

The cam is unique in that two parallel, noncontinuous grooves, provided with a diagonal crossover, are machined into the circumference of the cam hub. A follower pin, which controls the physical position of the servo valve spool, follows the groove as the cam rotates. When the servo valve is centered and closed, the follower pin is in the middle of the diagonal groove. This results in the hydraulic locking of the tilting box horizontal control lever, with the pump remaining in neutral stroke. As the cam rotates, the follower pin slides through the diagonal groove toward one of the parallel grooves. This action shifts the valve spool of the servo valve. The servo pump discharge then flows to one of the two single-acting actuators. This causes the other actuator to drain so that the main pump begins to be placed on stroke. As the tilting box tilts, it causes the sleeve around the valve spool to move in the same direction. Eventually, the sleeve matches the position of the spool and stops oil flow across the servo valve.

In order for the sleeve to match the position of the spool, the spool must first stop. Aside from the obvious physical limitations of the movement by the spool, the spool can be infinitely shifted from its centered closed position to its full open position in either direction. Remember, the amount of rotation by the cam proportionally shifts the spool; the cam rotates only as long as the hydraulic motor rotates, and the motor continues to rotate only as long as the double solenoids remain energized.

Recall that the rotary potentiometer is driven by the hydraulic motor, as is the cam. As the potentiometer rotates, it produces an electrical output, whose polarity is opposite to that of the signal generated by the electronic bridge circuit. Once the magnitude of the signals from the electronic bridge and the rotary potentiometer are equal, they cancel each other as they are of opposite polarity. This deenergizes the double-solenoid valve and returns it to its centered, closed position. With the solenoid valve closed, oil flow to the hydraulic motor stops, as will its rotation.

Rotation of the cam by the hydraulic motor also ceases, so that the original movement of the spool stops, allowing the sleeve to catch up. This action secures the flow of servo oil to the single-acting actuators and stops the tilting box from increasing its angle of tilt.

With the main pump still on stroke, the rams continue to slide through the cylinders, increasing the rudder angle. When the rams are moving, the helix screw, located atop the after set of rams, is forced to rotate. While the hydraulic motor rotates, the shaft from the helix screw, although rotating, provides no useful output. This is because both the hydraulic motor and helix screw outputs are directed to the planetary differential gear. Since the hydraulic motor begins to rotate first, its output is transferred to the cam by the planetary differential gear.

Once the hydraulic motor stops, the helix screw output becomes active as a function of the planetary differential gear. As this is the only input to rotate the cam, the cam rotates, but in a direction opposite to that originally established by the hydraulic motor. Therefore, the spool of the servo valve moves opposite to the direction from which it had originally shifted, and forces the tilting box angle to move back toward neutral stroke. As the tilting box regains neutral position, the rudder angle matches the angle originally designated by the helm, until a new command input occurs.

Emergency and Safety Conditions

When weather conditions intensify, the sea can create excessive forces on the rudder. These forces, known as rudder shock, are transferred to the rams, causing excessive pressure conditions to develop in the high-pressure side of the system. The relief valves, which are part of the distributor valves, protect the system from these forces, by dumping the pressurized oil to the low side of the system.

If while the ship is being steered, a failure occurs to the main remote steering gear control system, control can be transferred to the standby control at the steering stand. If both remote control systems fail, the steering gear can be controlled directly. This is accomplished by engaging the trick wheel to control the tilting box angle directly, as long as the pump prime movers are operable.

The emergency hand pump can be aligned to swing the rudder if both power pumps are lost by rotating the hand pump in one direction or the other. To line up the hand pump, the valves indicated at each end of the ram cylinders in Fig. 16-1 must be properly aligned. When hand pump steering is used, the single solenoid valve in the rotary actuator must be deenergized. This allows the hydraulic motor to be hydraulically locked in place to neutralize its effects on the system.

If extensive work is performed on the system, or the rudder, the distributor valves are generally insufficient for hydraulically locking the system for these repairs. In this case, the stop valves, indicated at each cylinder in Fig. 16-1, must be closed to hydraulically lock the rams in place.

CHAPTER 17

THE VANE-TYPE STEERING GEAR

For several decades, the ram-type steering gear was the workhorse controlling the ship's rudder. But, as ships have increased in size, more powerful steering gears have become necessary. However, as the power requirements of the steering gears have increased, so have the size and weight of these units. One solution to this problem of increasing sizes and weights is the vane-type steering gear. With it, substantial inroads in reducing the disadvantage of size posed by its older cousin have been made.

Each power unit for the vane-type steering systems (Fig. 17-1) consists of an electric motor, which simultaneously drives the main variable displacement pump and the constant flow replenishing pump. The replenishing pump provides for adding oil to the main system by way of check valves at each side of the main pump system piping. A portion of the replenishing pump flow is diverted to aid in controlling the actions of the main pump. Hydrostatic control pressure is also developed by the replenishing pump to shift the hydraulically piloted unit valve.

The functions of the unit valve are to provide a path to recirculate oil from one side of the main pump to the other, when that unit is in standby. Also, the unit valve aligns flow from the main pump to the vane motor. Since the unit valve can be shifted only when the replenishing pump is in operation, the steering gear power units can be changed over remotely by starting the electric motor, using the motor controllers located on the navigation bridge.

Once the power unit is started, the rudder angle is controlled in the following manner. By rotating the steering wheel, an electric potential is established to energize one of the two solenoids used to shift the three-position, spring-centered, directional control valve.

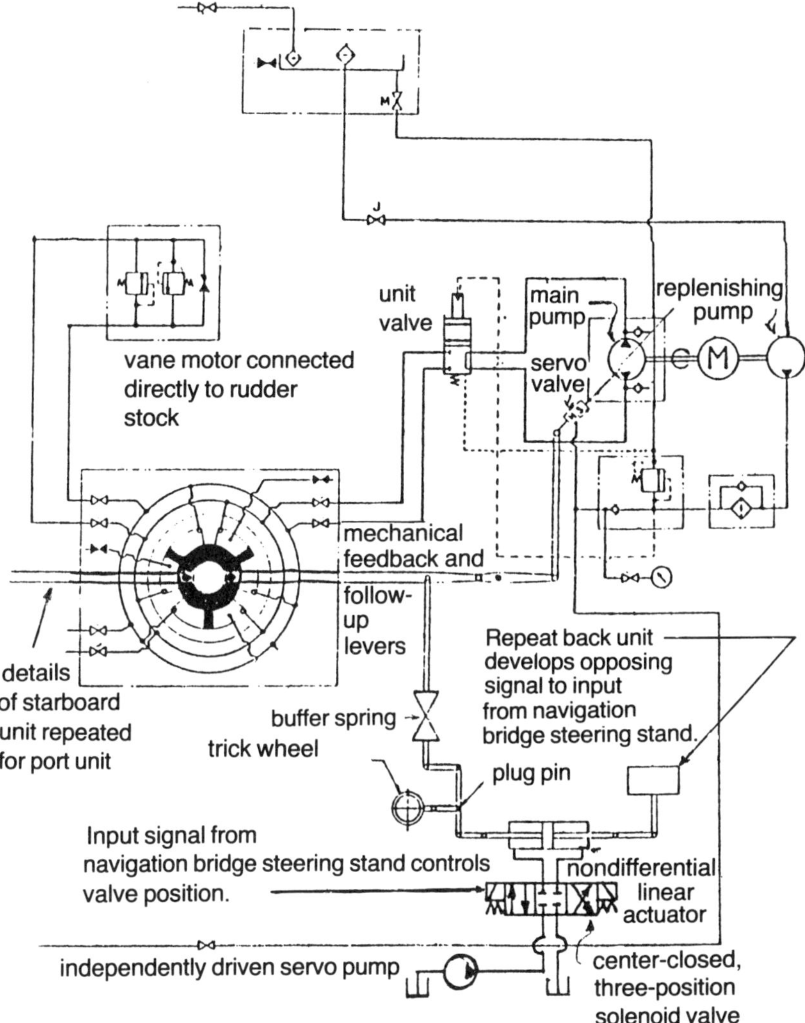

Fig. 17-1. Hydraulic schematic of vane steering gear

Oil flow, delivered by a second, separately driven constant flow servo pump, is directed across the solenoid directional control valve, to one end of the nondifferential linear actuator, with one end of the actuator piston rod connected to the electric repeat back unit, as indicated. The other end is connected to the stroke control linkage.

As the control piston shifts, the motion is transferred, via the buffer spring, to the control lever that pivots at the vane motor (see

Fig. 17-2). As the end of the lever nearest the pump moves, it causes the spool of the servo valve to slide in one direction. As the spool moves, it allows oil from the replenishing pump to flow through the servo valve sleeve to actuate the stroke control cylinders, similar to the method employed with the unitized steering gear described in chapter 16. By stroking the control cylinder, the angle of the tilting box changes. Flow is established from one side of the variable delivery pump to the vane motor to develop rotation.

Two actions occur simultaneously. First, as the hydraulic control cylinder shifts, it causes the repeat back unit to develop a signal proportional to the linear movement of the hydraulic control. However, the repeat back signal is opposite to the polarity of the control signal initially generated by the rotation of the steering wheel. Once the potential of the repeat back unit matches the original signal, the double solenoid is deenergized, allowing the control valve to return to its centered, closed position. This action hydraulically locks the control cylinder in place.

The mechanical linkage moves the servo valve spool proportionally to the movement of the control cylinder. As the tilting box angle increases, it simultaneously shifts the servo valve sleeve in the same direction that the spool had moved, but lagging behind the spool movement. Once the control cylinder is locked in place, the tilting box assumes an angle proportional to the distance moved by the control cylinder. Keep in mind that these movements are proportional to how far the steering wheel had been rotated.

The second set of actions takes place as the vane motor rotates. This action is initiated as the lever connected to the vane motor rotor is changed from the fulcrum to the point of pivot. Likewise, the end of the buffer spring rod changes from the point of pivot to that of the fulcrum. The combination of these shifts, as the vane motor continues to rotate, begins to shift the servo valve spool in a direction opposite to the originally designated command.

Again, the oil flow from the replenishing pump is permitted to flow across the servo valve to the stroke control cylinder, forcing the tilting box back toward neutral stroke. The sleeve also moves in the same direction as the spool, because of the mechanical interaction with the tilting box; yet it lags behind.

Shortly before the rudder achieves its designated angle, the levers stop changing position, and the servo valve spool is stopped. When the rudder reaches its designated angle, the sleeve catches

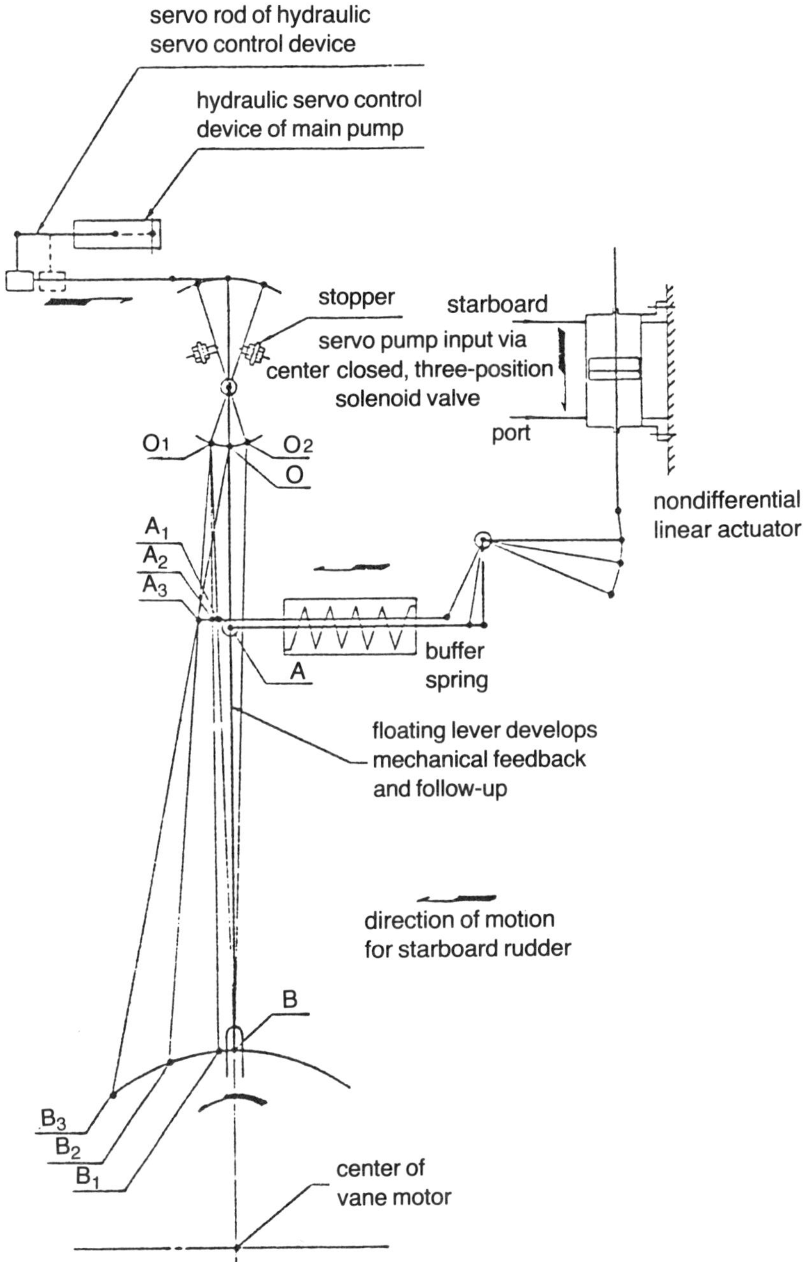

Fig. 17-2. Diagram of mechanical feedback and follow-up showing relative action during rudder movement

up to the spool position, as the spool has already stopped. The replenishing pump oil flow to the stroke control cylinder is blocked again, locking the tilting box in neutral stroke. As oil flow from the main pump is no longer in existence, rotation of the vane motor is stopped and locked in place until a new command is initiated by turning the steering wheel.

CHAPTER 18

THE CONTROLLABLE PITCH PROPELLER

On most engine-driven vessels, the control of speed and direction is a function of the engine speed and its direction of rotation. Although common in practice, this concept creates a set of problems that may result in a dangerous inefficient operating condition, particularly during maneuvering.

Engines operate most efficiently at the higher end of the rpm range. If the engine rpm can be kept at a constant and efficient operating speed the propeller pitch can be altered for the most efficient fuel consumption. With fixed-pitch propellers, however, when the direction of engine rotation is changed, there is a short period during which the engine is stopped. For steam-geared turbines, every second used to reverse the engines carries the ship closer to danger. The problem is further complicated by the fact that only 35 to 40 percent of the ahead power of the steam turbine is available for going astern.

For diesel engines that are directly reversed, this problem occurs when reversing the engine, since the engine must be completely stopped, then restarted in the opposite direction. If numerous bells for ahead-astern maneuvering occur rapidly, starting air may be depleted and may prevent restarting of the engine. Therefore, the use of controllable reversible pitch propellers can offer:

1. unidirectional shaft rotation and nearly constant engine speed, while controlling direction and speed of the vessel by changing the pitch angle of the blades
2. nearly 100 percent of power of ahead-astern operation for steam geared turbines

3. easier astern control on gas turbine engine plants
4. rapid astern thrust for diesel and steam-geared turbines since the engines do not have to be stopped in order to change thrust output

In the basic operation of the controllable reversible pitch propellers used aboard oceangoing vessels, the propeller blades rotate about an axis perpendicular to the axis of the main shaft. The blade angle change is effected by hydraulic pressure applied to a hub servo piston. The blades, connected by suitable linkage to the servo piston, rotate as the servo piston is forced to change its position.

Currently, there are three major manufacturers who have provided controllable pitch propeller systems for ships in the American merchant marine: Bird-Johnson, Lipps, and Escher-Wyss.

Although the following discussion is centered around the Bird-Johnson system it should be understood that each system is significantly different in how the blade pitch angle is modulated.

In this design the blades are positioned by the linear movement of a double-acting hydraulic piston (hub servo) located in the propeller hub (see Fig. 18-1). As the hub servo piston moves fore or aft, in response to the controlled hydraulic oil flow, the position of the cross head assembly is changed. The cross head assembly is designed with a sliding block arrangement for each propeller blade, to transfer the linear motion of the crosshead to rotate the blades.

The motion transfer occurs as the crosshead is forced to move in a fore/aft direction. The applied force is transferred to the side of the sliding block. (Each block accepts a large diameter pin connected to the periphery of the propeller base or crank ring. See Fig. 18-2.) As the linear force is applied to the sliding block, the force is concurrently transferred to the pin. The crank ring pin is forced to describe a circle about the propeller blade axis. During the linear movement of the crosshead, the applied force not only moves the sliding block linearly, but also forces it to slide athwart the crosshead axis. This combined action causes the crank ring, and therefore the blade, to rotate.

To change the position of the hub servo piston, i.e., the blade angle, a constant flow pump maintains oil flow at a moderate pressure to the hub. The pump discharge is initially fed to the oil distribution box (see Fig. 18-3) located by the engine reduction gear. Oil is then permitted to flow through the valve rod, located in the center of the main shaft, which shifts fore and aft during normal

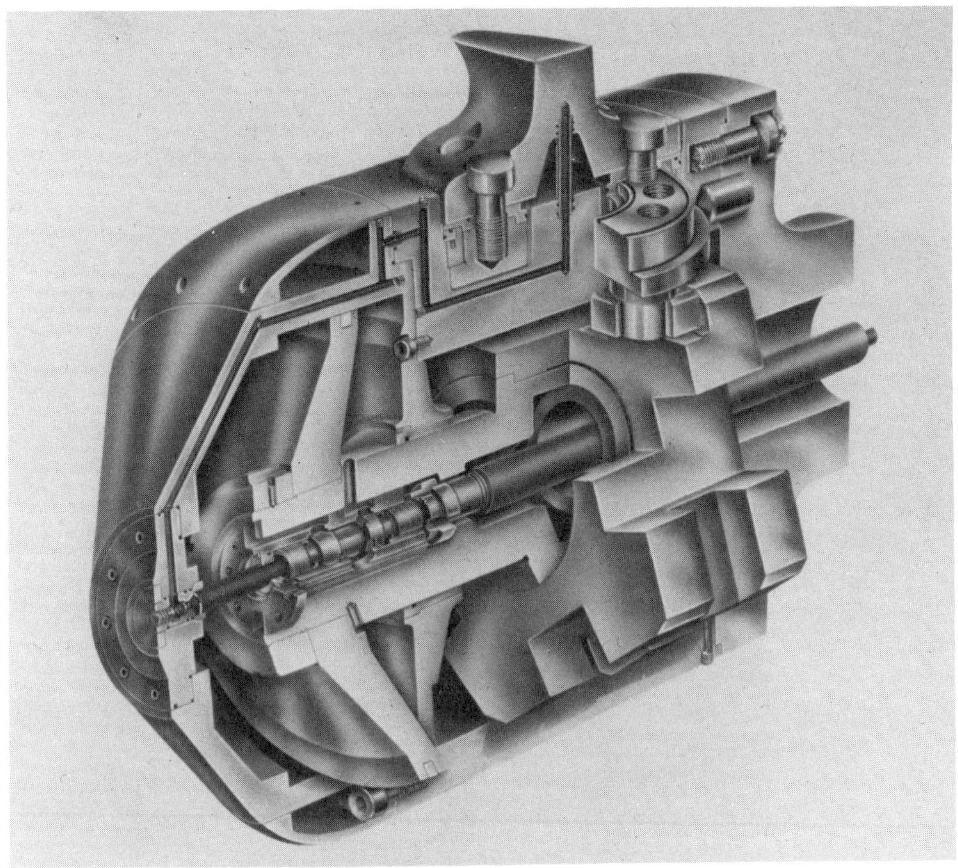

Fig. 18-1. Cutaway view of the controlled pitch propeller hub.

operation. The valve rod also controls the position of the valve spool, located in the horizontal center of the hub servo (see Fig. 18-4). The slide valve (valve spool) and valve rod, manufactured as one piece, are directly connected to the valve rod actuator (auxiliary servo piston) located in the forward end of the oil distribution box. When the valve rod actuator position is changed, a similar position is attained by the hub servo slide valve. Therefore, a change in the position of the hub servo slide valve controls the direction of oil flow to the appropriate side of the hub servo when blade pitch angle is to be changed.

Referring to the "valve rod assembly" diagram (see Fig. 18-3A), note the hollow box-shaped auxiliary servo piston at the forward end of the oil distribution box. The division of the auxiliary servo

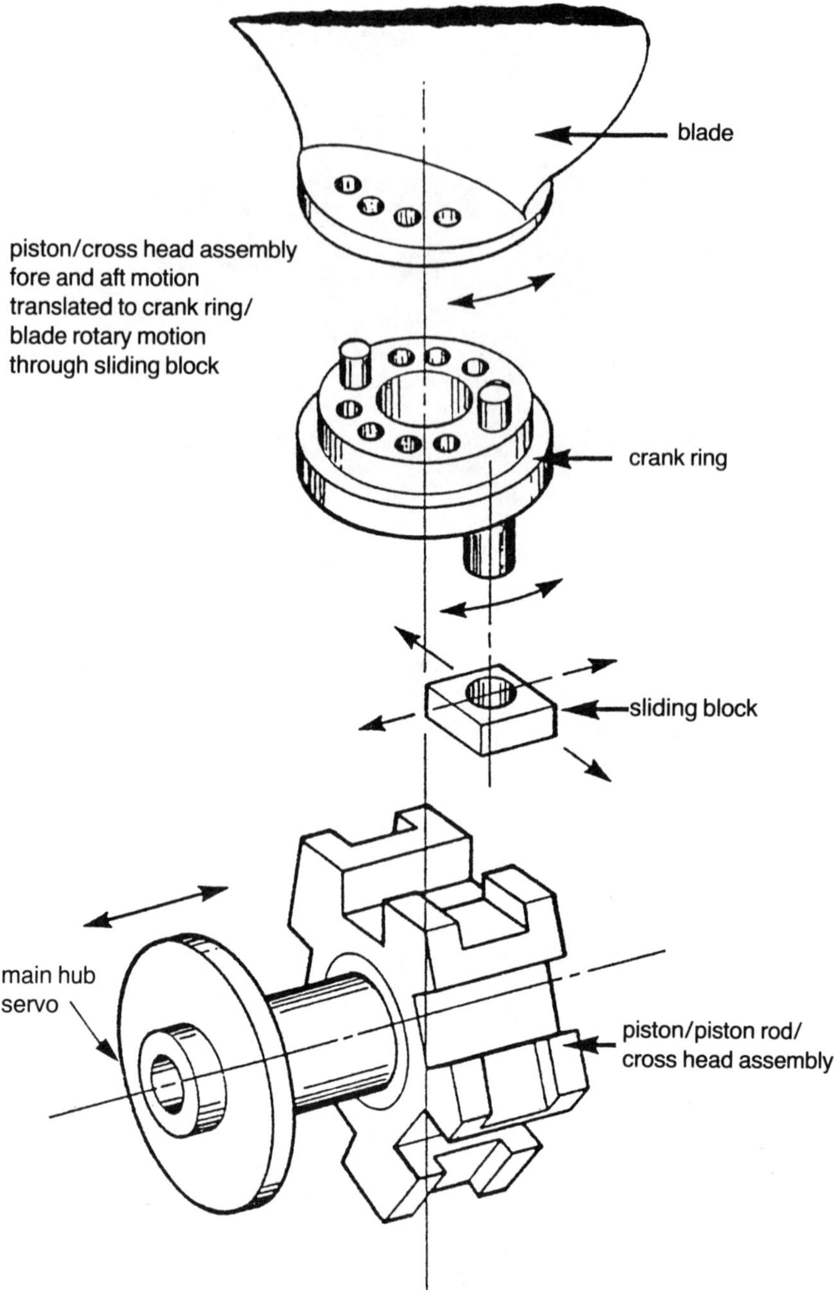

Fig. 18-2. Exploded view of cross head assembly

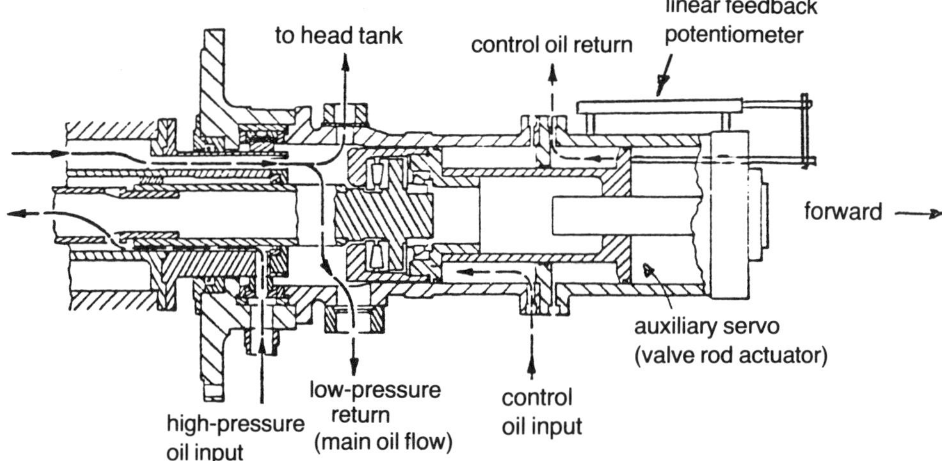

Fig. 18-3A. Oil distribution box showing the control rod in position for running astern

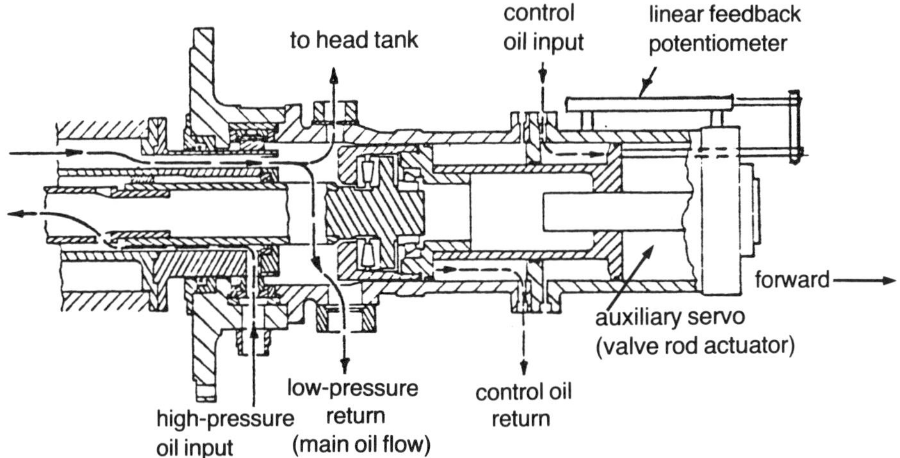

Fig. 18-3B. Oil distribution box showing the control rod in position for running ahead

cylinder, for positioning of the auxiliary servo piston, is provided by the diaphragm plate. Oil flow to either side of the diaphragm is provided at low pressure and controlled by a three-position directional valve. When control oil is fed between the right-hand side of the diaphragm and the lip at the right-hand end of the piston, the piston moves to the right. Conversely, when oil is channeled between

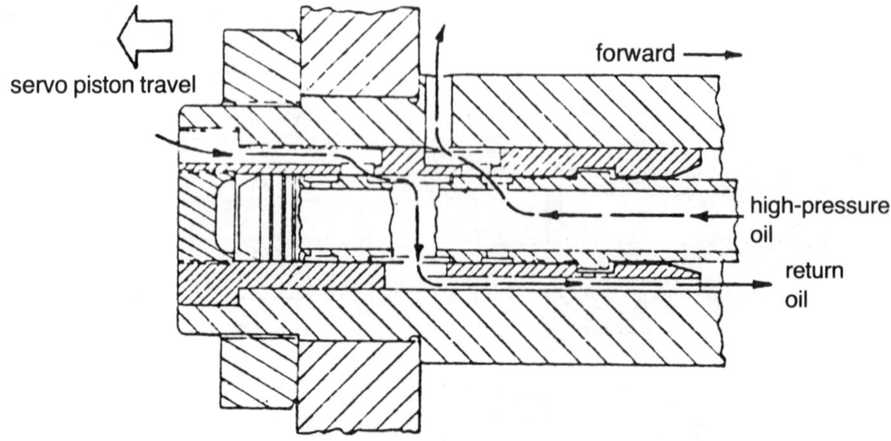

Fig. 18-4A. Valve slide in position for running astern

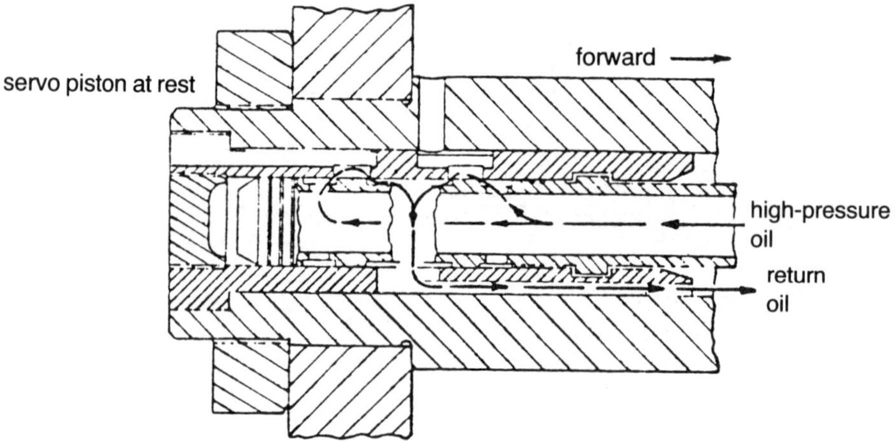

Fig. 18-4B. Valve slide in neutral position

the left-hand side of the diaphragm and the lip at the left-hand end of the piston, the piston moves to the left.

As the valve rod actuator moves forward, the regulating pin of the slide valve also moves forward and permits the relatively higher oil pressure to pass to the aft side of the hub servo piston. The force generated by the oil flow on the aft side pushes the hub servo piston and crosshead forward. This action rotates the blades to an ahead pitch angle. By reversing the flow to the forward side of the hub

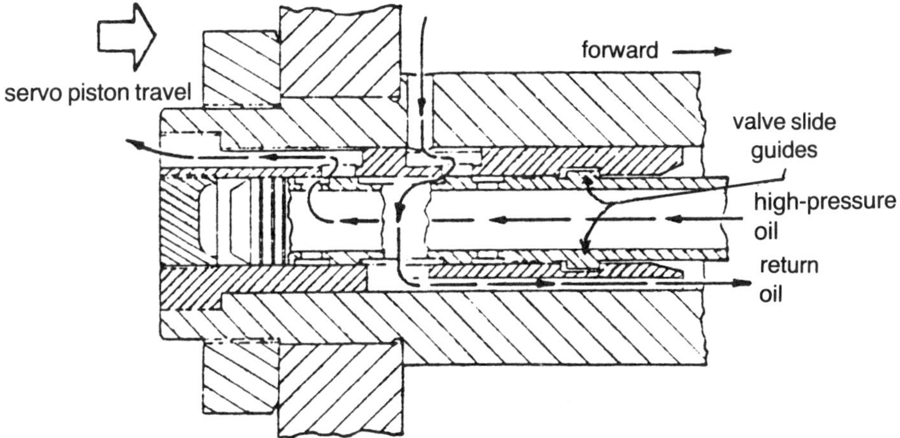

Fig. 18-4C. Valve slide in position for running ahead

servo piston, the movement of the hub servo piston and crosshead is reversed and brings the blade angle to an astern pitch.

When oil is fed to one side of the hub servo piston, the slide valve allows oil to pass from the opposite side of the hub servo piston to the low-pressure return annulus (see Fig. 18-5). This annulus is created by the outside of the valve rod and the inside of the main shaft.

The oil distribution box is designed to conduct a portion of the return flow from the annulus to the head tank and the remainder to the sump. A spring-loaded check valve, placed in the return line to the sump, is used to maintain a minimum 20 psi on the return side. The head tank, installed above the system, maintains an oil pressure 1½ times that of the water pressure exerted on the hub when the vessel is at its maximum draft. Thus, one function provided by the head tank is to prevent the leakage of seawater into the oil side when the system is secured or should any leakage occur across the blade seals.

In order to understand the remaining operation of the system, it will be helpful to refer to Fig. 18-6, the overall hydraulic schematic, and Fig. 18-7, the pressure control assembly. These diagrams indicate that there are two main pumps. Each pump is capable of developing constant flow rates at approximately 450 psi to the hub in addition to the approximately 200 psi control oil flow to the auxiliary servo piston.

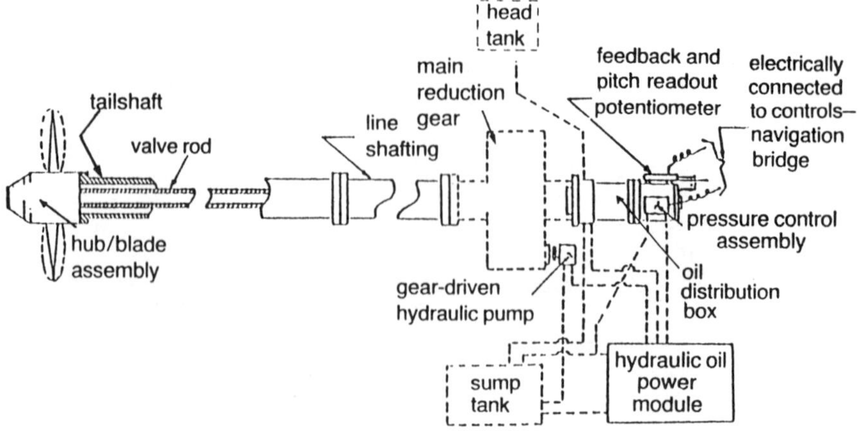

Fig. 18-5. CPP system diagram—overview arrangement

There are several arrangements that can be combined to operate the system. For purposes of the following discussion one of the two pumps is to be considered as being driven by a constant speed electric motor, while the other pump is to be considered as being driven by a power take-off from the main engine reduction gears. In addition, for the sake of the discussion, the reduction-gear-driven pump is to supply oil to the hub at sea for the purpose of pitch angle maintenance.

During maneuvering, either pump is capable of maintaining adequate oil flow to the hub, but the electric pump is to act as the main pump, while the reduction-gear-driven pump is automatically unloaded to the sump. Primarily, the only time that the two pumps operate in parallel is during the change of blade pitch angle.

All of the necessary control operations are carried out by the pressure control valve manifold. In order to understand the operation of the control arrangement of the pressure control valve assembly, consider that the electric pump is started prior to sailing to provide continuous oil flow to the hub as well as to warm up the oil by circulating it through the system.

Once the electric motor is started and oil flow established to the pressure control manifold, a portion of the oil flow is tapped off from the main discharge and passes through the check valve in line G. The check valve nearest the reduction-gear-driven pump (pump A) blocks the flow from bleeding off to line A. Oil passes through the indicated reducing valve to develop the control oil flow at approximately 200 psi for position control of the valve rod actuator.

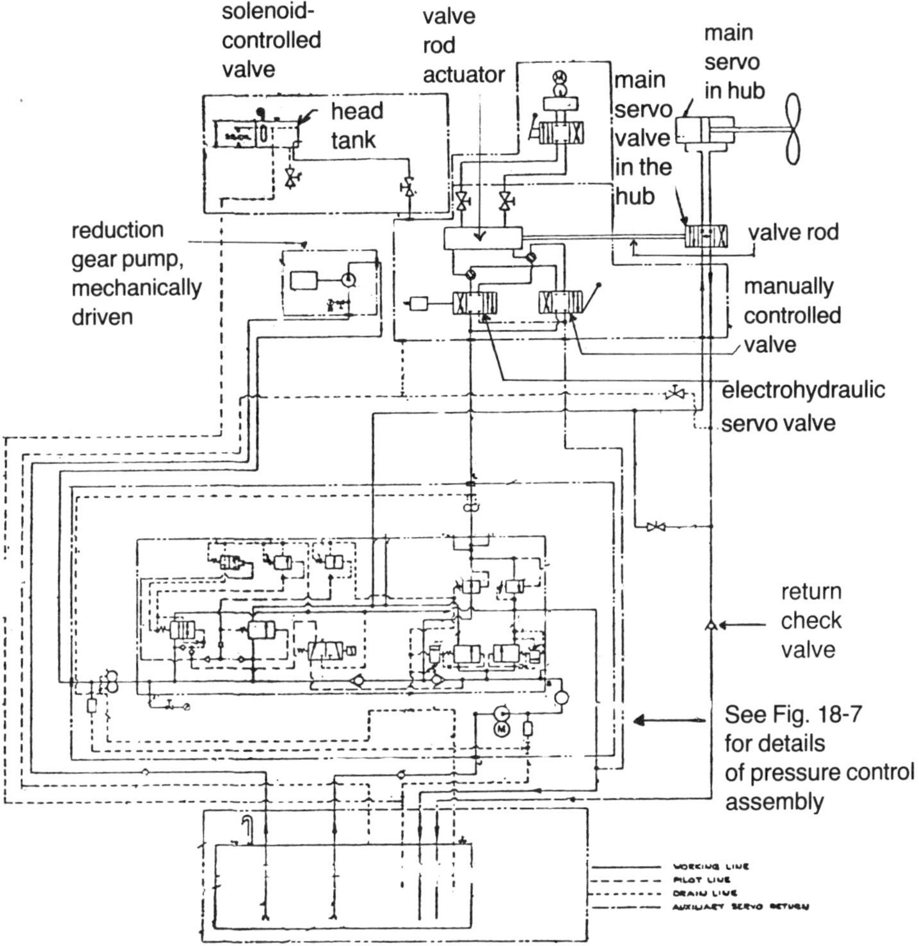

Fig. 18-6. Main hydraulic schematic for controllable pitch propeller

The actuation of the sequence valve for pump B is controlled by its pilot valve. The use of the pilot enables the main valve to be properly sized for the required flow rate, yet snap open only when setpoint pressure is achieved; the pilot prevents the valve from chattering as normal pump discharge is established. Since other main/ pilot valve combinations in the system open in a similar manner, it is necessary to understand this operation.

Note the sensing line arrangement associated with the pilot and the main valve. The graphic symbol indicates that the sensing line is provided prior to the main valve inlet to open the valve hydraulically. In addition, oil pressure from the inlet is used in conjunction

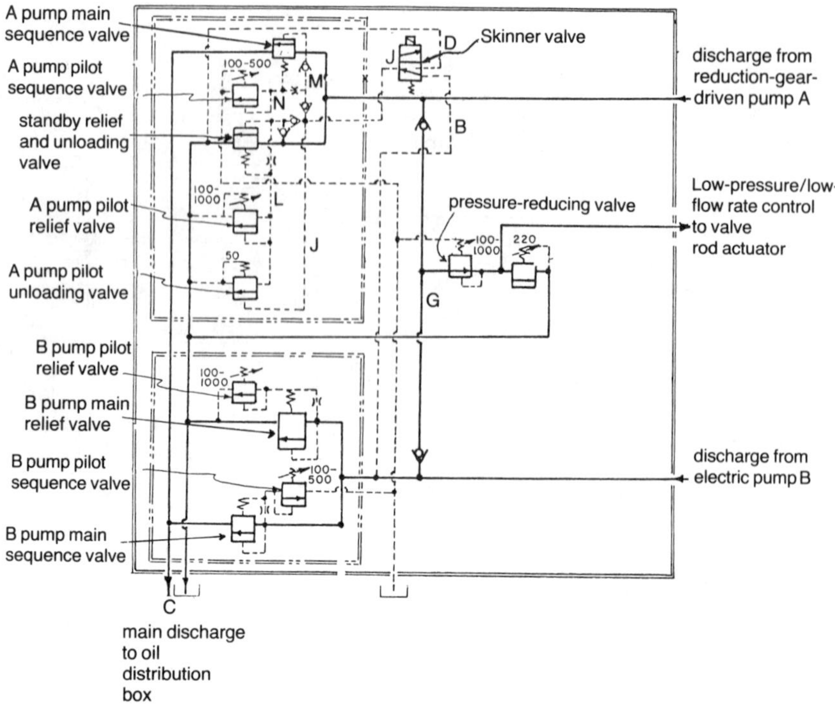

Fig. 18-7. Pressure control assembly diagram

with the indicated closing spring. As long as the oil pressure is equal in both lines, the spring alone keeps the valve closed. A fixed orifice is also provided in this passage to the spring side sensing port that is also the passage for actuating the incorporated pilot valve. The pilot spring force is adjusted to maintain the opening setpoint of the main sequence valve at 250 psi. Once the pilot opens, the pressure to the pilot inlet cannot rise above 250 psi. However, as the pump continues to establish its normal flow rate, the main stream pressure builds to force open the main sequence valve. Due to this interaction, the oil pressure necessary to open the main valve always remains higher than the combined closing force of the oil pressure and spring force. If the pump is secured or fails, the oil at the valve inlet flows rapidly across the main sequence valve, while the oil at the orifice outlet is maintained at approximately 250 psi, bleeding across the pilot at a slower rate. As a result, there is insufficient force acting against the combined closing force of the spring and the oil pressure at the pilot inlet to keep the main valve open.

If the discharge pressure from pump B rises above 495 psi, the setpoint of the relief valve pilot is exceeded. The main relief valve now opens to dump oil to the sump through line D in order to prevent the pressure from rising any further. The relief pilot/main valve operates in a similar manner to that previously described for the sequence pilot/main valve operation.

With the main engine now in operation, the reduction-gear-driven pump (pump A) is now able to produce flow. Until a pitch angle change occurs, the A pump discharge is unloaded to the sump. The following description should be helpful in understanding the purpose and function of the valve combinations in the pressure control assembly. The interaction of these valves is important for establishing control fluid flow, and loading and unloading of the standby pump when two pumps are operated in parallel, as well as the dual function of the A pump unloading and relief valve.

With the A pump discharge unloaded to the sump, it is necessary to review the existing opened and closed positions of the valves in the pressure control assembly. The position of the Skinner valve (solenoid two-position control, top center of Fig. 18-7) initiates the sequence of events for unloading and loading of the A pump when it is operated in parallel with the B pump. While the B pump discharge occurs primarily through line C, a restricted amount of oil flows from its discharge to be fed across the Skinner valve and on to line J, as long as the solenoid is de-energized, i.e., there is no change in pitch angle. As the amount of oil increases initially in line J, the pressure steadily rises to be exerted simultaneously to three distinct areas (line J, line M, and line L). As the pressure of the oil in line J increases, sufficient force is produced to overcome the 50 psi setpoint of the A pump unloading pilot valve.

At this point the oil in line L cannot become pressurized because the unloading pilot quickly opened. Consequently, the pressure in line L (below the fixed orifice) is insufficient to aid the force spring in keeping the main unloading valve closed. Since oil pressure in line J has risen, to keep the unloading pilot open, sufficient pressure is established and directed toward the main standby relief and unloading valve to force it open. The discharge from pump A now flows virtually unrestricted through the opened main unloading valve to the sump through line D.

As the ship is readied to get under way, the blade angle is increased to provide thrust, an action that can be initiated in one of three ways: an electric remote on the navigation bridge, a manual control at the oil distribution box in the engine room, and an emergency pitch control by separate pump unit. The remote control from the navigation bridge is the first to be discussed below.

A control lever on the navigation bridge is used to control the output of an electronic device that develops an output voltage proportional to the position of the control lever. Regardless of the magnitude of the generated signal the Skinner valve solenoid is energized. The primary signal is transmitted to energize the solenoid control valve at the oil distribution box. The direction of the control lever movement determines which of the two solenoids of the electrohydraulic servo valve is energized, hence in which direction the solenoid valve is opened. For example, the remote control can be set up to create a total voltage range of −15 volts to +15 volts, where +15 volts is proportional to 100 percent forward pitch, 0 volts to 0 pitch, and −15 volts to 100 percent astern pitch. Once the servo valve shifts, the 200 psi control oil flow is directed to the appropriate side of the valve rod actuator, causing it to move as previously described.

A linear potentiometer, installed at the forward end of the oil distribution box, changes its position in response to the movement of the valve rod actuator. As its position changes, a voltage proportional in magnitude to that produced by the remote is developed, but of opposite polarity. As the blades achieve the commanded angle, a null signal is established to the solenoid valve to de-energize and recenter it. This interaction cuts off further control oil flow to the valve rod actuator and hydraulically locks it in place. Shortly after the valve rod actuator stops moving, and hence the regulating valve pin stops as well, the hub servo piston only continues to move until the slide valve sleeve is in a position to stop flow to the hub servo. Thus the correct blade angle is developed in proportion to the original movement of the pitch control lever.

At the begining of the action just described, the Skinner valve is energized, and remains energized as long as the remote circuit and the linear potentiometer do not cancel out each other. As the Skinner valve shifts, the pressure buildup permitted through line B across the Skinner valve to line J is now blocked. Furthermore, the hydrostatic pressure in line J is bled to the sump through pilot line D, due to the new position of the Skinner valve. This action permits the unloading pilot to close. The oil pressure exerted on both sides of the main unloading valve equalizes as the pressure in line L rises as a result of the unloading pilot being closed. The discharge from the A pump also increases so that the spring force plus the oil pressure is greater than the oil pressure alone and keeps the main unloading valve closed.

As soon as the main unloading valve has closed, hydrostatic pressure in the A pump discharge rises and is simultaneously exerted at the inlet of the main A pump sequence valve. However, the main sequence cannot open until oil pressure is exerted via the check valve in line M and across the fixed orifice to open the sequence pilot. Until the pilot opens, the oil pressure on both sides of the main sequence valve is equal and opposing, so that the spring force keeps the main sequence valve closed. Once the A pump discharge rises to 250 psi, the oil pressure in line N is sufficient to open the A pump sequence pilot. This action prevents the oil pressure in line N from exceeding 250 psi. Since the spring force plus the pressure in line N are less than the force of the oil acting to open the main sequence, the main sequence valve snaps open.

With the main sequence valve now open, oil flow from the A pump combines with the B pump discharge, and flows to the hub assembly through line C. Rapid blade angle change is now possible since the flow rate to the hub is doubled.

Once the linear potentiometer feedback signal cancels the remote signal, the Skinner valve is de-energized. This permits the oil B pump discharge to recharge line J and open the pilot unloading valve. With the pressure in line L rapidly dropping, the pressure in J is greater than the closing spring force of the main unloading valve and this forces the valve open. The A pump discharge drops well below 250 psi, allowing the A pump sequence pilot to close. The A pump is again unloaded to the sump, through line D.

For purposes of this explanation, it is to be considered that after the vessel reaches cruising speed, pump B is to be secured. The A pump remains in continuous operation due to the power takeoff from the main engine. Since major pitch angle changes are not anticipated, the oil flow from the A pump is only to maintain pitch position and keep the system at normal temperature.

Since there is no discharge from the B pump, line J is no longer hydrostatically charged, and the A pump unloading pilot is permitted to close. This action causes the main unloading valve to close and the main sequence valve to open as previously described.

The A pump requires a relief valve and, by the use of a second pilot, the main unloading valve is able to fulfill this function. The unloading standby relief valve opens if oil pressure in line L exceeds the 495 psi setpoint of the pilot. Once the relief pilot opens, the combined oil pressure/spring force that was keeping the main valve closed drops below that of the oil pressure required to open the valve. Oil continues to pass across the valve until the pressure in the system has dropped below the opening setpoint. This means that the pilot closes first, allowing the oil pressure to aid the spring to close the valve off despite an equal pressure acting to keep the valve open.

If direct pitch control is required from the engine room, two four-way valves, located at the oil distribution box, are shifted from *auto* to *manual* position. This replaces the electrohydraulic solenoid valve in the control oil circuit with the manual three-position valve. The manual three-position valve, when shifted by the operator, is held in position until the desired pitch angle is achieved, as indicated by the pitch angle indicator at the forward end of the oil distribution box.

The maximum forward pitch angle is indicative of and proportional to the highest attainable pressure with the auxiliary servo piston at the forward end of its travel. Conversely, maximum astern pitch is the lowest pressure developed forward of the auxiliary servo piston when it is as far aft as possible. By observing the pitch indicator, the operator can close off the manual control valve to lock the blades, as automatic follow-up is not available.

If the system becomes completely inoperable, full ahead pitch can be maintained by connecting the emergency pump to the auxiliary servo cylinder. Once this is done the auxiliary servo piston is forced to its *full ahead* position carrying the valve rod and hub servo piston. The emergency pump is operated until the valve rod is "stretched" and full ahead pitch is achieved. As long as oil is maintained in the oil distribution box, and moderate speeds are maintained, the ship can be operated indefinitely in this mode.

CHAPTER 19

HYDRAULIC HATCH COVERS

As long as ships have been carrying cargo, it has been necessary to keep the cargo hatches sealed to protect them from the "elements" and to reduce the temptation of pilfering. Until the end of World War II, hatches were generally closed at each deck with a series of planks, known as "ceiling boards." Hundreds of these boards were required to cover all the hatches and tween decks. Consequently, the work of opening and closing the hatches and maintaining them was very time-consuming. As cargo-operating time needed to be shortened, the old system had to be changed, and hydraulic hatch covers came of age.

Currently, there are two basic systems in use. The first incorporates a limited rotation torque motor, while the second employs a system of linear actuators.

The Hydraulic Torque Motor System

Typical use of the torque motor hatch cover design is found aboard ships where one hold may be subdivided into three cells athwartships, in addition to the customary vertical division of upper and lower tween decks. In order to meet the needs of each hold, the configuration of the hatch cover panels varies in number and combinations. An understanding of the four-panel set (Fig. 19-1) is used to simplify the discussion of operation because the other combinations are based upon this one.

Each four-section hatch cover is operated by its own power unit. Every power unit comprises an electric motor, bolted and sealed to the outside of the oil sump used to hold four gallons of hydraulic oil.

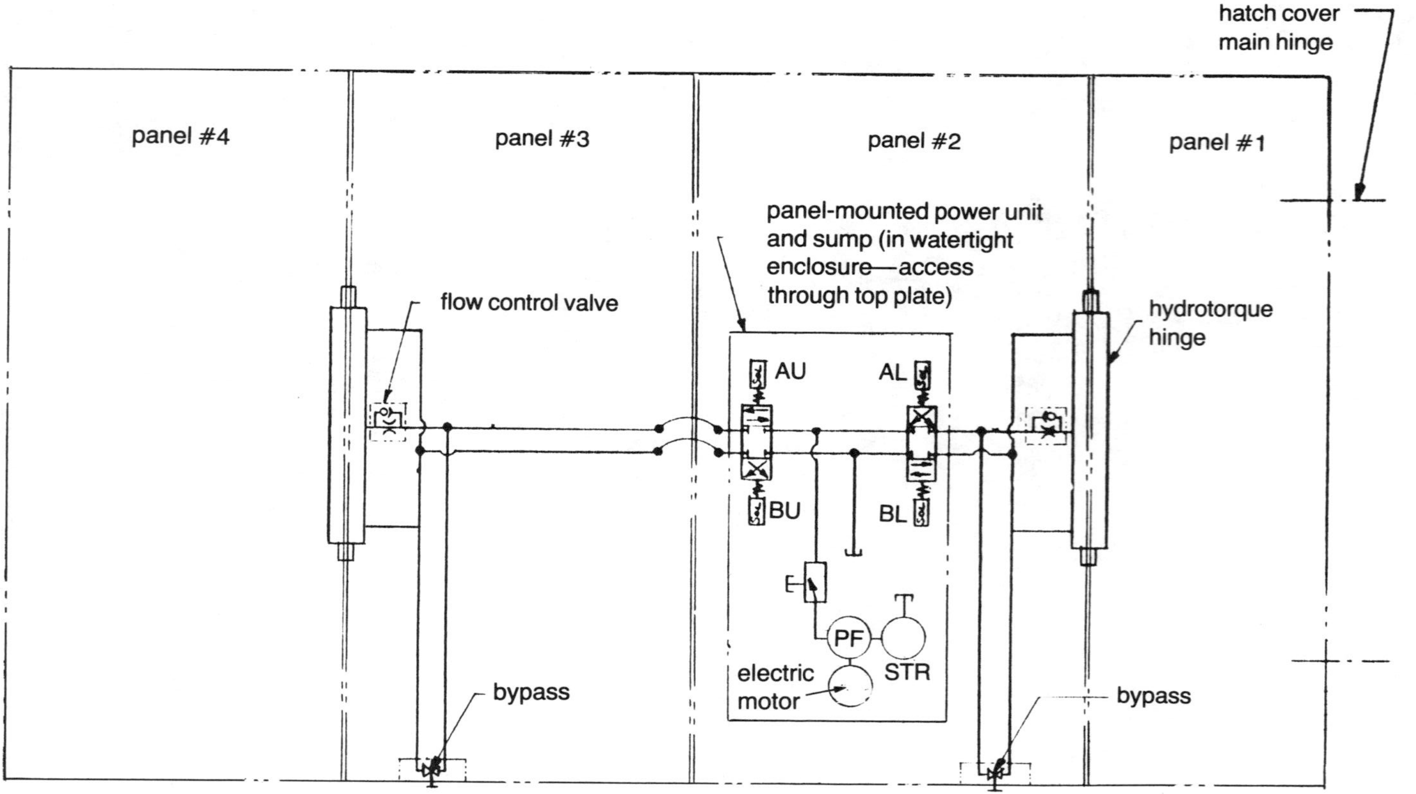

Fig. 19-1. Torque motor type hatch cover

An aluminum-cased spur gear pump, with suction strainer and relief valve, is bolted to the motor, and is accessible from inside the sump. A pair of double-solenoid valves is located in the discharge piping, as close as practicable to the outside of the sump, and is actuated by manual rotary and mechanical-limit electric switches. Each power unit is located in a protective covered well of the second hatch cover panel.

Each four-section hatch cover is hinged to the ship at the outboard end of the first panel. Although each subsequent panel is hinged to the next, the limited rotation hydraulic motor, or hydrotorque hinge, is installed between panels 1 and 2, and 3 and 4, with suitable piping completing the hydraulic circuit to the power unit.

The operation of the hatch cover is as follows: With electric power available to the control panel, you rotate the proper selector switch, which simultaneously starts the pump motor and energizes solenoid BL. This establishes maximum flow rate across the solenoid valve and the flow control valve unit to the hydrotorque hinge, located between panels 1 and 2. Unrestricted high-pressure oil flows to the center port of the hinge body and acts simultaneously on the opposing pistons (see Fig. 19-2). The outboard ends of each piston are externally splined to assure only linear movement without twisting. Internally, the ends of the pistons are machined with helical splines, or high-pitch threads, and mesh with a corresponding external helix on the rotating axles. As the entering high-pressure oil forces the two pistons apart, the axles rotate because of the inter-

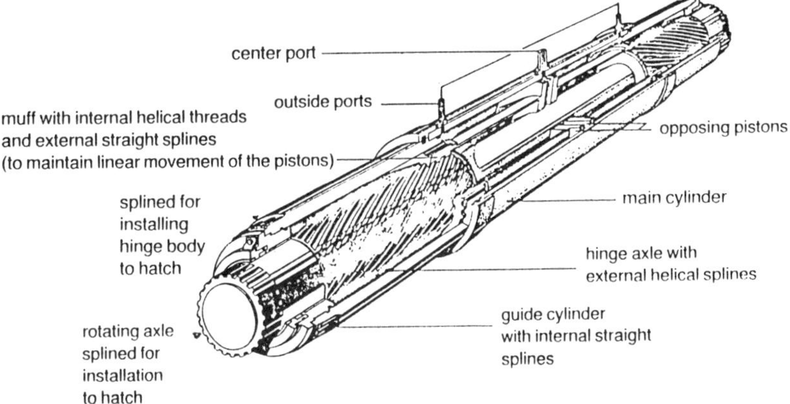

Fig. 19-2. Hydrotorque hinge

action promoted by the helical threads. With the body of the hinge splined to the folding hinge of one panel, and the rotating axle splined to the hinge half of the adjoining panel, the sections rotate to raise and fold together.

As panels 1 and 2 fold together, contact between the swing arm of the limit switch, and a striking plate on the opposite panel, causes solenoid BL to be de-energized, and solenoid AU to be energized. This action stops oil flow to the first hydrotorque hinge and allows flow to be established at the second hydrotorque hinge in order to raise panels 3 and 4. Releasing the spring-loaded rotary switch secures the power unit, and ends the opening operation.

When closing the hatches, the safety latches are first released. By rotating the selector switch to "close," the pump is rotated in the same direction as for the "opening" sequence. Since the limit switch has been shifted, solenoid AL is energized, permitting oil to flow to the outboard ends of the hydrotorque hinge, located between panels 3 and 4. The pistons are forced to move toward each other and rotate the axles opposite the original direction of rotation. The panels unfold and are lowered to the closed position.

It is important to realize that as the panels attain a slight angle to the horizontal, gravity causes them to drop in an uncontrolled manner. To prevent this from occurring, a flow control (restrictor valve) is installed in the return line (from the center port) to form a metered out circuit.

When you raise the hatch cover, oil is able to flow freely to the center hinge port across the check valve, positioned parallel to the variable restriction (needle valve). During the closing of the hatch cover, however, oil flow from the center port is blocked by the check valve. The only path the oil is able to take is across the partially opened needle valve, at a substantially reduced flow rate. "Runaway" is prevented because the speed when closing is controlled by the resulting "back pressure," and the restricted flow rate that is established by the needle valve.

If the power units become inoperable, you can open and close the hatches manually by the use of the ship's cargo gear, observing two precautions. First, be sure the bypass valves are opened to permit oil to leave the center port and flow into the two end ports of the hinge, and vice-versa. Now the cargo gear can be properly set up and attached to the lugs provided in order to raise the hatch covers. While lowering the hatch covers with the cargo gear, be *sure* you observe the second precaution. Raising the hatch cover requires only one winch and runner. For closing, however, while you use one winch to pull the hatch cover closed, be sure to use a second winch and runner to keep a strain on the rolling cover to prevent it from "running away."

The Linear Actuator System

The second of the two hatch cover systems, incorporating the use of linear actuators, differs widely from the first system in many respects. The most significant difference is found in the use of the two constant flow power units, each able to supply oil to half of the total number of hatches. A second difference is that the direction of fluid flow to the hatch covers is controlled by individual manually positioned directional valves. Aside from the obvious difference in the type of actuator used, small linear actuators are also used to jack open, and force the hatch covers to be tightly closed.

Each power unit is located under shelter and is a positive displacement generated rotor (gerotor) pump mounted atop a 180-gallon oil sump. Each is also provided with appropriate suction strainers, discharge filters, and a pressure switch. In addition, there is a minimum of three accumulators per power unit. The oil flow from each power unit is simultaneously fed to a series of control consoles, where the directional valves for controlling the opening and closing of the hatch covers are located.

For opening (raising) the hatch covers, oil flows unimpeded from the directional control valve toward the hatch cover by raising the control valve handle. Referring to the hatch cover circuit (Fig. 19-3), the flow is found to branch off and pass across the cam-operated two-position valve to the outrigger and truck-jacking cylinders with oil flow available to all of the cylinders at this point of the operation. However, because of the restrictions located in the supply lines, the jacking cylinders are actuated first. As a result of this action, the hatch cover is raised horizontally off its seat, which means that only the rolling friction of the wheels needs to be overcome during the opening of the hatch covers once the jacking has been accomplished.

Now that the jacking cylinders are fully retracted, oil continues to flow, at restricted rates, from the flow control valves to the main cylinders. The metered-in devices, A and B, are provided at each of

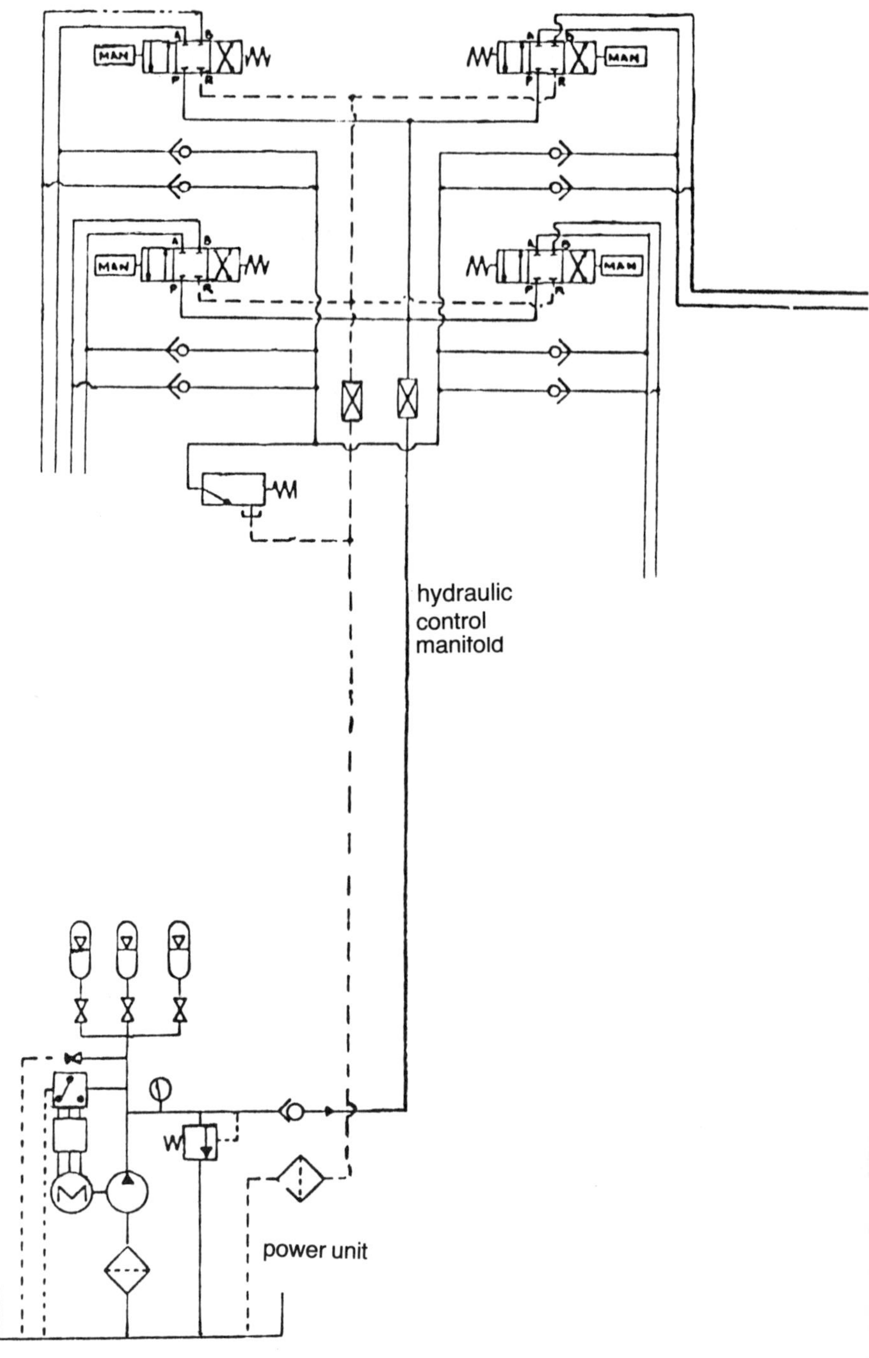
MAN
MAN
MAN
MAN
A
B
P
R
hydraulic
control
manifold
power unit

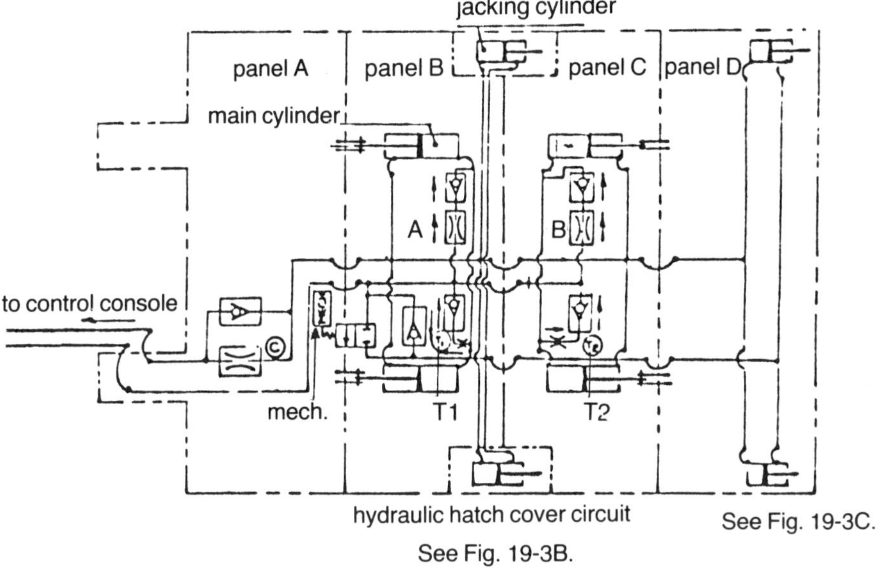

Fig. 19-3A. Linear actuator hydraulic hatch cover hydraulic circuit

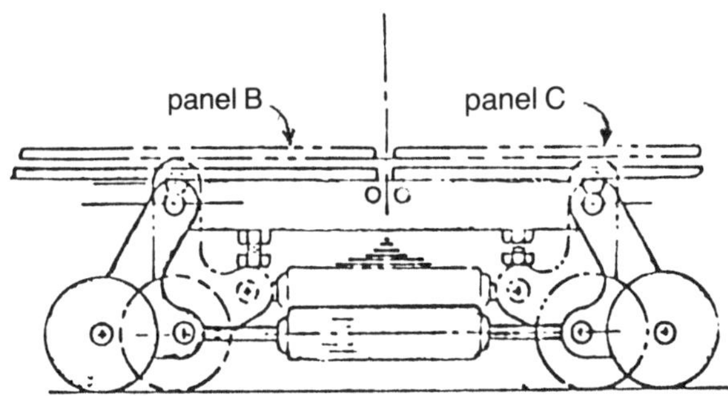

Fig. 19-3B. Truck jacking arrangement

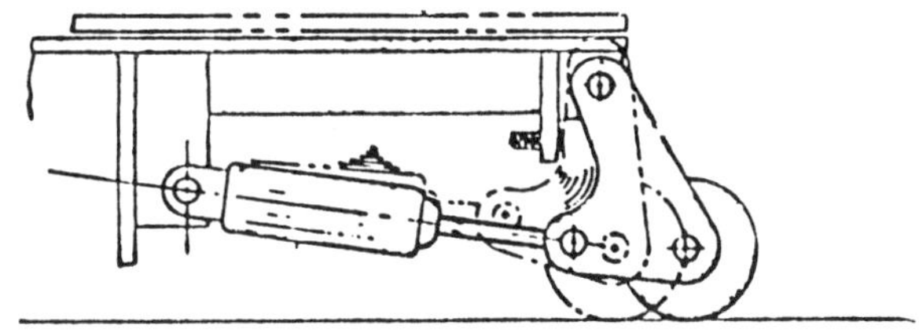

Fig. 19-3C. Outrigger jacking arrangement

the parallel pairs of cylinders to control the rate of opening. Also, note that flow control A is adjusted to enable panels A and B to be completely raised before panels C and D are. Once the panels have been raised, the operator releases the valve handle. Since the valves are spring-centered, releasing the handle closes the valve and cuts off additional flow to that hatch.

If no other hatch cover is to be opened, the pump discharge pressure continues to build until the pressure switch opens to shut down the pump at the 2,500 psi setpoint. If the pressure drops to less than 2,000 psi, the pressure switch would close and permit the pump to restart. In addition, the pump would continue to cycle on and off during the operation, as provided by the combined function of the pressure switch and the accumulators. This is done to prevent the pump from running continuously. Therefore, oil is stored under pressure in the accumulators to provide the oil flow necessary to open or close the hatches.

During the closing of the hatch covers, oil flow to the circuit is reversed by the directional control valve. At first, oil passes through the single flow control valve C before passing on to the rod end of each of the main cylinders. Oil leaving the cap end is prevented from passing across the flow control devices used to control the flow rate for opening. Instead, the oil has to pass across T1 and T2 since the path is blocked by both the two-position cam-actuated valve and the parallel check valve. Consequently, T1 and T2 act to meter-out the oil returning from the main cylinders. Furthermore, T2 is adjusted to allow panels C and D to lower before panels A and B.

As panels A and B become horizontal, the two-position valve is forced open mechanically. This action permits oil to be bled from the rod end of each jacking cylinder. As the jacking cylinders extend, the wheels swing away from their respective actuators, and lower the hatch cover onto their seats to complete the closing operation.

PART III

Troubleshooting

CHAPTER 20

TROUBLESHOOTING

Because of the numerous hydraulic systems, and the vast array of components utilized, several volumes could be written, covering detailed troubleshooting of these systems. As this is impractical for this handbook, all of the systems detailed in Part II, as well as in any other hydraulic system, are composed of similar basic components. Therefore, it is essential to understand the function and operation of the devices described in Part I. Although consistent and accurate troubleshooting depends primarily upon experience, the following concepts will be valuable to you, regardless of your current level of experience.

Those who are experienced at troubleshooting tend to react to conditions they have been exposed to in the past. But even these engineers and operators occasionally come up against a new problem. Whether the problem is new to the experienced, or new to the novice, the following steps in diagnosing a problem are important:

1. Know the system.
2. Operate the machinery.
3. Inspect the machinery.
4. List all possible causes for trouble.
5. Reach a conclusion.
6. Test the conclusion.

Knowing the System Is 90 Percent of Troubleshooting

From a logical point of view, you cannot determine what is wrong if you don't know what it is the system is supposed to do. When you understand what the system is supposed to do, and know the function of each component, then, and only then, can you begin to analyze why the system is not performing as it was designed to perform.

Operating the Equipment

When you know what operations the system is supposed to perform, go ahead and operate the equipment. Obviously, the system is not operating properly; otherwise, you would not be there trying to find out why it doesn't work. However, you must attempt to put the equipment through its paces, so that you can inspect it for the possible difficulties.

Inspecting the Machinery

As you operate the equipment, you listen for sounds that the machinery has made, as opposed to the sounds that it is currently making. Also, you look for telltale leaks and for the proper connection of the components, and observe what actions occur when operation is attempted.

Listing All of the Possible Causes

You may be fortunate and pick out the difficulty immediately. Unfortunately, system breakdown is not always that simple. Therefore, you need to make a list of the possible problems that you can associate with what you have observed. Compiling the list is probably the most difficult task you have. For, if only one or two conditions are considered to be responsible for the problems, making up a list impedes your progress. However, as you shall see, one set of conditions could all be responsible for the same ultimate malfunction. If you list the problems, that is, actually write them down, you will not mentally, or inadvertently, repeat checking out the difficulty. Nor will you compound the mistake by leaving out one possibility. Also, if there are, for instance, six possibilities, you may forget to check one out. *Write it down!*

Reaching a Conclusion

Once you've written down the problems, you can compare what actually exists with the possibilities you have listed. Then, you can begin to narrow down your list to the one or two probable faults.

Testing the Conclusion

Once you narrow down the possible difficulties, you can test your results. Even if you were wrong initially, at least you have eliminated that possibility and can go back and review your list. As you review your list, you may be stimulated to come up with another approach that you previously missed. But you are at least making progress. With these principles in mind, you can get down to business.

General Tips for Troubleshooting

The greatest problems occurring in any hydraulic system are associated with the pump. Most annoying is when someone simply did not provide electrical power to the prime mover, or when the sump level is inadequate. It is always a good idea, then, to check these two conditions first. Unless mechanical failures to the pump have been a recurring problem, leave the internal inspection of the pump until last. Another good habit to develop is to set up a maintenance and repair log for each system, so that you and the others who follow can check out the history of the system. When a problem develops, it is generally associated with fluid flow, and most likely traceable to the pump.

Usually, the pump becomes starved for oil. When it does, the noises that develop aid you in determining the problem. One common problem associated with a noisy pump is cavitation. Remember that cavitation is the compressing and subsequent collapsing of gas bubbles on the internal metal components of the pump as they are forced into the higher-pressure areas. The gas bubbles can result from air being drawn into the pump, or by the vaporizing of relatively high temperature oil as it passes through the suction line to the pump inlet, being subjected to a rapid decrease in pressure.

As mentioned before, a sump level that is too low allows air to be drawn into the pump suction. Although this tends to be a common occurrence, the condition is not always caused by an empty sump. Instead, the suction strainer may be partially exposed. At sea this happens as the apparent level in the sump shifts, because of the roll of the ship in "heavy" seas.

Other leading causes of cavitation are excessively high oil temperatures, a clogged suction strainer, dirty reservoir filler-breather cap, excessively high or low oil viscosity, or the pour point of the oil being too high for the existing operating conditions. The one thing all of these conditions have in common is that the oil does not flow in sufficient quantity to the pump, allowing the gas-laden oil to pass through the pump inlet.

In each instance, the lack of oil available to the pump suction results in an increase in fluid velocity as the pump continues to attempt to discharge its normal quantity. Keep in mind that suction velocity to the pump ranges from 2 to 4 feet per second, at less than 10 inches of mercury vacuum. As the oil velocity increases, the existing vapor pressure of the oil drops. If the temperature of the oil, corresponding to the normal vapor pressure, is higher than the existing temperature-pressure conditions, a small mount of oil flashes and becomes entrained with the oil entering the pump. As the vapor bubbles are compressed, they rupture, leaving pits or cavities on the internal pump surfaces.

Turbulent flow develops in the areas where there is pitting. Even if the cause of cavitation is corrected, once pitting has developed, the resulting turbulence continues to hamper the flow across the pump. As energy is already imparted to the pump, the turbulence also causes the energy transformation to the pump to develop as heat, rather than as useful potential energy. If severe enough, cavitation causes diminished oil flow to the system, with higher pump operating temperatures, wasted power, and additional cavitation within the pump.

Another group of causes that can lead to cavitation results from improper reassembly after replacement repairs have been carried out. Primarily, this group includes increasing pump speed or reversing its direction of rotation, excessive extension of the horizontal run of suction piping, or the increase in the required pump suction lift. Again, the velocity increase and accompanying pressure decrease lead to either fluid vaporization or pump starvation.

Since there are numerous conditions that can result in pump cavitation, you might wonder, "Where do I begin?" Good housekeeping (preventive maintenance) of hydraulic systems is essential and is always a good place to begin. The development of the maintenance and repair log, and keeping it up-to-date will help in providing you with valuable information. Infrequent entries indicate carelessness, just as detailed entries give you the specific history of the system. Hence, look for the obvious. First, determine the sump level, then check out the reservoir filler-breather cap. Once this has been done, drain a sample of the oil. If it is discolored and/or contains sludge and other contaminants, the entire sump should be drained, swabbed out, and refilled with clean oil. Once the sump has been drained, the inspection ports can be opened, and a closer inspection of the pump suction line, suction strainer, baffles, and returns can be carried out. In some cases, the pump is submerged in the sump. Therefore, it is a good idea to unbolt the pump, inspect the coupling device and casing for signs of cracks, and to check the motor speed and its direction of rotation without load. If all is found to be satisfactory, reassemble, and check the motor speed with a load. Do not forget to log all of the data for the tests that have been carried out.

Although cavitation can lead to internal damage of the pump, metal fatigue and wear to the moving internal parts from unnecessarily extended operation or poor lubrication are also likely to occur. Even more likely to cause pump damage is the misalignment of the pump to its prime mover, in addition to fluid contamination.

Misalignment generally results from careless pump installation with the prime mover. Eventually, damage to the coupling, and/or excessive side thrust to the bearings develops. In either case, the pump does not rotate at its required speed. As the energy of the prime mover cannot be properly transferred to the oil, the flow rate is diminished, and causes the system's load to stall in addition to its overheating.

Since materials used in the pumps are generally of sufficient production quality to withstand metal fatigue (premature breakage), fluid contamination through poor housekeeping is more apt to be the cause of damage to the pump. In the chapters covering fluids, filters, and oil storage, various aspects of contamination were discussed, and emphasis on the use of clean oil must be stressed. Improper conditioning of the oil can be the most destructive condition to the overall operation of the system, as well as to the pump.

Thus, the most detrimental condition leading to fluid contamination is the intrusion of moisture that mixes with the oil. If the moisture is allowed to collect and remain, emulsions and acids form.

As the oil begins to deteriorate, sludges, gums, varnishes, and additional acids are developed. System components now move with greater difficulty. Furthermore, lubrication becomes less adequate, with wear and oxidation attack of metal surfaces increasing. Continued oil breakdown occurs despite the capabilities and use of the filters and strainers that are provided to avoid these situations. In other words, the system falls apart.

Fortunately, piping and tubing, unlike other components in the system, do not develop numerous problems, other than leaking. When leaks occur, it is necessary to first determine why. Usually, replacing flange O-rings or gaskets, or tightening of the tubing connections are all that is necessary. When gaskets or O-rings are replaced, it is a matter of common sense for fluid flow and pressure to be reduced on the system, and the lines drained.

When tubing connections are to be tightened, it is very tempting to take up on them while under pressure—*don't*. First, it is impossible to tighten them properly, as the effects of the pressure in the system prevent this. Second, excessive stress, applied from one side of a coupling, may be all that is necessary to cause the coupling halves to fail completely, and separate.

Hoses, on the other hand, present another group of problems. If leaking, the best remedy is to replace the entire hose. When it is replaced, care must be used to prevent improper installation. Therefore, twists, kinking, too short, or even excessive lengths must be avoided and corrected. One problem that results as a matter of age, or improper assembly of the hose, is the separation of the inner layer. In this situation, oil, under pressure, passes between the inner and outer layers, allowing the hose to bulge or rupture. If the hose provides a flexible return path to the pump, the resulting internal restriction causes an increase in vacuum. The increase in vacuum is sufficient to collapse the inner layer and starve the pump of its oil supply.

When properly selected for service, linear actuators (cylinders) generally sustain failures only as a result of the seals' inability to maintain their integrity. Rod seals, more so than piston seals, tend to lose their integrity first, as a result of environmental exposure accompanied by external leakage. Also, seal materials tend to lose their elasticity and resilience over a period of time because of the constant application and relaxation of pressure, along with exposure to heat. Additionally, solid contaminants entrained in the oil can score the cylinder walls and rod. As chafing proceeds, the internal piston seals leak, and enough oil bypasses the pistons and stalls the load. If scored, these parts must be replaced; otherwise, the new seals are damaged and needlessly wasted.

Rotary actuators (hydraulic motors) usually sustain damage as a result of solid contaminants passing through the device. This leads to direct internal component failure, or simply results in poor lubrication, with eventual failure caused by seizing. As there are a variety of rotary actuators in use, there are many individual problems associated with each. The following discussion is directed primarily to the vane and axial piston motors.

Vane motors, for example, fail to operate as a result of the vanes being unable to extend. This develops as residue, faulty springs, or excessive wear to the vane's contact edge cause them to stick in their slots. The first two conditions only prevent rotation, while the last condition not only prevents proper rotation, but contributes to permanent damage of the casing.

Axial piston motors, on the other hand, are more susceptible to piston/cylinder wear due to contaminated oil. Tolerances are critical in these units in order for the oil to provide sealing. The slightest amount of impurity, regardless of size, causes scoring of the cylinder wall so that performance of the motor quickly drops off.

Remember, the casing of the motor is continuously drained to the sump to assist in lubrication. A low-pressure control valve may be installed to assist in maintaining continuous flow to prevent the oil temperature from rising. But, it may also be provided to make certain that enough oil remains in the casing to maintain lubrication. However, insufficient lubrication results if the valve fails to open; high oil temperatures occur if the valve fails to close. Ultimately, insufficient lubrication develops as the oil becomes "carbonized."

Regardless of the motor type, unusual side thrust to the shaft damages the bearings and the seals. Misalignment between the motor shaft coupling and the driven loaded shaft commonly results in this type of double damage. Usually, if oil leakage is found around the shaft, accompanied by laboring of the motor when loaded, extensive repair can be expected. Since the shaft seals leak because of wear, you should compare motor performance and noises, and inspect the bearings when complete overhaul is contemplated.

One problem, common to both the linear and rotary actuators, occurs when quantities of air become trapped within the confines of the hydraulic system. While air is a problem with regard to the operation of any system component, air greatly inhibits the movement of the actuators. Usually, the air in the system is characterized by jerky or erratic movement. This action is a result of the pressure exerted on the air, collected at the actuator, and compressed to the existing system pressure. As the actuator moves, the pressure of the air drops rapidly as it is allowed to expand. The actuator temporarily ceases its movement until the pressure of the air sufficiently builds to produce motion of the actuator. Therefore, the constant repetition of this condition produces the hesitating movement.

Fortunately, system failures are not always related to mechanical difficulties of the major components. Even though the system is totally inoperable, the problem may be related to the pressure, directional, and/or flow control devices.

Pressure control devices, regardless of function, are afflicted by similar problems:

1. weakened or broken valve springs
2. cuts developed on the face of the valve seat or disk
3. orifice, or balance hole, in the piston becoming blocked
4. improper spring compression, or pressure setting of the device
5. dirt accumulation on the valve seat, that keeps the valve open
6. valve sticking, or jammed, in the valve body

Relief valves with weakened springs, too low a pressure setting, or blockage in the orifice of the balanced piston valve, allow the valve to open prematurely. Despite the pump's developing its normal flow rate, and with the valve wide open, oil bypasses directly to the sump, without moving the load. With pressure from the load maintained on the system, it is insufficient to merely check out the pump discharge pressure. Instead, the sound of oil passing across the relief valve is more important (usually characterized by a high-pitch whine).

Where solid contaminants have scored the valve seat, or other related conditions exist, only the flow rate is affected as the valve bypasses small quantities of oil to the sump. Again, the load, controlled by the system, may maintain what appears to be normal pressure; however, the load moves very slowly, as less oil is able to flow to the actuator.

Following along the same line of improper operation for relief valves, a sequence valve allows the second sequence of operation to occur prematurely if the valve spring is weakened, the valve seat or disk is scored, or the setpoint is adjusted too low. On the other hand, if the sequential event fails to occur, the valve spring compression is either excessive, or the valve is jammed in its seat.

Should the counterbalance valve experience the same type of problem as the previously described pressure control valves—opening prematurely, or failing to close—the vertical load can drop. The speed of the falling load is an indication of the existing malfunction. For instance, if the internal piston seals leak, the load slowly creeps down. Therefore, it is necessary to listen to the counterbalance valve. If the sound of oil passing across the counterbalance is evident, the problem is the valve. If the sound of flowing oil is not evident, the problem is likely to be that of the piston seals. If the pressure setting is excessive, the load is unable to be lowered.

With regard to the unloading valve, any of the previous problems that allowed the valves to open prematurely prevents the double pump unit from developing proper working pressure. Otherwise, partial leakage across the valve, as was the case of the relief valve, diverts some of the flow to the sump, so that working pressure is not properly reestablished.

Reducing valves, however, react in the opposite fashion to their counterparts. The greater the flow rate across the valve, the higher the resultant downstream pressure. This results because a higher quantity of oil now exists between the reducing valve and the load. Therefore, the valve must close off to limit flow rate to the downstream side, hence the reduction in required pressure. If the spring is weakened, or the spring compression is insufficient, the valve closes, blocking the oil flow to the downstream side, with the pressure in this section of the system too low or nonexistent. If the spring compression is excessive, or the valve is jammed in the open position, higher than required flow across the valve exists, with downstream pressure being excessive.

Flow control valves, despite their simplicity, easily hinder the operation of any system. These controls generally incorporate an adjustable needle valve, or other type of spring-loaded device that is used in parallel or in series with a check valve to enhance operation. Primarily, the difficulties involving these devices either limit the speed, or allow the operation to occur too quickly. Before you speculate on the problem associated with the flow control, you must first determine what type of flow control circuit is employed. After that determination, you will have a more reasonable idea as to whether the flow rate is insufficient, excessive, or due to the pump.

As long as the oil in the system is kept reasonably clean, contaminants cannot block the oil flow across the flow control device. Regardless of metered-in, or metered-out type circuits, ultimately the increase in restriction causes the reduced flow rate to slow the actuator speed to a "crawl." Consider that minor vibrations within the system can cause the threaded valve stem to "creep" and the valve to open. Hence, higher than required flow rates occur, and the actuator moves faster. Where actuators are operated in parallel, excessive flow control valve openings give a false impression. For instance, if one of the two flow control valves installed in parallel is opened wider than the other, particularly where sequential movement is important, it may be assumed that the slower actuator flow control is too restrictive. However, the flow control that permits faster actuation is opened too wide, and the oil in the parallel circuit is thus flowing first to the point of least resistance. Therefore, further restriction of that valve will help to bring the system closer to the operating specifications.

Directional control valves experience the greatest difficulty with respect to their means of actuation, or positioning devices (i.e., detent and centering springs). While scuffing of the spool O-ring seals results in greater than desired internal/external leakage, this condition rarely results in complete operational failure.

Manual control levers are the least likely to cause a problem, except for those instances in which they become physically detached from the spool or rotary cartridge. As the operator is in direct contact with this control, this problem is picked up rather easily.

Solenoid actuation presents other difficulties, in that the problem may be the solenoid coil itself, or its switching device (limit switch). Fortunately, regardless of the actual problem, solenoids can be manually overridden by inserting a narrow diameter rod through the end cap in order to force the spool into its required operating position. Should a solenoid fail to shift by its designed remote means, a simple continuity test on the coil, with a multimeter, indicates whether or not the coil is itself at fault. Using the multimeter to determine current flow, with the control or limit switch closed, the answer to any problem existing between the source and the coil is obtained.

Hydraulic pilots, by themselves, result in few problems. However, some of these devices incorporate a needle valve to control bleed-off of hydrostatic pressure when deenergized. Consequently, the same problems that occurred with the flow controls may be repeated here. For instance, if the needle valve is opened too wide, insufficient back pressure is developed to force the valve into position. On the other hand, if the needle valve is closed too far, or foreign contaminants block off the flow across it, the hydrostatic pressure does not bleed off, thereby keeping the valve spool in its shifted position.

All directional control valves utilizing springs to return the valve spool may fail if the spring becomes weakened or broken. As this usually allows the valve to remain in its last position, reversal of the system does not occur. In situations where an open-centered valve is employed, spring failure may be indicated by the lifting of the relief valve after the actuator has stopped. You should also keep in mind that broken springs may prevent the valve spool from shifting completely. Therefore, the relief valve lifts, accompanied by the failure of the actuator to move.

While detent devices as a rule do not fail, realize that physical damage to the detent mechanism may occur. If the detent fails, you should notice the imprecise movement of the valve. Although it is rare, the detent device may keep the valve from shifting if the broken pieces find their way in between the spool and the body.

Servo controls, as was the case with directional, pressure, or flow control devices, are affected most by contaminated oil, faulty operation of the springs, or damaged seals of the servo piston. The basic ideas previously discussed apply here, as well, but it should be obvious that the problems can be very complex. Since servo controls aboard ship are primarily used with variable displacement pumps and motors, they must be suspected as a cause of the initial source of trouble.

For instance, if system pressure remains high, as the load increases, the fault may lie with the spring-loaded secondary valve not shifting to block flow to the primary valve, nor allowing oil to bleed off the servo piston. The reasons for this condition stem from excessive spring compression, jammed valve spool, or some leakage that prevents adequate build-up of hydrostatic pressure to the pilot of the secondary valve spool. On the other hand, if the flow rate or the working pressure of the system is low, the adjusting spring may be weak or broken, or the setpoint too low. These conditions allow the secondary valve spool to shift prematurely and cut off flow to the primary valve. Thus the required increase in the angle of the tilting box would remain very shallow; and the oil flow to the system would be held to a minimum.

In nearly everything we do, we prefer that they are "easy" or that an "easy method" is available. Unfortunately, you will find that, initially, hydraulic systems and their components present many stumbling blocks to your efforts to understand them. If you persist in your study of hydraulics, then consistently apply what you have learned, it will become "easy."

If you still feel a need to follow an easy-to-remember rule, simply remember the term "flow." The ability of the system to establish flow, at the required flow rate, is the key to a successful system operation. Despite the fact that the ability to maintain proper pressure within the system is important, without the existence of proper flow, the operation of the system, and required pressure conditions, will be impossible.

Appendices

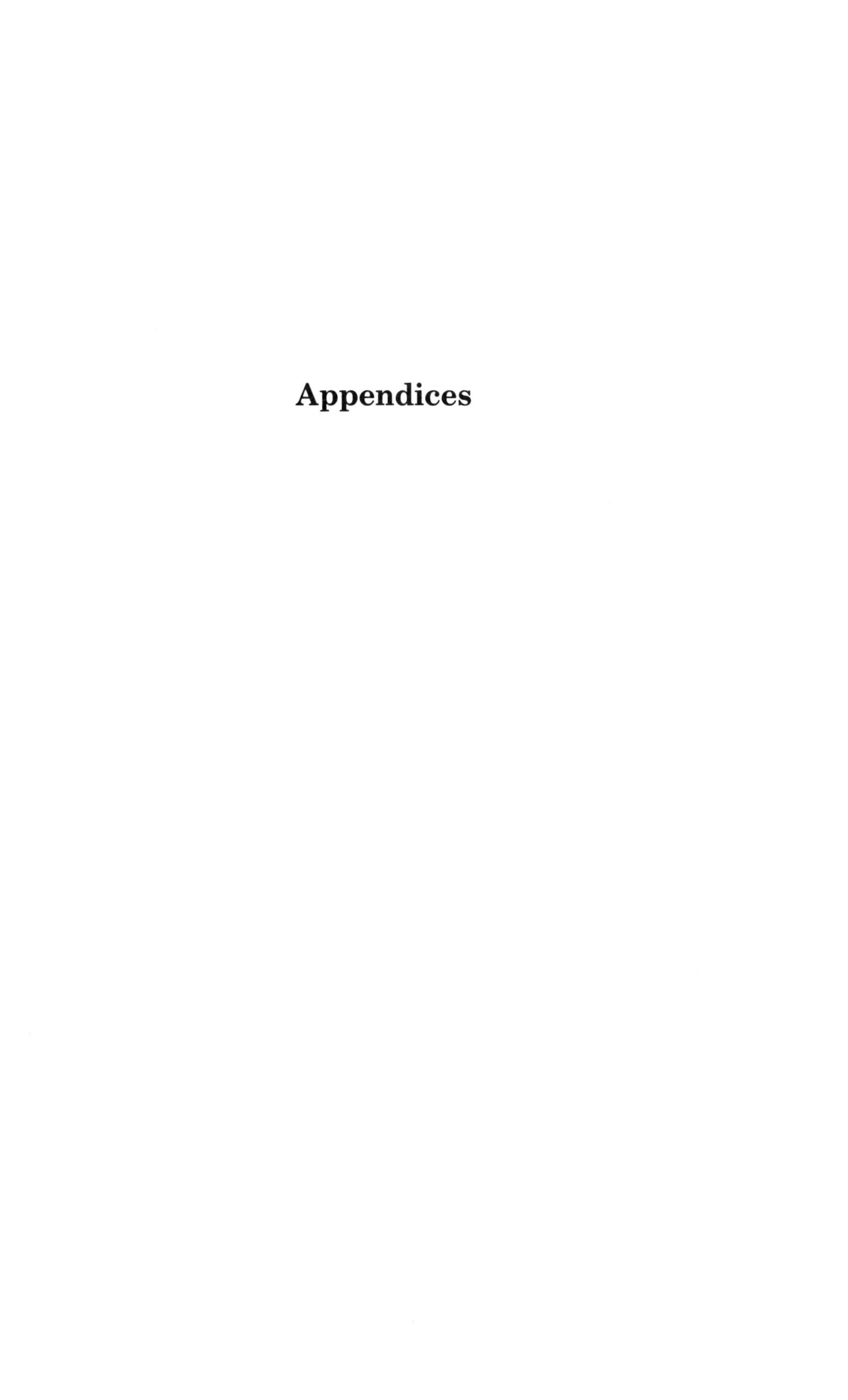

A. Graphic Symbols for Hydraulic Schematics

As it is with most engineering disciplines, schematic diagrams are used to represent the general arrangement of the components, and to show the flow from the components within the overall system. Also, the schematic representation for each discipline has its own "jargon." So it is with hydraulics as well. The following examples represent the basic symbology commonly used by manufacturers, according to the American National Standards Institute (ANSI), in order to compose schematics of their systems.

Since each manufacturer will design and use components peculiar to their systems, they in turn will develop their own symbols to represent those components. Consequently, while all of the symbols ever used in hydraulic schematics would be impracticable to list, the following list does include the more commonly used symbols. Therefore, by grasping the reason as well as the form of the symbol, understanding of the schematics in this text will aid in the understanding of any hydraulic schematic that will have to be "translated."

As the following list is studied, and compared with the schematics in Part II, note that the symbols are either simple geometric shapes, or a combination of shapes. Also, rules of usage of the shapes are simple, and are relatively few.

I. *Straight lines—all* lines, regardless of form, should be straight and meet at right angles.

A. *Solid lines*—main lines, constantly charged high side or return side pressure. ————————

B. *Mechanical enclosure or linkages* ——— - - ——— - -

C. *Pilot lines*—those lines that indicate the use of hydraulic oil to actuate a component within the system.

D. *Drain lines*—those lines used to drain off oil or return it to storage, generally at pressures less than 30 psi.

II. *Circles*—always used to denote rotation.

A. *Pumps*—arrowheads, pointed towards the periphery of the circle, will indicate the direction of flow, and whether or not the flow from the pump is reversible.

1. *Constant flow pump*—single direction of rotation, constant output and pressure.

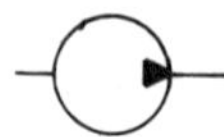

2. *Variable flow pump*—flow rate can be varied in one direction only.

3. *Bidirectional flow pump*—constant flow will occur in either direction.

4. *Variable delivery pump*—flow rate and the direction of flow from the pump can be varied, due to the construction of the pump.

B. *Hydraulic motors—all* circles with arrowheads pointing towards the center.

1. *Unidirectional motor*—one direction of rotation, speed controlled by pump flow rate or control valve.

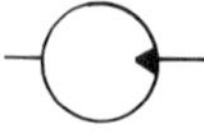

2. *Bidirectional motor*—rotation can occur in either direction and is controlled by the direction of flow from the pump or the directional control valve.

3. *Pressure-compensated motor*—a bidirectional motor whose speed will be varied in one direction by the use of a pressure compensating device automatically as loads increase.

4. *Torque motor*—torque-producing motor that rotates less than 360 degrees.

C. *Electric motors*—a circle with an "M" to differentiate this device from that of a hydraulic motor.

M

III. *Squares*—each square represents a valve envelope or valve position.

A. *Number of squares*

1. *Single square*—generally represents a pressure control device, of a simple form, that is basically opened or closed.

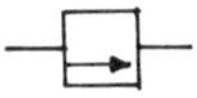

2. *Two squares*—indicate valves that will be manipulated into one of two positions.

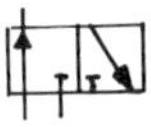

3. *Three squares*—valves that have three distinct operating positions.

B. *Number of paths and direction of flow*—the number of ways the oil will flow across the valve, and the relative direction it will flow across the valve.

C. *Control of the valve position*

1. *Electric solenoid*

2. *Manual control*

3. *Mechanical actuation*

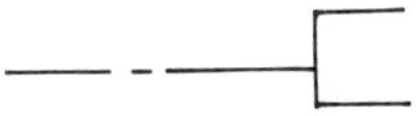

4. *Cam actuation*

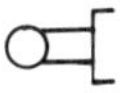

5. *Spring return or centered*

6. *Hydraulic pilot actuation*

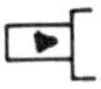

7. *Detented valve*

D. *Check valve*

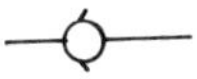

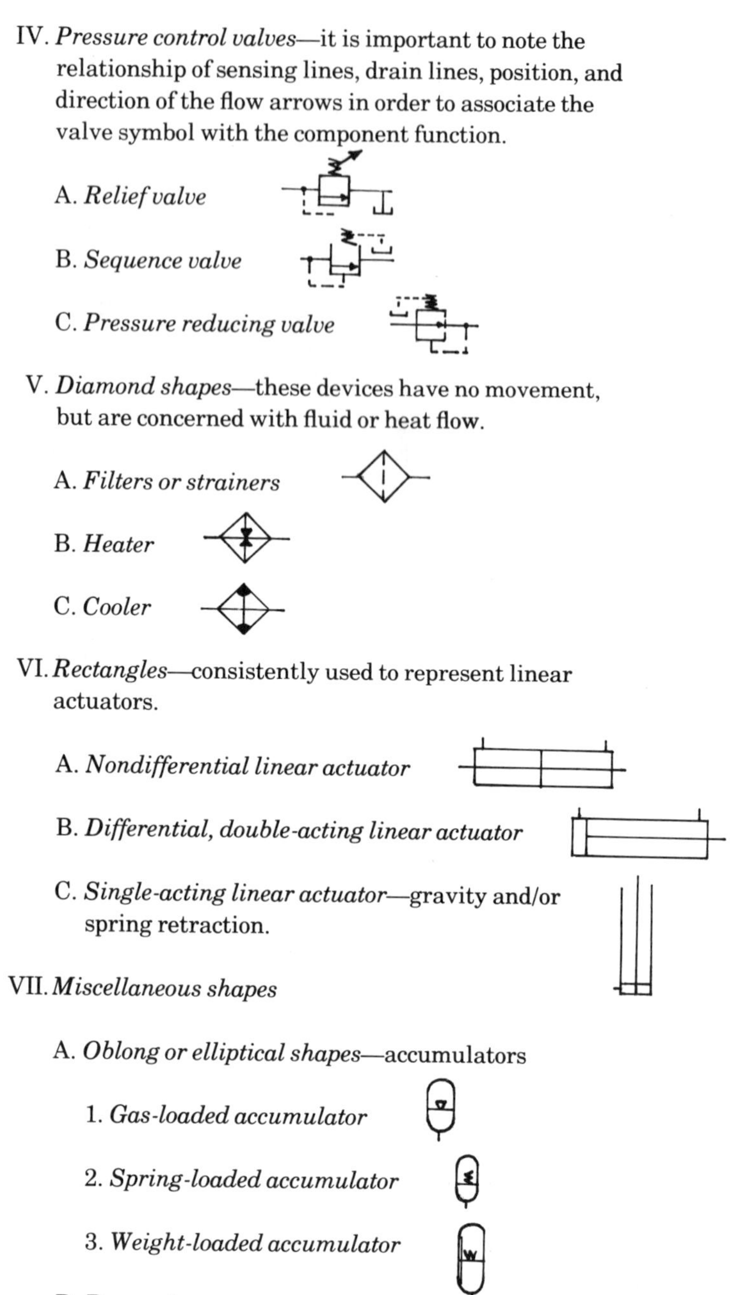

IV. *Pressure control valves*—it is important to note the relationship of sensing lines, drain lines, position, and direction of the flow arrows in order to associate the valve symbol with the component function.

A. *Relief valve*

B. *Sequence valve*

C. *Pressure reducing valve*

V. *Diamond shapes*—these devices have no movement, but are concerned with fluid or heat flow.

A. *Filters or strainers*

B. *Heater*

C. *Cooler*

VI. *Rectangles*—consistently used to represent linear actuators.

A. *Nondifferential linear actuator*

B. *Differential, double-acting linear actuator*

C. *Single-acting linear actuator*—gravity and/or spring retraction.

VII. *Miscellaneous shapes*

A. *Oblong or elliptical shapes*—accumulators

1. *Gas-loaded accumulator*

2. *Spring-loaded accumulator*

3. *Weight-loaded accumulator*

B. *Reservoirs*

1. *Open or vented reservoir*

2. *Closed or pressurized reservoir*

C. *Measuring instruments*

1. *Pressure gauges*

2. *Thermometers*

3. *Flow meter*

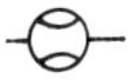

D. *Simple flow control devices*

1. *Fixed orifice*

2. *Variable orifice*

B. Fluid Power Formulas

FORMULA FOR:	WORD FORMULA:	LETTER FORMULA:
FLUID PRESSURE *In Pounds/Square Inch*	PRESSURE $= \frac{\text{FORCE } (pounds)}{\text{UNIT AREA } (Square\ Inches)}$	$P = \frac{F}{A}$ or $psi = \frac{F}{A}$
CYLINDER AREA *In Square Inches*	AREA $= \pi \times \text{RADIUS}^2\ (Inches)$	$A = \pi r^2$
	$= \frac{\pi}{4} \times \text{Diameter}^2\ (Inches)$	$A = \frac{\pi D^2}{4}$ or $A = .785D^2$
CYLINDER FORCE *In Pounds, Push or Pull*	FORCE = PRESSURE (psi) x NET AREA *(Square Inches)*	F = psi x A or F = PA
CYLINDER VELOCITY or SPEED *In Feet/Second*	VELOCITY $= \frac{231 \times \text{FLOW RATE } (GPM)}{12 \times 60 \times \text{NET AREA } (Square\ Inches)}$	$v = \frac{231Q}{720A}$ or $v = \frac{.3208Q}{A}$
CYLINDER VOLUME CAPACITY *In Gallons of Fluid*	VOLUME $= \frac{\pi \times \text{RADIUS}^2\ (Inches) \times \text{STROKE } (Inches)}{231}$	$V = \frac{\pi r^2 l}{231}$
	$= \frac{\text{NET AREA } (Square\ Inches) \times \text{STROKE } (Inches)}{231}$	$V = \frac{A\,l}{231}$ l = *Length of Stroke*
CYLINDER FLOW RATE *In Gallons Per Minute*	FLOW RATE $= \frac{12 \times 60 \times \text{VELOCITY } (Feet/Sec) \times \text{NET AREA } (Square\ Inches)}{231}$	$Q = \frac{720vA}{231}$ or $Q = 3.117vA$
FLUID MOTOR TORQUE *In Inch Pounds*	TORQUE $= \frac{\text{PRESSURE } (psi) \times \text{F.M. DISPLACEMENT } (Cu.\ In./Rev.)}{2\pi}$	$T = \frac{psi\ d}{2\pi}$ or $T = \frac{Pd}{2\pi}$
	$= \frac{\text{HORSEPOWER} \times 63025}{\text{RPM}}$	$T = \frac{63025\ HP}{n}$
	$= \frac{\text{FLOW RATE } (GPM) \times \text{PRESSURE } (psi) \times 36.77}{\text{RPM}}$	$T = \frac{36.77QP}{n}$ or $T = \frac{36.77Q psi}{n}$
FLUID MOTOR TORQUE/100 psi *In Inch Pounds*	TORQUE/100 psi $= \frac{\text{F.M. DISPLACEMENT } (Cu.\ Inches/Revolution)}{.0628}$	$T_{100psi} = \frac{d}{.0628}$
FLUID MOTOR SPEED *In Revolutions/Minute*	SPEED $= \frac{231 \times \text{FLOW RATE } (GPM)}{\text{F.M. DISPLACEMENT } (Cu.\ Inches/Revolution)}$	$n = \frac{231Q}{d}$
FLUID MOTOR POWER *In Horsepower Output*	HORSEPOWER $= \frac{\text{TORQUE OUTPUT } (Inch\ Pounds) \times \text{RPM}}{63025}$	$HP = \frac{Tn}{63025}$
PUMP OUTLET FLOW *In Gallons/Minute*	FLOW $= \frac{\text{RPM} \times \text{PUMP DISPLACEMENT } (Cu.\ In./Rev.)}{231}$	$Q = \frac{nd}{231}$
PUMP INPUT POWER *In Horsepower Required*	HORSEPOWER INPUT $= \frac{\text{FLOW RATE OUTPUT } (GPM) \times \text{PRESSURE } (psi)}{1714 \times \text{EFFICIENCY } (Overall)}$	$HP_{IN} = \frac{QP}{1714Eff}$ or $\frac{GPM \times psi}{1714Eff}$
FLOW RATE THROUGH PIPING *In Feet/Second Velocity*	VELOCITY $= \frac{.3208 \times \text{FLOW RATE THROUGH I.D. } (GPM)}{\text{INTERNAL AREA } (Square\ Inches)}$	$v = \frac{.3208Q}{A}$
COMPRESSIBILITY OF OIL *In Additional Required Oil To Reach Pressure*	ADDITIONAL VOLUME $= \frac{\text{PRESSURE } (psi) \times \text{VOLUME OF OIL UNDER PRESSURE}}{250{,}000}$	$V_A = \frac{PV}{250{,}000}$ [Approximately ½% Per 1000 psi]

GAS LAWS FOR ACCUMULATOR SIZING

Where "P" = psia *(ABSOLUTE)* = psig *(GAUGE PRESSURE)* + 14.7 psi

FORMULA FOR:	WORD FORMULA:	LETTER FORMULA:
PRESSURE OR VOLUME *w/Constant "T" (Temperature)*	ORIGINAL PRESSURE x ORIGINAL VOLUME = FINAL PRESSURE x FINAL VOLUME	$P_1 V_1 = P_2 V_2$ [Isothermic]
PRESSURE OR TEMPERATURE *w/Constant "V" (Volume)*	ORIGINAL PRESSURE x FINAL TEMPERATURE = FINAL PRESSURE x ORIG. TEMP.	$P_1 T_2 = P_2 T_1$ [Isochoric]
VOLUME OR TEMPERATURE *w/Constant "P" (Pressure)*	ORIGINAL VOLUME x FINAL TEMPERATURE = FINAL VOLUME x ORIGINAL TEMP.	$V_1 T_2 = V_2 T_1$ [Isobaric]
PRESSURE OR VOLUME *w/Temperature Change Due To Heat of Compression*	$\text{ORIGINAL PRESSURE} \times \text{ORIGINAL VOLUME}^n = \text{FINAL PRESSURE} \times \text{FINAL VOLUME}^n$	$P_1 V_1^n = P_2 V_2^n$
	$\frac{\text{FINAL TEMP.}}{\text{ORIG. TEMP.}} = \left(\frac{\text{ORIG. VOLUME}}{\text{FINAL VOLUME}}\right)^{n-1} = \left(\frac{\text{FINAL PRESSURE}}{\text{ORIG. PRESSURE}}\right)^{n-1/n}$	$\frac{T_2}{T_1} = \left(\frac{V_1}{V_2}\right)^{n-1} = \left(\frac{P_2}{P_1}\right)^{n-1/n}$

FOR NITROGEN THE EXPONENT "n" = 1.4 For full adiabatic conditions i.e., the "Full Heating" theoretical condition
"n" = 1.3 For rapid cycling (most heating normally experienced)
"n" = 1.1 For "Normal" cycling
"n" = 1.0 Where gas time to return to normal temp. before discharge or recharge

C. Basic Seal Materials

BASIC SEAL MATERIALS (ELASTOMERS)

The following is a brief list of the various elastomers used in seals. The trade names shown are representative and typical, but not a complete listing.

BUNA N (NITRILE) (NBR)

Trade Names:

Chemigum	Goodyear Tire & Rubber Co.
Butaprene	Firestone Tire & Rubber Co.
Paracril	Naugatuck Chemical
Hycar	Goodrich Chemical Co.

Copolymer of butadiene & acrylonitrile. Excellent w/petroleum products. −65 to +250°F. For low temperatures it is necessary to sacrifice some high temperature resistance. Superior in compression set, cold flow, tear and abrasion resistance. Inferior in resistance to ozone, sunlight or weather.

Generally recommended for:	Not recommended for:
General purpose	Halogenated hydrocarbons
Petroleum	Phosphate ester
Water	Ketones
Diester	Acids
Water-Glycol	Brake fluid

FLUOROCARBON (FPM) (VITON)

Trade Names:

Fluorel and Kel-F	Minnesota Mining & Mfg. Co.
Viton	E.I. duPont

A linear copolymer of vinylidene fluoride and hexafluoro propylene (approximately 65% fluorine). Excellent for high vacuum. Compatible and recommended with most fluids and gases. −20 to +350°F (to 600°F for short periods).

Generally recommended for:	Not recommended for:
Petroleum	Ketones
Silicate ester	Skydrol 500, 7000
Diester	
Halogenated hydrocarbons	
Most phosphate esters	

ISOPRENE RUBBER-SYNTHETIC (IR) (POLYISOPRENE)

Trade Names:

Ameripol SN	Goodrich-Gulf Chemicals, Inc.
Coral	Firestone Tire and Rubber Co.
Natsyn	Goodyear Tire and Rubber Co.
Shell IR	Shell Chemical Co.

The same chemical composition as natural rubber. (For properties, refer to Natural Rubber).

BUNA S (SBR) (GRS)

Trade Names:

Plioflex	Goodyear Tire & Rubber Co.
Ameripol	B.F. Goodrich Chemical Co.
ASRC	American Synthetic
Copo	Copolymer Rubber & Chemical Corp.
FR-S	Firestone Tire & Rubber Co.
Gentro	General Tire

BUNA S (SBR) (GRS) Continued

Originally a substitute for natural rubber. Composition, styrene and butadiene rubber. Little used for hydraulic seals (except brake systems). −65 to +200°F.

Generally recommended for:	Not recommended for:
Automotive brake fluid	Ozone
Some alcohols	Petroleum
Water	
Ketones	

BUTYL RUBBER (IIR)

Trade Names:

Enjay Butyl	Enjay Chemical Company
Hycar (2202)	B.F. Goodrich Chemical Co.

Copolymer of isobutylene and isoprene. −65 to +225°F. Used for inner tubes. Excellent resistance to gas permeation. Particularly useful for high vacuum.

Generally recommended for:	Not recommended for:
Phosphate ester	Petroleum
Ketones	Diester

SILICONE RUBBER (SI)

Trade Names:

Silastic	Dow Corning Corporation
(No trade name)	General Electric
(No trade name)	Union Carbide & Carbon

Made from silicone, oxygen, hydrogen and carbon. Resistance to temperature extremes. −135 to +500° for short periods. Recommended temperature, 400°F. Retention of properties at high temperatures is superior to other elastic materials. Fluorosilicone combines the good temperature properties of silicone with basic fuel and oil resistance. Not recommended for dynamic sealing because of poor tear and tensile strength. Higher than normal mold shrinkage.

Generally recommended for:	Not recommended for:
High-aniline point oils	Most petroleum
Chlorinated di-phenyls	Ketones
Some water glycols	Some phosphate esters

TETRAFLUOROETHYLENE (TEF) (not an elastomer)

Trade Names:

Teflon	E.I. duPont Co.

Rigid tetrafluoroethylene resin. Extremely low friction. Compatible and recommended with most fluids and gases. Will cold flow under high loads. −320 to +500°F.

CHLOROPRENE RUBBER (CR) (NEOPRENE)

Trade Names:

Neoprene	E.I. duPont Company

Homopolymers of chloroprene (chlorobutadiene). −65 to +250° F. Should be spring loaded for low temperatures.

Generally recommended for:	Not recommended for:
Refrigerants (Freons)	Phosphate ester fluids
High aniline point petroleum	Ketones
Silicate ester	

ETHYLENE PROPYLENE RUBBER (EPM) (EP) (EPR)

Trade Names:

Nordel	E.I. duPont Co.
Enjay EPR	Enjay Chemical Co.
Olethene	Avisum Corp.

An elastomer of ethylene and propylene monomers (Ethylene Propylene Copolymers). Excellent w/Skydrol 500 and phosphate esters. −65 to +300°F.

Generally recommended for:	Not recommended for:
Phosphate ester	Petroleum
Steam (to 400°F)	Diester
Water	
Ketones	

CORFAM

Trade Name:

Corfam	E.I. duPont Co.

Totally new material made of corfam poromeric substrate impregnated with adiprene polyurethane rubber. High abrasion, oil, fuel resistance. Also available with silicone or teflon coating. Finished seals are waterproof. −65 to +212°F.

Generally recommended for:	Not recommended for:
General purpose	High test gasoline
Petroleum	Hot detergent water
Hot water	Phosphate
Water/glycols	
Water/oil emulsion	
Water/soluble oil	

NATURAL RUBBER – NATURAL POLYSOPRENE (NR)

Principal source: the tree Hevea Brasiliensis. Petroleum oils are the greatest enemy of natural rubber compounds.

Generally recommended for:	Not recommended for:
Brake fluid	Petroleum
Water	Water/oil
	Phosphate esters
	Silicate esters

POLYURETHANE

Trade Names:

Disogrin	Pellon Corp.
Adiprene	E.I. duPont Co.

Diisocyanate with polyesters or polyethers. Superior mechanical and physical properties. Good resistance to petroleum products. Difficult to mold or cast. Some have poor compression and permanent set properties. Tend to soften excessively at temperatures above 250°F and in hot water.

Generally recommended for:	Not recommended for:
Petroleum	Hot water
Water/oil (moderate temp.)	Acids
Phosphate ester	Ketones
	Chlorinated hydrocarbons

The above charts are for general information and are presented without prejudice. They should not be taken as a warranty or representation for which legal responsibility is assumed. They are offered only for your convenience, consideration, investigation, and verification.

D. Fluid Motor Torque

• FIGURES SHOWN ARE INCH POUNDS EXCEPT AS NOTED

RPM	HORSE POWER												
	1	2	3	4	5	6	7	8	9	10	15	20	25
1	63,025	126,050	189,076	252,100	315,125	378,150	441,175	504,200	567,225	630,250	945,375	[illegible]	[illegible]
2	31,512	63,025	94,538	126,050	157,563	189,075	220,588	252,100	283,613	315,125	472,688	630,250	787,813
3	21,009	42,017	63,025	84,036	105,042	126,050	147,058	168,067	189,075	210,083	315,125	420,167	525,208
4	15,756	31,512	47,269	63,025	78,781	94,538	110,294	126,050	141,806	157,563	236,344	315,125	393,906
5	12,605	25,210	37,815	50,420	63,025	75,630	88,235	100,840	113,445	126,050	189,076	252,100	315,125
6	10,506	21,009	31,513	42,017	52,521	63,025	73,529	84,033	94,538	105,040	157,563	210,083	262,604
7	9,004	18,007	27,011	36,016	45,018	54,021	63,025	72,029	81,032	90,036	135,054	180,071	225,089
8	7,878	15,756	23,634	31,512	39,391	47,269	55,147	63,025	70,903	78,780	118,172	157,563	196,953
9	7,003	14,006	21,010	28,011	35,014	42,017	49,019	56,022	63,025	70,030	105,042	140,056	175,069
10	6,303	12,605	18,908	25,210	31,512	37,815	44,118	50,420	56,723	63,025	94,538	126,050	157,563
20	3,151	6,303	9,454	12,605	15,756	18,908	22,059	25,210	28,316	31,512	47,269	63,025	78,781
25	2,521	5,042	7,563	10,084	12,605	15,126	17,647	20,168	22,689	25,210	37,815	50,420	63,025
30	2,101	4,202	6,303	8,403	10,504	12,605	14,705	16,807	18,908	21,009	31,513	42,017	52,521
40	1,576	3,151	4,727	6,303	7,878	9,454	11,029	12,605	14,181	15,756	23,634	31,513	39,391
50	1,261	2,521	3,782	5,042	6,303	7,563	8,824	10,084	11,345	12,605	18,908	25,210	31,513
60	1,050	2,101	3,151	4,202	5,252	6,303	7,353	8,403	9,454	10,504	15,756	21,009	26,260
70	900	1,801	2,701	3,601	4,502	5,402	6,303	7,203	8,103	9,004	13,506	18,007	22,509
75	840	1,681	2,521	3,361	4,202	5,042	5,882	6,723	7,563	8,403	12,605	16,806	21,008
80	788	1,576	2,363	3,151	3,939	4,727	5,515	6,303	7,090	7,878	11,817	15,756	19,695
90	700	1,400	2,101	2,801	3,501	4,202	4,902	5,602	6,303	7,003	10,504	14,006	17,507
100	630	1,261	1,891	2,521	3,151	3,782	4,412	5,042	5,672	6,303	9,453	12,605	15,756
150	420	840	1,261	1,681	2,101	2,521	2,941	3,361	3,781	4,202	6,303	8,403	10,504
200	315	630	945	1,261	1,575	1,891	2,206	2,521	2,836	3,151	4,727	6,303	7,878
250	252	504	756	1,008	1,260	1,531	1,765	2,017	2,269	2,521	3,782	5,042	6,303
300	210	420	630	840	1,050	1,261	1,471	1,681	1,891	2,101	3,151	4,202	5,252
350	180	360	540	720	900	1,080	1,261	1,441	1,621	1,801	2,701	3,601	4,502
400	158	315	473	630	788	945	1,104	1,261	1,418	1,576	2,364	3,151	3,939
450	141	280	420	560	700	840	980	1,120	1,261	1,401	2,101	2,801	3,501
500	126	252	378	504	630	756	882	1,008	1,134	1,261	1,891	2,521	3,151
550	115	229	344	458	573	688	802	917	1,031	1,146	1,719	2,292	2,865
600	105	210	315	420	525	630	735	840	945	1,050	1,576	2,101	2,626
650	97	194	291	388	485	582	679	776	873	970	1,454	1,939	2,424
700	90	180	270	360	450	540	630	720	810	900	1,351	1,801	2,251
750	84	168	252	336	420	504	588	672	756	840	1,261	1,681	2,101
800	79	158	236	315	393	473	551	630	709	788	1,182	1,576	1,970
850	74	148	222	297	371	445	519	593	667	741	1,112	1,483	1,854
900	70	140	210	280	350	420	490	560	630	700	1,050	1,400	1,751
950	66	133	199	265	332	398	464	531	597	663	995	1,327	1,659
1000	63	126	189	252	315	378	441	504	567	630	945	1,261	1,576
1100	57	115	172	229	286	344	401	458	516	573	860	1,146	1,432
1200	53	105	158	210	263	315	368	420	473	525	788	1,050	1,313
1300	48	97	145	194	242	291	339	388	436	485	727	970	1,212
1400	45	90	135	180	225	270	315	360	405	450	675	900	1,125
1500	42	84	126	168	210	252	294	336	378	420	630	840	1,050
1600	39	79	118	158	197	236	276	315	355	394	591	788	985
1700	37	74	111	148	185	222	260	296	334	371	556	741	927
1800	35	70	105	140	175	210	245	280	315	350	525	700	875
1900	33	66	100	133	166	199	232	265	299	332	498	663	829
2000	32	63	95	126	158	189	221	252	284	315	473	630	788
2100	30	60	90	120	150	180	210	240	270	300	450	600	750
2200	29	57	86	115	143	172	201	229	258	286	430	573	716
2300	27	55	82	110	137	164	192	219	247	274	411	548	685
2400	26	53	79	105	131	158	184	210	236	263	394	525	657
2500	25	50	76	101	126	151	176	202	227	252	378	504	630
2750	23	46	69	92	115	138	160	183	206	229	344	458	573
3000	21	42	63	84	105	126	147	168	189	210	315	420	525
3250	19	39	58	78	97	116	136	155	175	194	291	388	485
3500	18	36	54	72	90	108	126	144	162	180	270	360	450
3750	17	34	50	67	84	101	118	134	151	168	252	336	420
4000	16	32	47	63	79	95	110	126	142	158	236	315	394
4250	15	30	44	59	74	89	104	119	133	148	222	297	371
4500	14	28	42	56	70	84	98	112	126	140	210	280	350
4750	13	27	40	53	66	80	93	106	119	133	199	265	332
5000	13	25	38	50	63	76	88	101	113	126	189	252	315
6000	11	21	32	42	53	63	74	84	95	105	158	210	263
7000	9	18	27	36	45	54	63	72	81	90	135	180	225
8000	8	16	24	32	39	47	55	63	71	79	118	158	197
9000	7	14	21	28	35	42	49	56	63	70	105	140	175
10000	6	13	19	25	32	38	44	50	57	63	95	126	158

E. Electric Motor Horsepower Required to Drive a Hydraulic Pump

	PUMP PRESSURE PSI										
GPM	100	200	250	300	400	500	750	1000	1250	1500	2000
½	.04	.07	.09	.10	.14	.17	.26	.34	.43	.52	.69
1	.07	.14	.17	.21	.28	.34	.52	.69	.86	1.03	1.37
1½	.10	.21	.26	.31	.41	.52	.77	1.03	1.29	1.54	2.06
2	.14	.28	.34	.41	.55	.69	1.03	1.37	1.72	2.06	2.75
2½	.17	.34	.43	.52	.69	.86	1.29	1.72	2.15	2.58	3.43
3	.21	.41	:52	.62	.83	1.03	1.54	2.06	2.57	3.09	4.12
3½	.24	.48	.60	.72	.96	1.20	1.80	2.40	3.00	3.60	4.81
4	.28	.55	.69	.82	1.10	1.37	2.06	2.75	3.43	4.12	5.49
5	.34	.69	.86	1.03	1.32	1.72	2.57	3.43	4.29	5.15	6.86
6	.41	.82	1.03	1.24	1.65	2.06	3.09	4.12	5.15	6.18	8.24
7	.48	.96	1.20	1.44	1.92	2.40	3.60	4.81	6.01	7.21	9.61
8	.55	1.10	1.37	1.65	2.20	2.75	4.12	5.49	6.86	8.24	11.0
9	.62	1.24	1.55	1.85	2.47	3.09	4.63	6.18	7.72	9.27	12.4
10	.69	1.37	1.62	2.06	2.75	3.43	5.15	6.86	8.58	10.3	13.8
11	.76	1.51	1.89	2.27	3.02	3.78	5.66	7.55	9.44	11.3	15.1
12	.83	1.65	2.06	2.47	3.30	4.12	6.18	8.24	10.3	12.4	16.5
13	.89	1.79	2.23	2.68	3.57	4.46	6.69	8.92	11.2	13.4	17.8
14	.96	1.92	2.40	2.88	3.84	4.81	7.21	9.61	12.0	14.4	19.2
15	1.03	2.06	2.57	3.09	4.12	5.15	7.72	10.3	12.9	15.4	20.6
16	1.10	2.20	2.75	3.30	4.39	5.49	8.24	11.0	13.7	16.5	22.0
17	1.17	2.33	2.92	3.50	4.68	5.83	8.75	11.7	14.6	17.5	23.3
18	1.24	2.47	3.09	3.71	4.94	6.18	9.27	12.4	15.4	18.5	24.7
19	1.30	2.61	3.26	3.91	5.22	6.52	9.78	13.0	16.3	19.6	26.1
20	1.37	2.75	3.43	4.12	5.49	6.86	10.3	13.7	17.2	21.6	27.5
25	1.72	3.43	4.29	5.15	6.86	8.58	12.9	17.2	21.5	25.8	34.3
30	2.06	4.12	5.15	6.18	8.24	10.3	15.4	20.6	25.7	30.9	41.2
35	2.40	4.81	6.01	7.21	9.61	12.0	18.0	24.0	30.0	36.0	48.0
40	2.75	5.49	6.86	8.24	11.0	13.7	20.6	27.5	34.3	41.2	54.9
45	3.09	6.18	7.72	9.27	12.4	15.4	23.2	31.0	38.6	46.3	61.8
50	3.43	6.86	8.58	10.3	13.7	17.2	25.7	34.3	42.9	51.5	68.6
55	3.78	7.55	9.44	11.3	15.1	18.9	28.3	37.8	47.2	56.6	75.5
60	4.12	8.24	10.3	12.4	16.5	20.6	30.9	41.2	51.5	61.8	83.4
65	4.46	8.92	11.2	13.4	17.8	22.3	33.5	44.6	55.8	66.9	89.2
70	4.81	9.61	12.0	14.4	19.2	24.0	36.0	48.0	60.1	72.1	96.1
75	5.15	10.3	12.9	15.4	20.6	25.7	38.6	51.4	64.3	77.2	103.0
80	5.49	11.0	13.7	16.5	22.0	27.5	41.2	54.9	68.6	82.4	109.8
90	6.18	12.4	15.4	18.5	24.7	30.9	46.3	61.8	77.2	92.7	123.6
100	6.86	13.7	17.2	20.6	27.5	34.4	51.5	68.6	85.8	103.0	137.3

THIS CHART IS BASED ON THE FORMULA $HP = \frac{GPM \times PSI}{1714 \times EFFICIENCY}$ (from page 22). FOR THE PURPOSES OF THIS CHART PUMP EFFICIENCY WAS ASSUMED TO BE 85%.

AS HORSEPOWER VARIES DIRECTLY WITH FLOW OR PRESSURE, MULTIPLY PROPORTIONATELY TO DETERMINE VALUES NOT SHOWN. FOR INSTANCE, AT 4000 PSI MULTIPLY 2000 PSI VALUES BY 2.

F. Hydraulic Cylinder Speeds

INCHES/MINUTE

PISTON DIAMETER	ROD DIAMETER	FLOW – GPM										
		1	2	3	5	10	12	15	20	25	50	75
1	**—**	**298**	**596**	**894**	**1490**							
	1/2	392	784	1176	1960							
1-1/2	**—**	**130**	**260**	**392**	**654**	**1308**						
	5/8	158	316	476	792	1584						
	1	235	470	706	1176	2352						
2	**—**	**73**	**146**	**221**	**368**	**736**	**883**	**1120**				
	3/4	85	170	257	428	956	1025	1283				
	1	97	184	294	490	980	1175	1465				
	1-3/8	139	278	418	697	1394	1673	2090				
2-1/2	**—**	**47**	**94**	**141**	**235**	**470**	**565**	**675**	**940**	**1175**		
	1	56	112	168	280	560	672	840	1120	1400		
	1-3/8	67	134	203	339	678	813	1015	1355	1695		
	1-3/4	92	184	277	463	926	1110	1385	1850	2310		
3	**—**	**32**	**64**	**98**	**163**	**326**	**392**	**490**	**653**	**817**		
	1	36	72	110	184	368	440	551	735	920		
	1-1/2	43	86	131	218	436	523	655	872	1090		
	2	58	116	176	294	588	705	882	1175	1470		
3-1/2	**—**	**24**	**48**	**72**	**120**	**240**	**288**	**360**	**480**	**600**	**1200**	
	1-1/4	27	54	82	137	274	330	411	548	685	1370	
	1-3/4	32	64	96	160	320	384	480	640	800	1600	
	2	35	70	107	178	356	428	534	712	890	1780	
4	**—**	**18**	**36**	**55**	**92**	**184**	**220**	**276**	**368**	**460**	**920**	
	1-1/4	20	40	61	102	204	244	306	408	510	1020	
	1-3/4	22	44	68	113	226	273	339	452	565	1130	
	2	24	48	73	122	244	294	366	488	610	1220	
	2-1/2	30	60	90	150	300	362	450	600	750	1500	
5	**—**	**12**	**24**	**35**	**58**	**116**	**141**	**174**	**232**	**290**	**580**	**870**
	1-1/2	13	26	39	64	128	155	193	258	320	640	960
	2	14	28	42	70	140	168	210	280	350	700	1050
	2-1/2	16	32	47	78	156	188	235	315	390	780	1170
	3	18	36	55	92	184	220	275	365	460	920	1380
	3-1/2	22	44	66	111	222	266	333	444	555	1110	1665
6	**—**	**8**	**16**	**24**	**41**	**82**	**98**	**123**	**162**	**202**	**404**	**606**
	1-3/4	9	18	27	45	90	107	135	180	225	450	675
	2-1/2	10	20	30	50	100	118	150	200	250	500	750
	3	11	22	33	54	108	130	165	206	270	540	810
	3-1/2	12	24	37	62	124	148	185	245	310	620	930
	4	15	30	44	73	146	176	220	295	365	730	1095
8	**—**	**4**	**8**	**14**	**23**	**46**	**55**	**69**	**92**	**115**	**230**	**345**
	3-1/2	5½	11	17	28	56	68	85	115	140	280	420
	4	6	12	18	30	60	73	90	122	150	300	450
	5	7½	15	22	38	76	90	114	150	185	375	555
	5-1/2	8½	17	26	43	86	104	129	172	215	430	645
10	**—**	**3**	**6**	**9**	**15**	**30**	**35**	**44**	**60**	**73**	**146**	**220**
	4-1/2	3½	7	11	18	36	44	55	75	92	184	275
	5	4	8	12	20	40	47	60	80	100	200	300
	5-1/2	4½	9	13	21	42	50	63	84	105	210	315
	7	5½	11	17	29	58	69	87	115	145	290	435

THIS CHART IS BASED ON THE FORMULA $V = \frac{231 \times GPM}{\text{EFF. CYL. AREA (SQ. INCHES)}}$.

SHADED HORIZONTAL LINES ARE CYLINDER EXTENSION SPEEDS WHERE THE FLUID ACTS ON THE ENTIRE CYLINDER AREA. NON-SHADED AREAS ARE RETRACTION SPEEDS WHERE THE FLUID ACTS ON THE PISTON LESS THE ROD AREA.

BIBLIOGRAPHY

Basic Hydraulics for Marine Engineers. New York: Marine Engineers Beneficial Association, Districts One and Two, n.d.

Controllable Pitch Propeller. Walpole, Mass.: Bird-Johnson Co., 1973.

Electro-Hydraulic Hatch Covers. Port Deposit, Md.: Wiley Manufacturing Co., 1965.

Fluid Power (Navpers 16193-B). Washington, D.C.: Government Printing Office, 1970.

Fluid Power Handbook and Directory. Cleveland, Ohio: Hydraulics and Pneumatics, 1972/73.

Industrial Hydraulics Manual (935001-A). Troy, Mich.: Vickers Division of Sperry Rand, 1970.

Knak, Christen. *Diesel Motor Ships Engineering and Machinery.* Copenhagen: GED Gad Publishers, 1979.

Operating Manual for Hydraulic Hatch Covers. Cleveland, Ohio: The Lewis Welding and Engineering Corp., n.d.

Operations Manual for Anchor Windlass. Everett, Wash.: Western Gear Corp., Heavy Machinery Division, 1971.

Operations Manual for Constant Tension Mooring Winch. Everett, Wash.: Western Gear Corp., Heavy Machinery Division, 1971.

Operations Manual for Mitsui-AEG Steering Gear. Tokyo: Mitsui Engineering and Ship Building Co. Ltd., 1970.

Operations Manual for Steering Gear. Western Gear Corp., Heavy Machinery Division, 1971.

Pippenger, John J., and Hicks, Tyler G. *Industrial Hydraulics Manual.* New York: McGraw-Hill, 1979.

Shaft Alley Watertight Door. Glen Head, N.Y.: Walz and Krenzer, 1963.

Ship Stores Crane. Rome, N.Y.: Pettibone Corp., n.d.

Standard Industrial Hydraulics Questions and Answers. New York: McGraw-Hill, 1967.

Stewart, Harry L., and Storer, John M. *Fluid Power.* Indianapolis, Ind.: Howard W. Sams, 1968.

INDEX

ABOUT THE AUTHOR

Perry Stutman was teaching shipboard hydraulics systems at a professional maritime school when a visiting bookseller asked for his order. Stutman replied that the book he wanted for his course hadn't been published by anyone. The salesman responded, "Well, then, why don't you write it yourself?" And so this book had its beginning.

The author received a B.S. in environmental science from Towson State University in Maryland, has taught and been assistant head in the marine engineering department at the Calhoun M.E.B.A. Engineering School, has given seminars at the major U.S. ports on "Inert Gas and Crude Oil Washing for Tank Vessels," contributed articles to *American Marine Engineer,* and in addition has served as first assistant engineer aboard oceangoing dry cargo vessels.

Besides being a certified diver, licensed pilot of single-engine planes, and active racing sailor on his sloop in the Chesapeake Bay, he has served on a log canoe race committee and as chairman of Baltimore's Inner Harbor Sailing School.